HITLER AND THE NAZI DARWINIAN WORLDVIEW

Hitler and the Nazi Darwinian Worldview is a powerful reminder of the central role Darwin's ideas played in opening the way for the depraved minds of Hitler and his henchmen to conceive and carry out some of the most shocking crimes in world history. Well documented in the writings of the participants themselves as well as in the accounts of both American and German historians, this book is a sobering study of the evil fruits of a false belief.

STEVEN E. WOODWORTH, Ph.D., Associate Professor of History, Texas Christian University, Fort Worth, Texas

A challenging read! Before delving into this book readers should brace themselves for encountering a blistering attack against Adolf Hitler's mid-twentieth-century German quest to produce a "superior race." This philosophy culminated in the so-called Final Solution, the extermination of approximately 6 million Jews and over 5 million other people who belonged to what German scientists judged were "inferior races," including blacks, Slavic peoples, especially Poles and Russians and Ukrainians, Gypsies and some Asiatic races—essentially all peoples in the world except Aryans (Western Europeans). The Nazis also killed the disabled and were anti-Church fanatics. Bergman's new book contains an extensive bibliographic collection of writers who have recognized that the German conquest had its foundational doctrines solidly based upon Darwinian evolutionary thinking.

WAYNE FRAIR, Ph.D., Professor Emeritus of Biology, The King's College, New York

If you think that there was only a superficial connection between evolution and Nazism, be astonished at the facts when reading this book. Learn how evolutionary theory animated so many aspects of Nazi ideology. Realize why Hitler's "Christianity" was purely tactical in nature and why evolutionary theory played a major role in driving erstwhile devout Christians into hardened Nazis.

JAN PECZKIS, M.A., Author, teacher and lecturer

Professor Jerry Bergman's book is certainly much needed, and I am in total agreement with his overall theme. I found the book interesting and engrossing, especially the second part. I heartily recommend it.

EMERSON THOMAS MCMULLEN, Ph.D., Associate Professor, Department of History, Georgia Southern University, Statesboro, Georgia

If you want to be informed about the details of what happened to cause World War II, and we all should, Jerry Bergman's latest exposé is required reading. Long before I got to the end of the book, it was obvious that Charles Darwin's ideas were deeply embedded in the minds of Adolf Hitler and his henchmen. While Darwin certainly wasn't the only culprit, one has to wonder how much less horrific things might have been without Darwinism.

MILT MARCY, author and lecturer

A reasonable attempt to help a popular audience understand the Darwinian influences on leading Nazi officials.

RICHARD WIEKART, Ph.D., Professor of History, California State University, Stanislaus

HITLER
AND THE NAZI
DARWINIAN
WORLDVIEW

HOW THE NAZI EUGENIC CRUSADE FOR A SUPERIOR RACE CAUSED THE GREATEST HOLOCAUST IN WORLD HISTORY

Jerry Bergman

joshua
press

p r e s s

www.joshuapress.com

Published by
Joshua Press Inc., Kitchener, Ontario, Canada
Distributed by
Sola Scriptura Ministries International
www.sola-scriptura.ca

First published 2012

Cover and book design by Janice Van Eck

The publication of this book was made possible by the generous support of The Ross-Shire Foundation

Library and Archives Canada Cataloguing in Publication

Bergman, Jerry, 1946–
    Hitler and the Nazi Darwinian worldview : how the Nazi eugenic crusade for a superior race caused the greatest holocaust in world history / Jerry Bergman.

Includes bibliographical references.
Also issued in electronic format.
ISBN 978-1-894400-49-7

    1. Social Darwinism—Germany—History—20th century. 2. Darwin, Charles, 1809–1882—Influence. 3. Eugenics—Germany—History—20th century. 4. Racism—Germany—History—20th century. 5. Holocaust, Jewish (1939–1945). 6. Hitler, Adolf, 1889–1945—Philosophy. 7. Hitler, Adolf, 1889-1945—Political and social views. 8. National socialism—Philosophy. 9. Nazis—Germany—Biography. I. Title.

DD256.6.B47 2012   943.086   C2012-906171-9

To my wife Dianne, the love of my life,
and our children, Aeron, Christine, Scott and Mishalea,
and our grandchildren, Kearstin, Bryn, Bryson, Sienna,
Owen, Abigail, Mackenzie, Mia and Josie.

Contents

"There was an ideological dimension to Hitler's foreign policy, an ideological level which saturated these geopolitical ideas.... The new greater German Reich—Greater German Empire that...was to dominate the European continent—was to be a racially pure empire.... Germany was...[the Nazis believed] the last best racial hope of mankind."[1]

—*Thomas Childers, Professor of History, University of Pennsylvania*

1 Thomas Childers, *World War II: A Military and Social History* (Chantilly: The Teaching Company, 1998), 27–28.

Foreword

Amazingly, though we live in an age of overwhelming amounts of information, people still swallow some ridiculous notions about one of history's most famous sets of villains: Hitler and his Nazi henchmen. One of the most bizarre is that somehow Darwinism was not at the front and centre of Nazi ideology. My late mother, who grew up under the National Socialist German Worker's Party government, confirmed the all-pervasive influence of evolution on that society's aberrations as a "given." She would have been surprised to hear that anyone could deny something so patently obvious.

Yet the myth persists in some circles, as does the perhaps even more "off the wall" idea that Hitler was somehow a Christian! At least the latter idea has some grains of reality as its possible seed material—Hitler did on numerous occasions try to pull the wool over the church's eyes while he was actively working to destroy it.

This thoroughly documented work by Dr. Bergman is therefore both timely and welcome. It adds to the recent spate of scholarly books that together should hammer the remaining nails into the coffin of such urban myths.

Bergman's unique approach is to make his point not just from Hitler's own writings and actions, but from examining one by one the lives, actions and statements of those of his disciples closest to him. The result is both fascinating and chilling. Much still has the power to surprise and shock, even for those who, like myself, think they are thoroughly familiar with what went on in the Third Reich.

All in all, a very important, interesting and most readable book.

–Dr. Carl Wieland
Physician, author and managing director of CMI

Preface

Harvard-trained historian Robert G. L. Waite stated in the preface of his book, *The Psychopathic God* (1977), that the appeal of Adolf Hitler as the leader of Nazi Germany still piques the interest of many people. At the time that he was writing his book, he was able to make the astounding observation that between 1945 (Hitler's suicide) and 1975, "There were already 50,000 serious works about Hitler and his Reich."[1] On a current website, "Adolf Hitler and Popular Culture," one is able to find Hitler featured in video games, television comedy, theatre and films. This site also mentions that, according to WorldCat—the world's largest library catalogue—there are 553 fictional works related to Adolf Hitler.[2] The public's fascination regarding this fiendish dictator seems insatiable.

Within the first decade of this century, historian Richard Weikart, in his books, *From Darwin to Hitler* (2004) and *Hitler's Ethic: The Nazi Pursuit of Evolutionary Progress* (2009), has written about a much-neglected topic—the influence of evolutionary ideology on Hitler and

---

1 R.G.L. Waite, *The Psychopathic God* (New York: Basic Books, 1977), xi.

2 See http://en.wikipedia.org/wiki/Adolf_Hitler_in_popular_culture under subsection, "Novels"; accessed September 5, 2012.

the rise of Nazism. In the wake of Dr. Weikart's publications, Jerry Bergman has investigated the impact of evolutionary thought on the lives of Hitler's henchmen, such as Dr. Josef Mengele, Martin Bormann and Hermann Göring, to name a few.

As is characteristic of all of Dr. Bergman's works, *Hitler and the Nazi Darwinian Worldview* has been thoroughly researched. It is highly significant that the first foreign translation of Charles Darwin's *On the Origin of Species* occurred in Germany. After having read this book, Ernst Haeckel, a recent graduate in medicine from the University of Würzberg, became an ardent disciple of Darwinism. In time, he would not only become Germany's foremost biologist, but also the "Father of German Evolutionism." This status provided him with an ideal platform to promote his version of Darwinism, which focused on the theory of German racial superiority.

In the 1920s, Adolf Hitler established this heinous philosophy as a foundational tenet for his Nazi Party. As Führer of Germany, he instituted the Nuremberg Racial Laws (1935), which he called "The Laws for the Protection of German Blood and German Honor."[3] Much to the chagrin and horror of the world, those unilaterally declared to be racially inferior by this law were eventually systematically exterminated in the gas chambers of Auschwitz, Treblinka, Belzec and more. Dr. Bergman cogently illustrates that Hitler's henchmen had two defining characteristics. First, they viewed Hitler as a demi-god. Second, they not only became totally obsessed with the Nazi worldview but were completely convinced that the only viable option for the purification of the "Aryan Race" was the total implementation of the "Final Solution."

As a retired history teacher, I particularly enjoyed the chapter titled, "Darwinism and Biology textbooks in Nazi Germany." All textbooks in Nazi Germany had to be approved by the educational authorities and were required to reflect the prevailing worldview and its concomitant values. Their textbooks were Darwinian to the core and were purposefully designed to instill in the minds of young German students that they were indeed a superior race.

---

3   Waite, *The Psychopathic God*, 26

It is no wonder that when the Hitler Youth—thoroughly indoctrinated—were sent into the battlefield during World War II, they fought with such intensity and ferocity.

Today, as in the past, universities control the educational system. As proponents of evolutionism, their influence is felt from the primary grades to teachers' colleges. To validate their nefarious doctrine, they loudly proclaim it not to be religious. Unfortunately, they have convinced the general public, especially the media, of this untruth.

Many Allied soldiers sacrificed their lives to defeat Nazi Germany so that Hitler's henchmen could be brought before an International Court of Justice to be sentenced and punished for their dastardly crimes against humanity. Dr. Bergman's book serves as a warning that this same naturalistic worldview that spawned the atrocities of World War II persists to this day. It is growing in intensity, year by year. As Nazism detested Christianity, twenty-first-century secular humanism is no different. In its many manifestos, it preaches peace and tolerance, but underlying lurks a theme of intolerance toward Christianity!

–Dr. David Herbert
Historian and author

Acknowledgements

The many people who read the manuscript, in whole or part, include historian Dr. David Herbert; Dr. Steven E. Woodworth, Associate Professor of History at Texas Christian University; Dr. Thomas McMullen, Associate Professor of History at Georgia Southern University; Dr. Wayne Frair, Professor Emeritus at The King's College, New York; Dr. Richard Weikart, Professor of History at California State University, Stanislaus; Dr. Carl Wieland, David Buckna, Bryce Gaudian and Jan Peczkis. I also want to thank Dr. Bert Thompson, Mary Ann Stewart, Clifford Lillo, Peter Beach, Milt Marcy and the many reviewers. I especially want to thank Bernard Kirk and Dr. Wieland for help in translating German into English. For help in translating the German quotes, I am thankful to Professor Richard Weikart whose work, published and unpublished, I relied on heavily, especially for the section documenting the teaching of Darwinism in Nazi German textbooks. Dr. Weikart also edited the entire manuscript. Needless to say, any mistakes or errors that remain are mine. I have found that translations are not always straightforward and disagreement exists in the best translation of certain expressions.

A note on sources

As is true of any historical study, the reliability of my sources varies. In general, I have used sources that are well recognized by Hitler scholars as very accurate. The veracity of the English translation of *Hitler's Secret Conversations* and *Hitler's Table Talk* (compiled by a supporter of Hitler who had his own agenda) has been questioned. Whereas these works are quoted a few times in this book, my conclusions do not rely on them but are well supported by numerous other sources. As research on Hitler progresses I will revise this work to reflect the latest scholarship.

Introduction

~~~~~~

"The leader of Germany [Adolf Hitler] is an evolutionist
not only in theory but, as millions know to their cost,
in the rigor of its practice."
—SIR ARTHUR KEITH, PHYSICAL ANTHROPOLOGIST

Almost every high-school student knows that one of Hitler's
primary goals was producing a superior race based on the
Darwinian idea of ever-advancing progression of life, upward
from molecules to humans, caused by natural selection.
What is not as widely known, however, is how central this goal was
to the entire Nazi movement. Hitler scholar and Yale University Professor Emeritus Fritz Redlich, when asked what was the centrepiece
of Hitler's worldview, answered his social Darwinism and his anti-
Semitism, both which flowed from his Darwinian worldview.[1]

This volume takes a fresh look at the most influential Nazi leaders,
viewing each one through the lens of Darwinian thought. Nazi is the
English abbreviation for *Nationalsozialistische Deutsche Arbeiterpartei* or,

---

1   Fritz Redlich, *Hitler: Diagnosis of a Destructive Prophet* (New York: Oxford University Press, 1998), 340.

in English, The National Socialist German Workers' Party. The conclusion from the academic literature? Almost all Nazi leaders were enslaved to Darwinian ideas and ideals, and almost all were strongly opposed to Christianity to the degree that they eventually wanted to eradicate it from Europe.[2]

This is not a judgement but a well-documented fact. The German Führer was "an evolutionist; he has consciously sought to make the practice of Germany conform to the theory of evolution."[3] Nor should the outcome of his worldview surprise us. As an international committee of psychologists stated in a 1935 manifesto, "war is the necessary outcome of Darwin's theory."[4] Darwin's ideas about race are very clear in his 1871 book, *The Descent of Man*, which has been called a racist tome from cover to cover. On page two Darwin wrote

> The sole object of this work is to consider, firstly, whether man, like every other species, is descended from some pre-existing form; secondly, the manner of his development; and thirdly, the value of the differences between the so-called races of man.[5]

He then added, to make his intention clear, that it must "be enquired whether man, like so many other animals, has given rise to varieties and sub-races, differing but slightly from each other, or to races differing so much that they must be classed as doubtful species?"[6] Darwin added that by applying his survival of the fittest theory, the eventual result of the differences between the races was that "the civilized races of man will almost certainly exterminate, and replace throughout the world the savage races"[7] The result will be that

---

2   Gertrude Himmelfarb, *Darwin and the Darwinian Revolution* (New York: Doubleday, 1959).

3   Arthur Keith, *Evolution and Ethics* (New York: G.P. Putnam's Sons, 1946), 10, 203.

4   Arthur Keith, *Essays on Human Evolution* (London: Watts & Co., 1946), 46.

5   Charles Darwin, *The Descent of Man, and Selection in Relation to Sex* (London: John Murray, 1871), 2–3.

6   Darwin, *The Descent of Man*, 9–10.

7   Darwin, *The Descent of Man*, 201.

Charles Darwin (1809-1882)

Darwin's *On the Origin of Species* influenced many in the late nineteenth and early twentieth century and his survival of the fittest theory of evolutionary progress propelled the Nazi eugenics theorists forward as they looked to create a master Aryan race.

The break between man and his nearest allies will then be wider, for it will intervene between man in a more civilized state—as we may hope, even than the Caucasian and some ape as low as a baboon instead of now between the negro or Australian [Aborigine] and the gorilla.[8]

Darwin "clung to the idea that the human races were distinctly different and basically unchangeable."[9] Furthermore, "according to Charles Darwin, the 'strong' were bound to be victorious, and the 'weak' to perish."[10] Furthermore, as will be documented, Darwin's own words condemned him as a racist:

When the *Beagle* arrived in Tierra del Fuego at the southernmost tip of South America, Darwin was astonished and horrified at the sight of the savages who ran out to meet the boat. "It was without exception," he wrote in his diary of the voyage, "the most curious and interesting spectacle I had ever beheld. I could not have believed how wide was the difference, between savage and civilized man. It is wider than between a wild and domesticated animal, inasmuch as in man there is a greater power of improvement."[11]

Darwin's conclusions about the inferiority of certain human races openly influenced his theory of evolution.[12] In *The Descent of Man*, where Darwin added that on seeing the Fuegians "absolutely naked and bedaubed with paint, their long hair...tangled, their mouths, frothed with excitement, and their expression...wild, startled, distrustful," the idea immediately occurred to him: "such were our

---

8   Charles Darwin, *The Descent of Man, and Selection in Relation to Sex*, 2nd ed. (London: John Murray, 1874), 178.

9   John Jackson, Jr. and Nadine M. Weidman, *Race, Racism, and Science: Social Impact and Interaction* (Santa Barbara: ABC-CLIO, 2004), 71.

10   Brigitte Hamann, *Hitler's Vienna: A Dictator's Apprenticeship* (New York: Oxford University Press, 2010), 200, 203.

11   Jackson and Weidman, *Race, Racism, and Science*, 71.

12   Stefan Kühl, *The Nazi Connection: Eugenics, American Racism, and German National Socialism* (New York: Oxford University Press, 2002).

[primitive evolutionary] ancestors."[13] Also, Darwin's direct experiences
with what he called

> savages provided him with further proof of their inalterable racial
> difference. When a party of Fuegian natives Christianized and
> civilized in England, returned on board the *Beagle* as missionar-
> ies to their native land, the Fuegians reverted to their savage ways,
> convincing Darwin that racial habits and racial natures were
> entrenched and basically unchangeable. The conversion the sav-
> ages had undergone had been superficial and fleeting, while their
> suitability to their native way of life, and their clear inferiority,
> were permanent. All that remained of racial evolution for Dar-
> win, as for Wallace, was the extermination of the inferior races
> by the superior [races].[14]

These ideas spread to many nations including in Canada and the
United States.[15] For example, in the first half of the nineteenth century
the United States was "infatuated" with

> eugenics and its promise of strengthening the human race by
> culling the "unfit" from the genetic pool. Along with the "feeble-
> minded," insane, and criminal, those so classified included
> women who had sex out of wedlock (considered a mental illness),
> orphans, the disabled, the poor, the homeless, epileptics, mas-
> turbators, the blind and the deaf, alcoholics, and girls whose
> genitals exceeded certain measurements. Some eugenicists advo-
> cated euthanasia, and in mental hospitals, this was quietly car-
> ried out on scores of people through "lethal neglect" or outright
> murder. At one Illinois mental hospital, new patients were dosed
> with milk from cows infected with tuberculosis, in the belief that
> only the undesirable would perish. As many as four in ten of
> these patients died. A more popular tool of eugenics was forced

---

13 Darwin, *The Descent of Man*, 2nd ed., 404.

14 Jackson and Weidman, *Race, Racism, and Science*, 71.

15 Jane Harris-Zsovan, *Eugenics and the Firewall: Canada's Nasty Secret* (Winnipeg:
Shillingsford, 2010).

sterilization, employed on a raft of lost souls who, through mis-behavior or misfortune, fell into the hands of state governments. By 1930, California was enraptured with eugenics, and would ultimately sterilize some twenty thousand people.[16]

These ideas were greatly expanded by Ernst Haeckel and other scientists in Germany. Charles Darwin and his cousin Francis Galton were not the originators of eugenics and racism, but served to popularize it enormously and give it scientific respectability as no other men in history did. Hitler was a voracious reader but, as far as we know, never read Darwin's works, but he did read those of Darwin's German disciples, such as Ernst Haeckel and others who popularized Darwin's theory. Hamann wrote that

> Hitler did not usually gain his knowledge directly from such philosophers and theoreticians as Darwin...but instead from reports in newspapers, pamphlets, and popular periodicals, which regurgitated the main theses of the writers who happened to be in vogue [such as Darwin was in Germany then].[17]

Waite believed that most of Hitler's knowledge about Darwinism and his anti-Semitic ideas came from newspapers, magazines pamphlets and other popular writing since they were very popular topics then.[18] It is well documented that Ernst Haeckel and the German scientific establishment had a major influence on the Nazi leadership. Furthermore, it was Darwin himself who was responsible for popularizing, on a global scale, the ideas of evolution via survival-of-the-fittest natural selection. Although anti-Semitism existed in Europe long before Hitler, one major difference existed in Hitler's anti-Semitism, namely it was based squarely on race and reflected the influence of Darwinism.[19]

---

16 Laura Hillenbrand, *Unbroken: A World War II Story of Survival, Resilience, and Redemption* (New York: Random House, 2010), 11.

17 Hamann, *Hitler's Vienna*, 233.

18 Robert Waite, *The Psychopathic God* (New York: Basic Books, 1977), 66–71.

19 Thomas Chiders, *The Nazi Voter: The Social Foundations of Fascism in Germany, 1919–1933* (Chapel Hill: The University of North Carolina Press, 1983).

Ernst Haeckel (1834-1919)

Haeckel was one of Darwin's most devoted disciples in Germany, popularizing Darwin's theories and influencing Hitler, the Nazi Party leadership and a whole generation of German scientists, professors and doctors.

Clearly, Darwin's ideas played a critical role in the Nazi movement, even though many of Hitler's disciples likely never even read Darwin in the original English. Reasons why include they were not fluent in reading English and their anti-British sentiment. Furthermore, parts of the German translations of Darwin were not always very faithful to the original English. Nonetheless, Darwin's critical influence on German biologists, especially Haeckel, is well established.

HITLER'S DISCIPLES WERE ANTI-SEMITIC

Cutting-edge ideas often are introduced to cultures through the educational system, and that was certainly the case when it came to nurturing the seeds of anti-Semitism and eugenics in the land that would ultimately become Nazi Germany. In fact, one of the world's very first formal anti-Semitic and eugenic organizations was The Association of German Students, established in 1881.[20] Many of its members eventually became German professors who were careful to indoctrinate their students, including many future pastors, into this new Darwinian way of thinking. These pastors, in turn, passed the ideas on to their own congregations.

This was not universally true, of course. Especially in the early years of Hitler's rule, the church, particularly the so-called "Confessing Church" was the only source of major opposition to Nazism.[21] But there were many faithful church members who remained self-protectively silent and, in general, the churches as a whole for several reasons did relatively little to help Hitler's victims.[22]

What's more, some church leaders openly rejected their Christian teachings in favour of the Nazi programme. As one Berlin pastor insisted, "The Jews belong to the Semitic race. Compared to the Aryan race, the Semitic race is inferior. For the Aryan people, particularly for the German people, contact with [the Jews] is fatal because…their different ways and their inferiority" damages Germany.[23]

---

20 Wolfgang Gerlach, *And the Witnesses Were Silent: The Confessing Church and the Persecution of the Jews* (Lincoln: University of Nebraska Press, 2000), 2.

21 Gerlach, *And the Witnesses Were Silent*.

22 Joseph Keysor, *Hitler, the Holocaust, and the Bible* (New York: Athanatos, 2010).

23 Gerlach, *And the Witnesses Were Silent*, 4.

Due to the influence of various academics and scholars,

Hitler came to view history as the struggle between the races, in which the strong defeat, dominate, or destroy the weak—a vulgarized view of social Darwinism in which war plays a fundamental role. This notion became the centre of Hitler's worldview and eventually contributed to unprecedented destruction.[24]

This worldview was in dynamic contrast to Christianity.

Ironically, this church support of Hitler's schemes did little to endear these churches to the Nazi leadership. Even though many Nazis were raised in suitably religious homes, most of Hitler's disciples were as virulently anti-Christian (they were especially opposed to the Catholic church) as they were anti-Semitic, thanks to the influence of their anti-Christian professors, the "theological liberalism that was really secular philosophy disguised by religious language" and their involvement in the anti-Christian Nazi movement.[25] Of course, Hitler's influence was critical as well. As Jewish author Ray Comfort remarked, "Hitler trained his disciples well. Each of then parroted his spiritual convictions for the sake of the Reich."[26] Unfortunately, some clergy today likewise have sold out to the Darwinism that was the foundation of Nazi thought.

In fact, as we will document, the Nazi leadership planned to destroy Christianity after the war and replace it with a German church worshipping Hitler and the Nazi Party with elements of pre-Christian paganism. A 150-volume U.S. government report titled, The Nuremberg Project, was prepared under the direction of General William Donovan to document Nazi war crimes for the Nuremberg War Crimes Trial. Part of the 150 volumes was a 108-page report titled, The Nazi Master Plan, which concluded the Nazis "sought to eliminate the Christian Churches in Germany" after the war.[27]

---

24 Redlich, *Hitler: Diagnosis of a Destructive Prophet*, 274.
25 Ray Comfort, *Hitler, God & the Bible* (Washington: WND Books, 2012), 132.
26 Comfort, *Hitler, God & the Bible*, 147.
27 Copy in Cornell University archives, section IIC3c1.

HITLER'S INNER CIRCLE

In 1939, Oswald Dutch published a prophetic book titled, *Hitler's 12 Apostles*. In it, he described the men he felt to be the most important in the inner circle of Nazi Germany. This book inspired me to research each example given to determine which disciples of Hitler were influenced by Darwinism and which were anti-Christian. It turned out that most of his leading disciples were influenced by Darwin and most were anti-Christian.

This book was written to tell the rest of the story, with only slight variations on the men Dutch chose to investigate. With the benefit of hindsight, I have been able to select those men who were at the core of the Nazi movement from its early days and who managed to retain Hitler's favour for most of the twelve years that he ruled Germany. Most historians would agree that the people I selected—Heinrich Himmler, Joseph Goebbels, Herman Göring, Julies Streicher and Reinhard Heydrich, among others—were the Führer's nearest and most important disciples.

IS DARWIN REALLY TO BLAME?

Darwinism was far from the only cause for World War II and the Holocaust. There were many other contributing factors, including Germany's humiliating loss of World War I, what Germans regarded as the enormous war reparations required by the Treaty of Versailles that they claim plunged Germany into a severe economic depression, and hyperinflation.[28] These factors have all been discussed in detail in scores of other works and are not the focus of this book. Instead, this book exposes Darwinism's catastrophic influences on the Nazi movement and its leaders. The written historical record makes these influences abundantly clear.

Historian and philosopher Rabbi Shmuel Boteach stressed in his book, *Moses of Oxford*, that Darwinism's influence on Hitler is well-documented. He quoted two famous men as follows:

---

28 Peter Longerich, *Holocaust: The Nazi Persecution and Murder of the Jews* (New York: Oxford University Press, 2010).

"The more civilized so-called Caucasian races have beaten the Turkish hollow in the struggle for existence. Looking to the world at no very distant date, what an endless number of the lower races will have been eliminated by the higher civilized races throughout the world."

"In nature there is no pity for the lesser creatures when they are destroyed so that the fittest may survive...."

These statements express such similar sentiments that the reader may initially suppose they were written by the same author. However, the author of the former was a scientist, Charles Darwin, and the author of the latter statement was a political leader who lived by Darwin's evolutionary ideology. His name: Adolf Hitler. Hitler was a spiritual and ideological student of Darwin and evolution. His entire concept of the Aryan master race evolved in response to the ethical implications of the theory of evolution.[29]

Boteach tells us that the first quote is by Charles Darwin,[30] and the second is from *Mein Kampf*. Rabbi Boteach said that, as a Jew, he had been "watching this debate on Darwinian evolution very closely" and had strongly encouraged others, especially Jews, to do the same. He applauded the Oxford University L'Chaim Society for having "sponsored numerous debates on Darwinism, which featured scientists of international renown to address this topic.[31] One reason for his concern, he said, was that:

too often in the past, "scientific" positions (which are contrary to Judaism) have been adopted without delving into the validity of those scientific assertions: this is bad for the truth if the theories are wrong, and the situation is worsened [from]...belief in

29 Shmuel Boteach, *Moses of Oxford: A Jewish Vision of a University and Its Life* (London: André Deutsch Ltd, 1995), 485.

30 See Charles Darwin, *The Life and Letters of Charles Darwin*, ed. Francis Darwin (New York: D. Appleton, 1896), 286.

31 Boteach, *Moses of Oxford*, 484.

false or inaccurate scientific dogma. Another, perhaps more important, reason to intensify the debate on this issue in particular is the way in which Darwinism can sometimes be manipulated to promote dangerous morals and ethics. [32]

Furthermore, Rabbi Boteach quoted Sir Arthur Keith—a man who entered World War II as a leading British evolutionist and who, after having endured terrible suffering, came out opposed to war. He was one who understood the truth about evolution. As Professor Keith wrote, evolution had been

> applied vigorously to the affairs of a great modern nation…Germany of 1942. We see Hitler devoutly convinced that evolution produced the only real basis for a national policy…. The means he adopted to secure destiny of his race and people [were] organized slaughter.[33]

As Keith stressed, Hitler used "evolutionary mentality" to solve an "evolutionary problem," and, as a eugenicist, his goals include the prevention of "the greatest racial sin, racial mixing" and the elimination of all inferior human races. In Hitler's mind, evolution and its ultimate end—a superior race—justified any available means, even the murder of over 11 million Jews and Christians, and the loss of 55 million more lives in the theatre of war (including the Pacific).[34]

Boteach approved of Oxford University's debates on evolution because of the unhealthy climate that he believed existed there—a climate that had produced a dogmatic, unquestioning acceptance, of the

> propositions necessitated by the Theory of Evolution. If it is unhealthy for an individual to jump blindly into religious doctrines and belief, and I have constantly told my students that it is, then the same is true of scientific theory as well. Judaism has

---

32 Boteach, *Moses of Oxford*, 484.

33 Arthur Keith, cited in Boteach, *Moses of Oxford*, 485–486.

34 Keith, *Evolution and Ethics*, 12.

a very proud intellectual tradition which should continue to govern all aspects of our life.[35]

The major opposition to Hitler's policies was Christianity, of which a central doctrine was the need to help the disenfranchised, the poor, the deformed, the handicapped and the mentally ill, all of those that the Nazi leaders wanted to eradicate.

THE NAZIS OPPOSITION TO CHRISTIANITY

The Nazi opposition to Christianity was somewhat muted at first, but their long-term goal was very clear and well articulated:

> From the beginning, the Nazi party had paid lip service to religious values, endorsing what it called a positive Christianity. What positive Christianity entailed, aside from opposition to Jews and Marxists, the Nazis never explained. Before taking power, Hitler studiously avoided conflict with the churches. Indeed, by supporting their independence and their proper role in the affairs of state, by opposing godless communism and espousing the moral regeneration of Germany, he appealed to thousands of individual Christians. "I need the Catholics of Bavaria just as I need the Protestants of Prussia," he avowed.[36]

Although Hitler was reared a Catholic, he "harbored little affection for the church" and privately voiced contempt for "hypocritical priests" and their "satanic superstition," and "his Nazi deputies sparred with the representatives of the Catholic Center Party in the Reichstag." He also was known to read anti-Catholic literature with much interest.[37] Although Hitler told the new Reichstag, "The rights of churches will not be diminished,"

he revealed his true feelings in private, explaining to intimates that he would tolerate the churches temporarily for political

---

35 Boteach, *Moses of Oxford*, 532.
36 George Constable, ed., *The New Order* (Alexandria: Time Life, 1990), 122–123.
37 Waite, *The Psychopathic God*, 69.

reasons. "But," he added, "that won't stop me from stamping out Christianity in Germany, root and branch. One is either a Christian or a German. One can't be both!"[38]

At this time, ironically, the "Lutheran church moved closer to Hitler—and to destruction."[39] Even "Catholic university students pledged their loyalty to the Führer and learned to execute the stiff Nazi salute."[40] In the meantime, around 1933, the

> resistance to Nazi interference in Lutheran affairs crystallized around the imposing figure of Martin Niemöller, an influential pastor in Berlin. Niemöller...sympathized with Hitler's call for national revival but balked when the Nazis tried to insert an article banning non-Aryan pastors into the Lutherans' cherished confession of faith. Niemöller circulated a letter calling on his colleagues to return to Holy Scripture.[41]

An example of Nazification of the German church was when the Lutheran Bishop appointed by the Nazis, Ludwig Müller, stated

> that the Old Testament of the Bible, "with its Jewish morality of rewards and its stories of cattle dealers and concubines," would be discarded, and that the New Testament would be cleansed of the ideas of the "Rabbi Paul."[42]

Not surprisingly this statement only drove more clergy into Niemöller's movement. By January 1934, his league had close to 7,000 members. Shaken by these developments, the Nazis resorted to using its growing police powers against the church, resulting in Gestapo agents "encouraging" parishioners, by force if necessary, to

---

38 Constable, ed., *The New Order*, 123–124.
39 Constable, ed., *The New Order*, 124.
40 Constable, ed., *The New Order*, 124.
41 Constable, ed., *The New Order*, 125–126.
42 Constable, ed., *The New Order*, 126.

denounce dissident pastors, who were then barred from the pulpit. On January 24, one offending Berlin minister was dragged from his bed by five young toughs and beaten. The next day, Hitler exercised his own brand of intimidation. He called Niemöller and eleven other Lutheran leaders to his office...his eleven colleagues hastily dissociated themselves from the Pastors' Emergency League. As Hitler recalled with satisfaction later, they "were so shaken with terror that they literally collapsed." That night, the Gestapo raided Niemöller's home. A few days later, a bomb exploded in his hallway. He was forced to take a leave of absence, and his less well-known associates were packed off to concentration camps.[43]

Niemöller did not cease his resistance against the Nazis. He was sent to a concentration camp in 1937, only days

after delivering a defiant sermon: "No more are we ready to keep silent at man's behest when God commands us to speak." Germany's Catholics, meanwhile, were learning for themselves what Hitler's pledge to respect religious traditions was worth. Not even an ironclad contract with the Nazi state could save the Catholic church from the brutal attentions of Nazi thugs. Early in 1934, the Nazis unleashed bands of Hitler Youth to bully Catholic youth groups into submission. The SS raided the other remaining Catholic organizations and forcibly disbanded them, confiscating their property. Undaunted, a few prominent German Catholics bravely protested Nazi policies that violated Church teachings.[44]

Although many Roman "Catholics in positions of authority went along with the regime and prayed quietly that conditions would improve" that hope largely ended on

June 30, 1934, when Hitler authorized the infamous Blood Purge.... On the long list of enemies abducted and shot, however, were

---

43 Constable, ed., *The New Order*, 126.
44 Constable, ed., *The New Order*, 126.

several outspoken Catholic activists and writers. In light of these murders, there could no longer be any doubt about Hitler's determination to silence Christians of conscience, whatever their denomination…. With the established churches effectively neutralized, the Nazis attempted to foster their own religion by replacing Christian rituals with secular ones that glorified the regime. The party issued guidelines for Nazi ceremonies "of a liturgical character, which shall be valid for centuries."[45]

Furthermore, in steps eerily similar to what is going on in the U.S. today, to reduce the influence of Christianity

the Nazis promoted a busy cycle of festivals that celebrated pagan and political turning points…. This new calendar was observed with particular zeal in Himmler's SS, which took the trend toward secular religion further by instituting its own rites for baptisms, weddings, and burials. A typical SS marriage ceremony took place by the light of torches, with changed refrains from a Wagnerian opera, a reading from Norse mythology, and a ritual exchange of bread and salt. Celebrants at SS "christenings" professed belief in the "mission of our German blood."[46]

As will be documented in this work, weaning of Americans from Christianity by banning public display of Christian symbols and ritual is remarkably reminiscent of what Nazi Germany did.[47] And Darwinism and its implications were a major impetus for these Nazi goals. As Keith concluded at the end of World War II, "Hitler is an uncompromising evolutionist, and we must seek…an evolutionary explanation if we are to understand his actions" against the Jews, the Christians, the handicapped, and against what he regarded as the misfits of society.[48] This is the goal of this volume.

---

45 Constable, ed., *The New Order*, 128.
46 Constable, ed., *The New Order*, 128–129.
47 Keysor, *Hitler, the Holocaust, and the Bible*.
48 Keith, *Evolution and Ethics*, 14.

01

The Holocaust: Government-sponsored mass murder inspired by social Darwinism

INTRODUCTION

In 1942, journalist Wallace Deuel wrote, "The Nazis are [now] engaged in the greatest programme of selective human breeding in all modern history. They have set out to change, by controlled procreation, the whole character of the German people."[1] Part of this programme of applying social Darwinism to society was the elimination of less fit humans, including Jews, Slavs and other "inferior" racial groups, a genocide programme collectively known today as the Holocaust.

The period of recent history called the Holocaust formally began in 1933 when Hitler assumed power in Germany. It ended only in 1945 when the Nazis were soundly defeated by the Allied nations. The term holocaust is from the Greek word *holokauston*, meaning "sacrifice by fire," and refers to the Nazis' persecution and planned total slaughter of all Jewish people in Europe. The Hebrew word *Shoah*, meaning "devastation, ruin or waste," is also used to refer to this historical genocide.

---

1   Wallace Deuel, *People under Hitler* (New York: Harcourt, Brace and Company, 1942), 180.

In addition to murdering Jews, the Nazis used Darwinian-inspired eugenics to justify the removal of several other "inferior races" and groups from the human gene pool. The categories the Nazis judged as "sub-human peoples" included Slavic peoples (especially Poles and Russians), Gypsies, Asiatic and Mongolian races and the disabled.[2] These peoples were labelled racially inferior and less evolved, and, consequently, were claimed to have a genetically corrosive influence on society. Anyone who actively resisted the Nazis, such as Jehovah's Witnesses and the communists, were often sent to forced labour camps to die or were murdered directly.[3]

The primary perpetrator of the Holocaust was a political party called the Nazis, an acronym for *Nationalsozialistische Deutsche Arbeit-erpartei* (in English, National Socialist German Worker's Party) and their supporters. The Nazis used a variety of terms to conceal their actual goals, which included the application of active social Darwinism to governmental policy, requiring the extermination of all inferior races. For example, the "Final Solution" phrase was a euphemism they used to refer to their plans to murder every Jew living in Europe.

THE GOD OF THE NAZIS

What the Nazis called Biologism (*Biologismus*) was "an essential feature of National Socialism," which acquired its ideological base largely by applying biology, specifically Darwinian evolution, to humans. The Nazis taught that both "the biological doctrine of race... and of the concept of 'Living Space,' [were], according to...Social Darwinism" fully

> justified by the "eternal struggle for existence" and the "right of the stronger." The theory of heredity had a particular impact, influencing National Socialist marriage law and providing a logic for the euthanasia program. The ideology of the "*Volk* Community"

---

2   Peter Longerich, *Holocaust: The Nazi Persecution and Murder of the Jews* (New York: Oxford University Press, 2010), 241.

3   Jerry Bergman, "The Jehovah's Witnesses' Experience in the Nazi Concentration Camps: A History of Their Conflicts with the Nazi State," *Journal of Church and State* 38, No. 1 (Winter 1996): 87–113.

was also derived from...biologism, which from the alleged primacy of species preservation over self-preservation inferred a natural law of the subordination of the individual to the community.[4]

The Nazis stressed that *Kampf* (often translated as "struggle") was "a central concept of National Socialist ideology." They taught that the basic force in human life was the struggle "among opposing powers and forces for dominance or destruction." To lend support to achieve this goal the Nazis appealed "to the authority of"

[Charles] Darwin ("struggle for existence"), and Nietzsche (struggle as the manifestation of the "will to power"). In the Social Darwinist sense, struggle was explained as the agent of political and racial selection.[5]

Darwin's 1871 book, *The Descent of Man*, influenced the Nazi "Theory of Descent" (*Abstammungslehre*) idea and explained the existence of

the present variety of species as the result of a process of natural selection. The struggle for existence allows only the best-adapted individuals to survive and reproduce, while the others are "culled out." In the biologistic worldview of National Socialism, the Theory of Descent became the model for human society, peoples, and races as well. Fantasies of master races and theories of racial value have their origins here.[6]

Darwinism influenced not only the development of the worldwide eugenics movement but also the academic elite's attempt to disenfranchise Christianity. As science historian Ronald Numbers concluded, in Darwin's "revolutionary essay *On the Origin of Species* (1859), Darwin aimed primarily 'to overthrow the dogma of separate creations'

---

4   Christian Zentner and Friedemann Bedürftig, eds., *The Encyclopedia of the Third Reich* (New York: Da Capo Press, 1997), 86.

5   Zentner and Bedürftig, eds., *The Encyclopedia of the Third Reich*, 488.

6   Zentner and Bedürftig, eds., *The Encyclopedia of the Third Reich*, 192.

and extend the domain of natural law throughout the organic world. He succeeded spectacularly."[7] As this book will document, in almost all cases, acceptance of Darwinism was accompanied by the rejection of Christianity, either as a cause or an effect. Many leading Nazis, such as Martin Bormann, were aggressively hostile to Christianity and what it stood for.

THE GERMAN SOCIETY FOR RACIAL HYGIENE

An important factor that contributed to the Holocaust was the support of many leading German academics. One example is The German Society for Racial Hygiene (*Deutsche Gesellschaft für Rassenhygiene*), an association founded in 1905 by Professor Alfred Ploetz to

> propagate the doctrine of racial purity as the sole means to stem the [genetic] decline of German *Volk*. It applied principles of animal and plant husbandry to human society ("social biology"), thus foreshadowing National Socialist racism (social Darwinism). It dissolved at the war's end in 1945.[8]

The *Gesellschaft für Rassenhygiene* was the major political organization behind the German racial policies and, as documented in Chapters 6 and 12, was supported by many leading scientists.

HITLER'S WORLDVIEW

Hitler was a committed Darwinist and "spoke repeatedly of his Darwinian worldview, such as in his book *Mein Kampf*," which documented that he "possessed an internally logical and consistent ideology and that he felt committed to its premises and goals to the end" of his life.[9] The basis of his worldview was "a central concept of National Socialist ideology," namely that the Darwinian "struggle for existence governed all beings," and involved "the right of the stronger applied to individuals as well as to communities" to suppress the racially inferior who

---

7   Ronald L. Numbers, *Science and Christianity in Pulpit and Pew* (New York: Oxford University Press, 2007), 53.

8   Zentner and Bedürftig, eds., *The Encyclopedia of the Third Reich*, 339–340.

9   Zentner and Bedürftig, eds., *The Encyclopedia of the Third Reich*, 192.

were destined for destruction. For the "sake of self-preservation" a "stronger race will displace the weak ones," and the "ridiculous fetters of so-called humanity" would break asunder, "in order to allow in its place the humanity of Nature, which destroys the weak in order to make way for the strong."[10]

Hitler was guided by the

> "nearly ironclad principle" of "Nature's will to live" in the "internal exclusivity of species among all living beings on earth." ...If unequal individuals were crossed, the offspring "no doubt will be superior to the racially inferior parental half, but not as advanced as the superior one. As a result it will later lose out in the struggle against a superior type. Such mating contradicts Nature's will to improve breeds." The result of this "ubiquitous instinct for racial purity in Nature is not only the sharp demarcations dividing individual races, but also their own internally uniform nature." These "iron laws of Nature" were also responsible for the evolution of human history, in which race and racial purity were allotted decisive significance.[11]

THE EXTENT OF THE HOLOCAUST

It is estimated that 55 million people died as a result of the Nazis war on those persons they regarded as "inferior races." Specifically, over 11 million people were murdered directly as part of the Holocaust, including over 5 million Slavic Christians and 6 million Jews. The Nazis murdered close to two-thirds of all Jews then living in Europe, including an estimated 1.1 million children, in their quest to create a superior race.

THE PERSECUTION BEGINS

The events leading up to the Holocaust were gradual and required a decade until the mass killing occurred by gassing in concentration camps. The beginning of the active Nazi persecution against Jews was

---

10 Zentner and Bedürftig, eds., *The Encyclopedia of the Third Reich*, 426–427.
11 Zentner and Bedürftig, eds., *The Encyclopedia of the Third Reich*, 426–427.

April 1, 1933, when the Nazis instigated their first formal action against German Jews by announcing a boycott of all Jewish-owned businesses. The first major formal step that would lead to the Holocaust was the Nuremberg Laws, passed on September 15, 1935, that began to exclude Jews from public life by the force of law. These laws stripped German Jews of their German citizenship and of all the rights of citizenship.

The Nuremberg Laws also prohibited marriages and extramarital sex between Jews and Germans because, in harmony with the racist eugenic policies of Nazi Germany, the Nazis believed the inferior genes of Jews would pollute the superior Aryan gene pool. The Nazis reasoned that reducing Jewish-Aryan contact as much as possible would lower the likelihood of sexual relations between the two "races," and, consequently, reduce the level of Aryan race degeneration.

The Nuremberg Laws also set the legal precedent for further anti-Jewish legislation and the anti-Jewish actions that soon followed. The Nazi leaders realized that they had to implement their genocide programme gradually to reduce public opposition, but ostensibly lawfully, to achieve their long-term eugenic goal of a pure, superior Aryan race. Additional anti-Jew laws included excluding Jews from parks, terminating them from civil service jobs (i.e., teaching and government work) and requiring Jews to register their property. One law even made it illegal for Jewish doctors to treat anyone other than Jewish patients. The wide-ranging set of anti-Semitic laws that were passed had the clear intent of, in Hermann Göring's words, "Aryaniz-ing" Germany.

Jews were also required to turn over all precious metals they owned to the government, as well as Jewish-owned bonds, stocks, jewellery and art works. Furthermore, pensions for Jews dismissed from civil service jobs were arbitrarily reduced. Next, Jews were physically seg-regated within German towns, their driver's licenses suspended, Jewish-owned radios were confiscated, a curfew to keep Jews off the streets between 9 P.M. and 5 A.M. in the summer, and between 8 P.M. and 6 A.M. in the winter was passed and laws protecting tenants were not applicable to Jewish tenants.[12]

---

12 Michael Burleigh and Wolfgang Wippermann, *The Racial State: Germany, 1933–1945* (New York: Cambridge University Press, 1991), 92–96.

The German Minister of the Interior also issued regulations prohibiting Jews from "acquiring, possessing, and carrying firearms and ammunition," as well as "stabbing weapons." Those possessing such weapons and ammunition were required to turn them over to the local police authority. This law would prevent Jews from defending themselves when the holocaust formally began. The noose was rapidly tightening around Jews, thus leading toward their eventual systematic murder in the Holocaust.

During the night of November 9, 1938, the Nazis incited a pogrom (a mob attack directed against a minority group characterized by killings and destruction of their property) against Jews in both Austria and Germany. This pogrom is now termed, *"Kristallnacht"* or the "Night of Broken Glass" because the windows of many Jewish-owned businesses were broken, showering the streets with glass. This night of violence included the pillaging and burning of close to 300 synagogues and massive looting of an estimated 7,500 Jewish-owned stores and shops. Thousands of Jews were also physically attacked, almost 100 were murdered, and approximately 25,000 to 30,000 were arrested and sent to concentration camps, mostly to Buchenwald.

This event is often regarded as the actual beginning of the Holocaust. The unlikely excuse used for the pogrom was the fact that a seventeen-year-old Polish Jew named Herschel Grynszpan, then living with his uncle in Paris, had murdered a German official in Paris. The main reason for Herschel's anger was the inhumane treatment his Jewish parents in Germany received from the Nazis.

Herschel's father, Zindel, was born in western Poland and moved to Hanover, Germany, in 1911 to establish a small store. On the night of October 27, the Grynszpan family's possessions were confiscated and they were forced to flee to Poland. When Herschel received news of his family's expulsion, he went to the German embassy in Paris on November 7 intending to assassinate the German Ambassador to France. After learning that the Ambassador was not in the embassy, he shot Third Secretary Ernst vom Rath. Rath was critically wounded and died two days later.

The assassination provided Hitler's Chief of Propaganda, Joseph Goebbels, with the excuse he needed to launch his pogrom against German Jews. Goebbels tried to spin Grynszpan's attack as a conspiratorial action against the Reich by "International Jewry" and, symbolically, against the Führer himself. Goebbels claimed they had received orders from the Führer that the "Jewish question be now, once and for all, coordinated and solved one way or another."[13]

The monetary cost of *Kristallnacht* was another problem for Germany because German insurance companies were legally required to pay for the damages to Jewish business and merchandise. The Nazis rationalized that the Jewish property was stolen from the German people and "it's insane to…burn a Jewish warehouse, then have a German insurance company make good [on] the loss." It was decided that, "since Jews were to blame for these events," they will "be held legally and financially responsible for the damages incurred by the pogrom. Accordingly, a "fine of 1 billion marks was levied for the slaying of vom Rath, and 6 million marks paid by insurance companies for broken windows was to be given to the state coffers."[14]

Consequently, the Jewish community was required to pay millions of Reichsmarks to Germany for the damage inflicted on them! After *Kristallnacht*, the persecution of Jews became more organized and far more widespread. This led to an exponential increase in the number of Jews sent to concentration camps.

By this time it was clear to Hitler and his top advisors that forced emigration of Jews was no longer a feasible option because almost no nation would accept them. Numerous concentration camps and forced labour camps were already in operation; therefore the Nazis decided to send them there. The "passivity of the German people in the face of the events of *Kristallnacht* made it clear that the Nazis would encounter little opposition—even from the German churches."[15] Although historian and professor Ronald Rychlak concluded that "Pope Pius XII did all within his power to negotiate peace and to save as many Jewish people as he could,"[16] he did far too little too late.

---

13 Douglas Brinkley, *World War II, 1939–1942: The Axis Assault* (New York: Times Books, 2003), 54.

14 Louis L. Snyder, *Encyclopedia of the Third Reich* (New York: Paragon, 1989), 201.

15 Mitchell Geoffrey Bard, ed., *The Complete History of the Holocaust* (San Diego: Greenhaven Press, 2001), 67.

16 Ronald Rychlak, *Hitler, the War and the Pope*, rev. ed. (Huntington: Our Sunday Visitor Books, 2010), 17.

Herschel Grynszpan (1921-1942)

Herschel's shooting of Ernst vom Rath gave the Nazis the excuse to launch their pogrom against German Jews.

After World War II began in 1939, the Nazis began ordering Jews to wear a yellow Star of David on their clothing so that they could be easily recognized and targeted for persecution. The German government recognized that most Jews could go underground or effectively blend into society because most German Jews in the 1930s were fully assimilated Germans. They often did not identify themselves as Jews first, but rather as Germans. Furthermore, in spite of the racial scientists claims, most German Jews were physically indistinguishable from Aryans.

The Nazis planned their holocaust very carefully and meticulously documented their activities because they believed the world would eventually celebrate their achievement of producing a superior race. They also wanted to prove to the world that they achieved what they saw as glorious work—such as finally eliminating the inferior parasitic races such as Jews.

THE NEXT STEP: GHETTOS

After World War II began, the Nazis began ordering all Jews to live within very specific regions of select large cities—these areas were called ghettos. Jews were forced out of their homes and relocated into smaller apartments inside these ghettos, often sharing them with other families.

Some ghettos started out as "open," meaning that the residents could leave the area during the daytime for work, but had to be back inside the ghetto before their curfew. Later on, all ghettos became "closed," trapping Jews within the confines of the ghetto walls. The major ghettos were located in the European cities of Warsaw, Lodz, Minsk, Riga, Vilna, Bialystok and Kovno. The largest ghetto was in Warsaw, Poland—at its height, in March 1941, its population reached almost 500,000.

In most ghettos, the Nazis ordered the Jews to establish a *Judenrat* (a Jewish council) to both administer Nazi demands and to regulate internal life in the ghetto. The organization allowed Nazis to effectively order deportations of large numbers of Jews from the ghettos to the concentration camps. When the "Final Solution" began, the larger ghettos loaded up to 1,000 people per day into cattle cars and sent them to either concentration or death camps.

Inside the Warsaw Ghetto
Young Jewish men being taken away (1941); after the Warsaw Uprising (1943).
Bundesarchiv, Bild 101I-134-0766-20 / photographer: Ludwig Knobloch;
Bundesarchiv, Bild 183-41636-0002 / photographer: unknown

To facilitate the Jews' cooperation, the Nazis repeatedly lied to them, such as telling them that they were being transported from the ghettos to work sites for labour when, in fact, they were being sent to their deaths, although the young and healthy were often worked to death. The Nazis eventually decided to murder all of the Jews remaining in the ghettos, "liquidating" them by boarding every one onto trains to be sent to death camps.

When the Nazis attempted to liquidate the Warsaw Ghetto on April 13, 1943, the remaining Jews fought back in what is now known as the Warsaw Ghetto Uprising. The Jewish resistance fighters had only a few small weapons yet held out against the Nazi regime for 28 days— longer than some European countries had been able to withstand Nazi conquest.

CONCENTRATION AND EXTERMINATION CAMPS

Although all Nazi camps are often referred to as "concentration camps," some camps were extermination camps, others labour camps, prisoner-of-war camps and transit camps. While concentration camps were designed to work and starve prisoners to death, extermination camps (also known as death camps) were built for the sole purpose of rapidly and efficiently killing large numbers of people. The six extermination camps were Auschwitz, Treblinka, Chelmno, Belzec, Sobibor and Majdanek. Auschwitz and Majdanek were both concentration and extermination camps. Auschwitz was the largest and most famous camp where an estimated 1.1 million people were systematically murdered.

One of the first concentration camps to be built was Dachau, in southern Germany, which opened on March 20, 1933. From 1933 until 1938, most of the inmates in this camp were political prisoners (i.e., people who spoke or acted in some way against Hitler or the Nazis, such as the communists and Jehovah's Witnesses) and those people that the Nazis labelled asocial.[17]

Life within Nazi concentration camps was often inhumane and cruel. Prisoners were given inadequate rations of food and other life

17 Detlef Garbe, *Between Resistance & Martyrdom: Jehovah's Witnesses in the Third Reich*, trans. Dagmar G. Grimm (Madison: The University of Wisconsin Press, 2008).

necessities, yet were forced to do hard physical labour for up to 12 hours a day. Eventually most were worked to death. Prisoners often slept with three or more people on each crowded wooden bunk, lacking mattresses and pillows. Both torture and death were frequent. At several Nazi concentration camps, Nazi doctors conducted painful, often lethal, medical experiments on prisoners against their will. One of the most well-known examples was the race medical experiments carried out by Dr. Josef Mengele, the subject of chapter 7.

Prisoners transported to the extermination camps were told to undress under the pretense of taking a shower to delouse them. Rather than taking a shower, the prisoners were actually herded into gas chambers, the doors locked, and then the innocent victims were murdered by poisonous gas. The prisoners at Chelmno were herded into gas vans instead of gas chambers. The purpose of the camps was to achieve the goal of a superior race by "breeding," a

term that originally referred only to the systematic increase and eventual improvement of animals and plants, but that Charles Darwin applied to humans. "With the exception of the human case, no breeder is so ignorant as to allow his worst animals to reproduce." In this sense, the term "breeding" was taken up by Houston Stewart Chamberlain and *völkisch* theorists such as Josef Lanz for their program of racial biology.[18]

Although Darwin evidently did not foresee the particular application of his ideas that the Nazis would adopt (i.e., slaughtering people) it was a very logical application of the ideas in his writings, especially his 1871 book, *The Descent of Man.*

The National Socialists strove for the "rebirth" of the nation "through the conscious breeding of a new human.... Racial breeding and pure breeding will be and must be the sole religion and church of the future."[19] The extent of the Nazi fanaticism was, according to Nazi ideologist Richard Walther Darré, Hitler's Minister for Food and Agriculture, such that they believed "only a few noble sires" were required

---

18 Zentner and Bedürftig, eds., *The Encyclopedia of the Third Reich*, 111.
19 Zentner and Bedürftig, eds., *The Encyclopedia of the Third Reich*, 111.

to raise the whole level of breeding and transmit noble traits to the offspring." Because mankind was also "naturally subject to the same laws of breeding," National Socialist leaders wanted, alongside the "exclusion of the worst," the artificial Selection of the "best Germans by dint of blood." Himmler in particular attempted after 1932 to fill the SS with a "racial selection of men."[20]

Hitler's "biologistic assumptions are the most extreme [example of] Social Darwinism," but his racial conceptions go back to at least as far as Count Arthur de Gobineau (1816–1882)

as popularized in Germany primarily by Houston Stewart Chamberlain. Agreements are obvious between *Mein Kampf* and Theodor Fritsch's *Handbuch der Judenfrage* (*Handbook of the Jewish Question*), which Dietrich Eckart called "our whole intellectual arsenal." In 1920…during his years in Vienna, Hitler was influenced by the racial ideas of Josef Lanz, as published in his *Ostara* journal. At the center of Lanz's ideas was the "blue-blond," the "Aryan race" as the "masterpiece of God," while the "dark races," among which were the Jews, were the "botched job of the Demon." Moreover [the Nazis believed], "everything hateful and evil [stemmed] from racial mixing."[21]

Hitler made his "Social Darwinist and racial-hygienic pronouncements" very clear and believed that they justified his brutal evolutionary "ideology of a struggle for existence." In his confluence of social Darwinist, racist, anti-Semitic and racial-hygienic ideas, Hitler thought he possessed a worldview that was grounded in natural science."[22]

THE MONSTERS BEHIND THE HOLOCAUST

It often is assumed that those who carried out the orders to murder over 11 million innocent non-combat men, women and children must have been monsters. This label actually separates these humans from

---

20 Zentner and Bedürftig, eds., *The Encyclopedia of the Third Reich*, 111.
21 Zentner and Bedürftig, eds., *The Encyclopedia of the Third Reich*, 429.
22 Zentner and Bedürftig, eds., *The Encyclopedia of the Third Reich*, 429.

ourselves, causing many to conclude that normal people never would have voluntarily carried out the crimes of the Nazis.

In fact, as we will document, many of the high level Nazi officers were outwardly very normal, family-oriented human beings. Interviews with Himmler's family show that Himmler and other leading Nazis were in many ways normal, if not exceptional, persons. The story of Joseph Goebbels' courtship of his wife is suitable for a touching Hollywood story. They were an attractive family that won the hearts of many within in the Reich. According to historians Rochus Misch (*Der Letzte Zeuge*) and Bernd Freytag von Loringhoven (*Mit Hitler im Bunker*), Goebbels and his wife killed their children, then themselves. Magda Goebbels said she could not bear to live in, or to have her children live in, a world without Hitler.

Himmler and the other leading Nazis also travelled fairly freely within both German and European society and were, as a whole, well liked by the German-speaking population.[23]

Himmler's daughter, Gudrun, his brother, Gebhard, and other family members found it very difficult to reconcile the public post-war image of Himmler as a monster with the kind and affectionate man that they knew and loved for almost five decades. For this reason, Roger Manvell and Heinrich Fraenkel strove in their research to "try to achieve this reconciliation, to try to understand why this simple, unassuming man became a mass-murderer convinced of the essential rightness of his actions."[24]

As will be documented, the Holocaust was an essential step required "in order to fulfil a false dream of racial purity which obsessed both Himmler and his master" Adolf Hitler.[25] No theme has dominated the Holocaust and the entire Nazi movement more than racism and the quest to achieve a pure superior race, a goal inspired by the eugenic ideas of Darwinism.

This is best illustrated by the fact that, forced to make a choice between winning the war or exterminating the Jews, Hitler chose

---

23 Roger Manvell and Heinrich Fraenkel, *Heinrich Himmler: The Sinister Life of the Head of the SS and the Gestapo* (New York: Skyhorse Publishing, 2007), xi-xii.

24 Manvell and Fraenkel, *Heinrich Himmler*, xiii.

25 Manvell and Fraenkel, *Heinrich Himmler*, xiv.

extermination of the Jews. The fact is, "Hitler believed that killing Jews was more important than winning the war."[26] Hitler was confident that the world would some day thank him for eliminating this inferior parasitic race, even if Germany lost the war.

THE SLAVIC HOLOCAUST

The Nazi Party's first priority was the eradication of Jews. Not far behind was the elimination of most of the Slavic peoples, who were seen as an inferior race, and subjugate the rest, or deport them from territory controlled by, and designated for, Aryans.[27] One of the best examples of the Slavic Holocaust was exemplified by the siege of the Soviet city of Leningrad (now called by its original Christian name, St. Petersburg) that occurred from 1941 to 1944, just short of 900 days long.[28]

The purpose was not just to level the city, but to murder all of its over 3 million inhabitants by starvation. The Germans surrounded the city, then destroyed most of the food supplies and waited for the residents to starve to death.[29] This clear example of genocide was based squarely on race. As one Jewish writer wrote about the ordeal,

That Social Darwinistic language ("struggle for survival") showed how theory justified murder. The goal of a typical siege is to make the enemy surrender, but in Leningrad giving up and getting bread wasn't even an option: Germans set up a minefield outside one area of the city to keep civilians from leaving and stationed artillery at other points with orders to fire on groups trying to surrender. The goal was extermination.[30]

---

26 Max Domarus, *The Essential Hitler: Speeches and Commentary* (Wauconda: Bolchazy-Carducci, 2007), 412.

27 Richard Weikart, "Hitler's Struggle for Existence against Slaves: Racial Theory and Vacillations in Nazi Policy toward Czechs and Poles" in Anton Weiss-Wendt, ed., *Eradicating Differences: The Treatment of Minorities in Nazi-Dominated Europe* (Newcastle: Cambridge Scholars Publishing, 2010), 61–84.

28 John Barber and Andrei Dzeniskevich, *Life and Death in Besieged Leningrad, 1941–44* (New York: Palgrave Macmillan, 2005), and Harrison Evans Salisbury, *The 900 Days: The Siege of Leningrad* (New York: Da Capo Press, 1969).

29 Leon Goure, *The Siege of Leningrad* (Palo Alto: Stanford University Press, 1981).

30 Marvin Olasky, "Darwinian Siege," *World Magazine* (April 11, 2009): 22.

In this, the "most murderous siege in world history," surviving by cannibalism became the "last refuge of the starving."[31] The "racially motivated starvation policy" became an integral part of German plans to exterminate those whom German scientists determined belonged to an inferior race.[32]

One of the next groups the Nazis wanted to exterminate was the Asiatic peoples. Longerich notes that the "murder of 'Asiatic' people in the Soviet Union is one of the chapters in the history of the Nazi regime's policies of racial annihilation that have yet to be written."[33] The Nazis had just begun to work on achieving this goal and managed to begin the systematic murder of those people whose "external appearance made them appear to be 'elements of inferior value with a predominantly Asiatic look.'"[34]

THE DARWINIAN JUSTIFICATION FOR WAR

The Nazi motivation for war was also derived from the racism that required the creation of a Great German Empire that extended well beyond the boundaries of Germany to supply

> the German *Volk* the "Living Space" supposedly necessary for its survival. The goal of German foreign policy was to be an "eastern policy [*Ostpolitik*], in the sense of obtaining the necessary soil for our German *Volk* [namely] of Russia and the subject states surrounding it."[35]

The Nazis believed that this central "goal could be realized only through a war—of that, Hitler and the other National Socialists had no doubt."[36] The reason only war could realize this goal was because

---

31 Olasky, "Darwinian Siege," *World Magazine* (April 11, 2009): 22.

32 Jörg Ganzenmüller, *Das belagerte Leningrad 1941–1944* (Paderborn, Germany: Ferdinand Schöningh Verlag, 2005), 17, 20.

33 Longerich, *Holocaust*, 241.

34 Longerich, *Holocaust*, 241.

35 Zentner and Bedürftig, eds., *The Encyclopedia of the Third Reich*, 624-625.

36 Zentner and Bedürftig, eds., *The Encyclopedia of the Third Reich*, 624-625.

[the] racism of National Socialism was permeated...by a primitive Darwinism—the idea that "the most universal, implacable law of life" was the "struggle (of a people) for its existence...if necessary, with other peoples who stand in the way of its own development as a people." The war of conquest to acquire "living space" for the German *Volk* was further intended to gain mastery by the "Aryan" German *Volk* and its state over the racially "inferior" Slavic peoples and states of eastern and east-central Europe, and ultimately would lead to German World hegemony.[37]

Racism was even involved in the "living space" (*Lebensraum*) ideology because National Socialists believed that territorial expansion was

implied in the geopoliticians' Social Darwinist schemes.... According to them, it fell to a "master race" to promote the subjection and "displacement" of lesser nationalities and races, even to the extent of extermination. In Hitler's view, the Bolshevik Revolution had been nothing more than a Jewish takeover in Russia. But since Jews could never build a state, "the giant empire in the East was ripe for a collapse," which would become the "most powerful confirmation of the correctness of the *völkisch* racial theory." The Final Solution of the Jewish question was thus an integral part of the war for Living Space, which, in February 1945, Hitler was still calling "the holy mission of my life" and the "reason for my existence."[38]

SUMMARY

The Holocaust progressed from living restrictions to genocide over a ten-year period, partly because no other way existed in a highly educated, advanced, industrialized nation to murder over 11 million people without problems from Christians and others. The Nazis had to take one step at a time to achieve this goal, which included the systematic annihilation of what their scientists judged as inferior,

---

37 Zentner and Bedürftig, eds., *The Encyclopedia of the Third Reich*, 624-625.
38 Zentner and Bedürftig, eds., *The Encyclopedia of the Third Reich*, 554.

sub-human, less evolved races, including almost all peoples in the world except Aryans.[39]

Lastly, it is now well documented that Darwinism was a critical part, not only of the Holocaust, but also of World War II and the quest for *Lebensraum*, which translated into conquering nations and either expelling the people living on the land or murdering them to enable the "superior" race to repopulate the land.[40]

---

39 Longerich, *Holocaust*, 24, 31, 132, 142.

40 Alan Steinweis, *Studying the Jew: Anti-Semitism in Nazi Germany* (Cambridge: Harvard University Press, 2006).

Adolf Hitler (1889–1945)
Führer of Germany from 1934 to 1945, Hitler took Darwinism to new and horrific lengths in his efforts to "engineer" a master German race.

Bundesarchiv, Bild 146-1990-048-29A / photographer: unknown

Adolf Hitler:
A doctrinaire Darwinist

INTRODUCTION

A central goal of Hitler and his government was the development and implementation of eugenics to produce a "superior race," often called the Aryan, Teutonic or Nordic race. At the very least, this goal required preventing the "inferior races" from mixing with those judged superior in order to reduce contamination of the gene pool. Hitler believed that what we today recognize as the human gene pool could be improved by using selective breeding, similar to how farmers breed superior cattle.

In formulating his racial ideas, Hitler relied heavily on Darwinism, especially the elaborations by Darwin's German disciples such as Professors Fritz Lenz and Ernst Haeckel. The "superior race" belief was based on the theory of racial inequality within each species, a major presumption and requirement of Darwin's original "survival of the fittest" theory.

This philosophy culminated in the Final Solution, the extermination of 6 million Jews and over 5 million Poles and others who belonged to what German scientists judged were "inferior races," including

Slavs and Gypsies.[1] Hitler's writings and speeches reveal that Darwin's theory and the writings of Darwinists had a major influence on his views of race and eugenics.

THE INFLUENCE OF DARWINISM ON HITLER

Although it is unknown if Hitler read Darwin's original writings, he did read those of Darwin's disciples.[2] One of the leading German eugenicists was Fritz Lenz, professor of eugenics at the University of Münich. Lenz's publisher, Julius F. Lehmann, was a close personal friend of Hitler. Lehmann's published many books that promoted "social Darwinist racism, eugenics, and anti-Semitism" and these books

> probably had a significant influence on Hitler's worldview. By the 1890s Lehmann was a leading Pan-German nationalist, and in 1907–8 he became excited about eugenics as a means to reju-venate the German nation. Toward the end of World War I Lehmann began publishing a magazine…which promoted many ideas that found their way into Hitler's ideology. Whether it reflected ideas that Hitler already embraced from other sources, or whether it decisively influenced his thought is unclear.[3]

Furthermore, Lehmann "regularly gave Hitler copies of the books he published on eugenics and racism" some of which are now part of Hitler's personal library captured by the U.S. army after World War II and now housed in the Library of Congress in Washington, D.C. We know that Hitler read many books on eugenics, racism and related topics because he tended to mark up the books he read, even adding his penciled notes in some.[4]

---

1   Richard Lukas, *The Forgotten Holocaust: The Poles under German Occupation 1939–1944* (New York: Hippocrene Books, 1997).

2   Philipp Gassert and Daniel S. Mattern, *The Hitler Library: A Bibliography* (Westport: Greenwood Press, 2001).

3   Richard Weikart, "The Impact of Social Darwinism on Anti-Semitic Ideology in Germany and Austria. 1860-1945," in Geoffrey Cantor and Marc Swetlitz, eds., *Jewish Tradition and the Challenge of Darwinism* (Chicago: The University of Chicago Press, 2006), 112.

4   Ambrus Miskolczy, *Hitler's Library* (New York: Central European University

Hitler's personal library included books by the "notorious race theorist Hans F.K. Günther," the chair in social anthropology at the University of Jena.[5] Hitler probably read Günther's works in the 1920s, possibly even before writing *Mein Kampf*. In his account of the history of racial ideas, Günther honoured Darwin for encouraging his research in racial anthropology, even repeating many common race stereotypes, such as the claim that "Jews lacked creativity and originality, except perhaps in the field of music."[6] Furthermore, Günther

maintained that the racial antagonism that Germans feel toward Jews is not a cultural artifact but rather is rooted in the German's blood. This idea, that racial animosity was a biological instinct helping to preserve the race in the human struggle for existence, was a common theme in biological racism in the early twentieth century. Finally, he suggested the strict separation of Germans and Jews as the only viable solution to the racial problem. He called intermarriage *Rassenchande* (racial disgrace), a favorite term of the Nazis later when enforcing the Nuremberg Laws.[7]

Another Nazi who reportedly had a major influence on Hitler was the charlatan Kurt Lüdecke, who read in depth on the topic of eugenics, and foremost among his reading was Sir Francis Galton and his book titled *Hereditary Genius*.[8] While all of the books Hitler read are unknown, it is clear that he knew about Darwin and eugenics because social Darwinist eugenic ideals were openly espoused in his two published books (one published after Hitler committed suicide; the other, *Mein Kampf*, made Hitler a fortune), as well as in many of his public speeches that clearly

---

Press, 2003); Gassert and Mattern, *The Hitler Library*.

  5 Weikart, "The Impact of Social Darwinism," 112–114.

  6 Weikart, "The Impact of Social Darwinism," 113.

  7 Weikart, "The Impact of Social Darwinism," 113.

  8 Kurt Lüdecke, *I Knew Hitler: The Story of a Nazi Who Escaped the Blood Purge* (London: Jarrolds, 1938), 30.

reflect the influence, either directly or indirectly, of Günther, Lenz...and other racial thinkers of his time. As many scholars have explained, Hitler's world-view revolved around race. He viewed history as a Darwinian racial struggle, with the victors expanding at the expense of the losers. He spurned any moral codes—especially ones benefiting the weak and sick—that would interfere with the ability of the "Aryan" race to triumph in this struggle.[9]

Hitler often discussed the motor of evolution, survival of the strongest race and the need to eliminate the weakest, obviously reflecting the Darwinian survival of the fittest idea. This "truth," Hitler wrote, is "obvious" because interbreeding of two life forms that are

not at exactly the same level produces a medium between the level of the two parents. This means: the offspring will probably stand higher than the racially lower parent, but not as high as the higher one. Consequently, it will later succumb in the struggle against the higher level. Such mating is contrary to the will of Nature for a higher breeding of all life. The precondition for this does not lie in associating superior and inferior, but in the total victory of the former. The stronger must dominate and not blend with the weaker, thus sacrificing his own greatness.[10]

Hitler used this Darwinistic philosophy to support his belief that, contrary to Christianity, the strong must dominate the weak, and the evolution of life would be impossible if this "law of Nature" was not allowed to prevail. In the struggle for life, the weak succumb, and the right to propagate is given "by Nature" only to the strongest.[11] Struggle is the means by which a superior species survives and a weaker one

---

9 Weikart, "The Impact of Social Darwinism," 112–114.

10 Adolf Hitler, *Hitler's Secret Conversations, 1941–1944*, trans. Norman Cameron and R.H. Stevens; intro. H.R. Trevor-Roper, "The Mind of Adolf Hitler" (New York: Farrar, Straus and Young, 1953), 285. As noted, the English translation of the work must be considered with caution.

11 George L. Mosse, *Nazi Culture: Intellectual, Cultural, and Social Life in the Third Reich* (Madison: University of Wisconsin Press, 1981).

perishes. Hitler reasoned that this struggle results in a species evolving to a higher level. In Hitler's words, the weak inferior humans

> can view this as cruel, but...if this law did not prevail, any conceivable higher development of organic living beings would be unthinkable. Therefore, here, too, the struggle among themselves arises less from inner aversion than from hunger and love. In both cases, Nature looks on calmly, with satisfaction.... In the struggle for daily bread all those who are weak and sickly or less determined succumb, while the struggle of the males for the female grants the right or opportunity to propagate only to the healthiest. And struggle is always a means for improving a species' health and power of resistance and, therefore, a cause of its higher development.[12]

He added that nature abhors the

> blending of a higher with a lower race, since, if she did, her whole work of higher breeding, over perhaps hundreds of thousands of years, might be ruined with one blow. Historical experience offers countless proofs of this. It shows with terrifying clarity that in every mingling of Aryan blood with that of lower peoples the result was the end of the cultured people.[13]

Hitler's proof for the harm resulting from mingling Aryans with "less evolved," thus inferior, races was his claim that by far the largest part of the North American population consisted of Germanic races "who mixed but little with the lower colored peoples," and, as a result, manifested a "different humanity and culture from Central and South America, where the predominantly Latin immigrants often mixed with the aborigines on a large scale." Hitler believed this observation documented the adverse effect of racial mixture. Furthermore Hitler claimed that the

---

12 Adolf Hitler, *Mein Kampf* (Cambridge: Houghton Mifflin/The Riverside Press, 1962), 285.

13 Hitler, *Mein Kampf*, 286.

Germanic inhabitant of the American continent, who has remained racially pure and unmixed, rose to be master of the continent; he will remain the master as long as he does not fall a victim to defilement of the blood. The result of all racial crossing is therefore in brief always the following: (a) Lowering of the level of the higher race; (b) Physical and intellectual regression and hence the beginning of a slowly but surely progressing sickness.[14]

Hitler also used evolution to justify war by arguing that the natural law, by which he meant natural selection,

teaches us with every look into its working, into its events, that the principle of selection dominates it, that the stronger remains victor and the weaker succumbs. It teaches us, that what often appears to someone as cruelty, because he himself is affected or because through his education he has turned away from the laws of nature, is in reality necessary in order to bring about a higher evolution of living organisms.[15]

Hitler also wrote about the dangers of the "higher" more evolved races breeding with the "lower" races in a now infamous account:

With satanic joy in his face, the black-haired Jewish youth lurks in wait for the unsuspecting girl who he defiles with his blood, thus stealing her from her people. With every means he tries to destroy the racial foundations of the people he has set out to subjugate. Just as he himself systematically ruins women and girls, he does not shrink back from pulling down the blood barriers for others, even on a large scale. It was and it is Jews who bring the Negroes into the Rhineland, always with the same secret thought and clear aim of ruining the hated white race by the necessarily resulting bastardization, throwing it down from its cultural and political height, and himself rising to be its master. For a racially

---

14 Hitler, *Mein Kampf*, 286.

15 Cited in Richard Weikart, *Hitler's Ethic: The Nazi Pursuit of Evolutionary Progress* (New York: Palgrave MacMillan, 2009), 50.

pure people which is conscious of its blood can never be enslaved by the Jew. In this world he [the Jew] will forever be master over bastards and bastards alone. And so he tries systematically to lower the racial level by a continuous poisoning of individuals.[16]

Hitler reasoned that a "higher race would always conquer a lower" race because this is what the law of evolution demands.[17] In the 1933 Nuremberg party rally, Hitler explained that a higher race should rule a lower race because this is a "right which we see in nature and which can be regarded as the sole conceivable right" because it was founded on the scientific fact of evolution.[18] Evolution is clearly expressed in Hitler's analogy that human evolutionary progress is similar to climbing a ladder, noting that

it is impossible to climb higher without first taking the lower steps. Thus, the Aryan had to take the road to which reality directed him and not the one that would appeal to the imagination of a modern pacifist. The road of reality is hard and difficult, but in the end it leads where our friend [the pacifist] would like to bring humanity by dreaming, but unfortunately removes [humanity] more [away from the dream] than bringing it closer.[19]

Hitler also deduced that under conditions of limited reproduction, if the birth rate decreased, then the natural struggle for existence, which allows only the strongest and healthiest to survive, will be replaced by the mistaken anti-evolutionary desire to save the weakest and sickest. Hitler reasoned the result of this misguided approach is that the progeny of the strong who breed with the weak will cause the offspring to be inferior to the strong, resulting in the degeneration of the race. Therefore, the weaker race will eventually replace the stronger.

---

16 Hitler, *Mein Kampf*, 325.

17 Robert Clark, *Darwin: Before and After* (Grand Rapids: Grand Rapids International Press, 1958), 115.

18 *The Nuremberg Trials*, 14:279, cited in Joseph Tenenbaum, *Race and Reich* (New York: Twayne, 1956), 211–212.

19 Hitler, *Mein Kampf*, 295.

It is for this reason that the drive for life will decimate what Hitler described as the "so-called humaneness of individuals." In other words, the inferior races must be destroyed to make room for the superior races, and what Hitler believed was misplaced Christian humaneness will only interfere with this goal.

Historian Professor Richard Weikart documented that Hitler's "evolutionary ethic swept aside any humane impulses and provided a way to justify any action, no matter how abominable, if it promoted the interests of the 'best' humans."[20] In Hitler's words, if reproduction

> is limited and the number of births diminished, the natural struggle for existence which leaves only the strongest and healthiest alive is…replaced by the obvious desire to 'save' even the weakest and most sickly at any price; and this plants the seed of a future generation which must inevitably grow more and more deplorable the longer this mockery of Nature [evolution] and her will continues.[21]

As a result of his policy, Hitler concluded that the stronger race will replace the weaker one. Furthermore, the drive for survival will decimate the "fetters of the so-called humanity of individuals," resulting in the elimination of the weak and giving their place to the strong.

Hitler believed that humans were animals to which the genetic laws learned from livestock breeding can, and should, be applied. Instead of permitting natural forces and chance to control evolution, the government must control evolution in order to advance the human race. The first step to achieve this goal was to isolate the "inferior races" to prevent them from further contaminating the "Aryan" gene pool.[22] Inferior races included not only Jews but also Slavs (mostly Russians, Poles, Czechoslovakians and Ukrainians). Although the "Germans intended to eliminate the Jews before the end of the war, most Poles would work as helots [a class of serfs between a slave and freeman]

---

20 Weikart, "The Impact of Social Darwinism," 114.

21 Hitler, *Mein Kampf*, 132.

22 Leon Poliakov, *The Aryan Myth* (New York: Barnes & Noble, 1996).

until they too ultimately shared the fate of the Jews."[23] The reason was to "the Nazis, the Poles were *Untermenschen* (subhumans)...subjected to a program of extermination and enslavement."[24] The same fate awaited the Russians for the same reason.[25]

The widespread public support for this policy was partly a result of the belief common among the educated classes, that it was scientifically proven that certain races were genetically inferior. Hitler believed that he was simply applying facts proven by science to produce a superior race of humans as part of his plan for a better world. He believed that the "business of the corporate state was eugenics or artificial selection–politics as applied biology."[26] He even used his belief in human evolution to justify his own vegetarianism, noting that "monkeys, our ancestors of prehistoric times, are strictly vegetarian."[27]

As early as 1925, Hitler outlined in Chapter 4 of *Mein Kampf* his view that application of Darwinism to society was the *only* basis for a successful Germany to which the title of his most famous work—in English, *My Struggle*—alluded. Although the title refers to Hitler's own struggle, the Darwinian struggle for existence was an important theme of Hitler's writings. As Clark concluded, Adolf Hitler "was captivated by evolutionary teaching—probably since the time he was a boy. Evolutionary ideas—quite undisguised—lie at the basis of all that is worst in *Mein Kampf* and in his public speeches."[28] As an adult, Hitler "foresaw the biological evolution of Germans into supermen."[29]

Hickman adds it is no coincidence that Hitler firmly believed in Darwinism and "whatever the deeper, profound, complexities of his psychosis, it is certain" that the concept of struggle was important because his book, *Mein Kampf*, clearly set forth "evolutionary ideas, particularly those emphasizing struggle, survival of the fittest, and the

23 Lukas, *The Forgotten Holocaust*, 4.

24 Lukas, *The Forgotten Holocaust*, 4.

25 Leon Goure, *The Siege of Leningrad* (Palo Alto: Stanford University Press, 1981).

26 George Stein, "Biological Science and the Roots of Nazism," *American Scientist* 76, No. 1 (Jan–Feb 1988): 50–58.

27 Hitler, *Hitler's Secret Conversations*, 189.

28 Clark, *Darwin: Before and After*, 115.

29 George Victor, *Hitler: The Pathology of Evil* (Washington: Brassey's, 1998), 96.

extermination of the weak to produce a better society."[30] Furthermore, the conclusion that evolution can be directed by scientists to produce a "superior race" was the *central leitmotif* of Nazism. Although Hitler drew his racist ideology from many sources, the "concatenation of ideas and nightmares which made up the...social policies of the Nazi state, and to a considerable extent its military and diplomatic policies as well, can be most clearly comprehended in the light of its vast racial program."[31]

Weikart documented that Hitler "synthesized traditional anti-Semitic stereotypes into an overarching social Darwinist framework" and, as a result, Darwinist racism contributed

> several elements to anti-Semitic ideology. First, Darwinism entailed biological variation within species, and many, including Darwin himself, thought this meant racial inequality. Second, the Malthusian population principle and the struggle for existence suggested that human populations were expanding faster than the food supply, so masses of humans would necessarily die in each generation, with only the fittest surviving. Third, social Darwinism contributed to the rising fear of biological degeneration by the end of the nineteenth century. Fourth, Darwinism provided the foundation for eugenics, which was a key ingredient in the Nazi worldview. Finally, biological racism increased substantially after the advent of Darwinism. To be sure, Darwinism did not necessarily imply biological racism (just as it did not necessarily imply eugenics), but nonetheless Darwinism gave impetus to hereditarian thought, and most biological racists were also avid Darwinists.[32]

To Hitler, individuals are not only *far less important* than the race but, he added, certain races were animals that he "labeled subhumans." It was, therefore, "both legal and right to exterminate them in the collectivist and evolutionist viewpoint. They were not considered... persons in the sight of the German government."[33]

---

30 Richard Hickman, *Biocreation* (Worthington: Science Press, 1983), 51–52.
31 Tenenbaum, *Race and Reich*, vii.
32 Weikart, "The Impact of Social Darwinism," 115.
33 John Whitehead, *The Stealing of America* (Westchester: Crossway, 1983), 15.

As a result, the Darwinist movement, especially as developed by the father of German evolution, Ernst Haeckel, became one of the most powerful forces in the nineteenth- and twentieth-century German intellectual history, which served as a prelude to Nazism. Evolution caught hold in Germany faster and took a firmer grasp there than in any other place in the world, and when Germans referred to Darwinism, they often were thinking of Haeckel's interpretation of Darwinism.[34]

HITLER'S EUGENIC GOALS

Hitler's policies resulted from the idealistic goal of preventing "pollution" of the superior Aryan race by putative inferior races. He elaborated his Darwinian views by comparing the strong killing the weak to a cat devouring a mouse. The Jews, especially, must ultimately be eliminated so they will no longer pollute Aryan blood. Hitler admitted that one might be "repelled by this law of nature which demands that all living things should mutually devour one another," but the fact is that the "fly is snapped up by a dragon-fly, which itself is swallowed by a bird, which itself falls victim to a larger bird...to know the laws of nature enables us to obey them."[35] This is one example of many where

Hitler couched his rhetoric in primitive, Darwinian slogans about animals and their biological nature. To him the struggle of a species to survive meant constant war with another species until one of them was extinct. (Survival struggles of most species have no resemblance to genocidal warfare. Some species kill members of another species at hand, but they have no instinct to eradicate the species.) He believed Aryans were more than a national group—they were a genetically determined race, a species superior to others. And Germany's enemies—Jews and Slavs—were enemies by nature and evil by nature. They could not change, and the only sensible strategy was to eradicate them.[36]

---

34 Daniel Gasman, *The Scientific Origin of National Socialism* (New York: American Elsevier, 1971).

35 Hitler, *Hitler's Secret Conversations*, 116.

36 Victor, *Hitler: The Pathology of Evil*, 108.

Hitler then argued it is for this reason that governments must both understand and apply the "laws of Nature," especially the "survival of the fittest" law that originally produced the human races and also is the source of their further evolution. The government for this reason must aid in the elimination, or at the least quarantine, of inferior races. Hitler was especially determined to prevent Aryans from breeding with non-Aryans, a concern that eventually resulted in his Final Solution because

> Germans were the higher race, destined for a glorious evolution-
> ary future. For this reason it was essential that the Jews should
> be segregated, otherwise mixed marriages would take place.
> Were this to happen, all nature's efforts "to establish an evolution-
> ary higher stage of being may thus be rendered futile."[37]

Ironically, Hitler ignored his own race theory when it was convenient, and placed many Jews (most all were *Mischlinge*, part Jewish, but still Jewish according to the Nazi definition) in high positions to further his military goals.[38]

HITLER'S VIEWS OF BLACKS

Hitler strongly condemned both Africans and the missionaries who tried to convert them. He believed that as a result of religious teaching, humans "no longer bother to breed the best for posterity" and then are

> full of amazement at the small effect of the Christian faith in
> their own country, at the terrible "godlessness," at this physically
> botched and hence spiritually degenerate rabble, and try with
> the Church's Blessing, to make up for it by success with the
> Hottentots and Zulu Kaffirs. While our European peoples...fall
> into a condition of physical and moral leprosy, the pious mission-
> ary wanders off to Central Africa and sets up Negro missions

---

37 Clark, *Darwin: Before and After*, 115.

38 Bryan Mark Rigg, *Hitler's Jewish Soldiers: The Untold Story of Nazi Racial Laws and Men of Jewish Descent in the German Military* (Lawrence: University of Kansas, 2002).

until there, too…though primitive and inferior, human beings [degenerate] into a rotten brood of bastards.[39]

Hitler even claimed that the "Christian churches, instead of annoying Negroes with missions which they neither desire nor understand," and allowing inferior persons to have their own children, should instead "take pity on a poor little healthy [Aryan] orphan child and give him father and mother" rather then allowing Negroes to give birth to inferior children that

> will only bring unhappiness and suffering on himself and the rest of the world. The folkish state must make up for what everyone else today has neglected…. *It must set race in the center of all life. It must take care to keep it pure.*[40]

Hitler also wrote that the "boundless sins" of humanity are shown by one example, namely the fact "that some…Negro has…become a lawyer, teacher, even a pastor." He added that while what he called the

> idiotic bourgeoisie looks with amazement at such miracles of education, full of respect for this marvelous result of modern educational skill, the Jew shrewdly draws from it a new proof for the soundness of his theory about the *equality of men* that he is trying to funnel into the minds of the nations. It doesn't dawn on this depraved bourgeois world that this is positively a sin against all reason; that it is criminal lunacy to keep on drilling a born half-ape until people think they have made a lawyer out of him, while millions of members of the highest culture-race must remain in entirely unworthy positions…. The same pains and care employed on intelligent races would a thousand times sooner make every single individual capable of the same achievements.[41]

---

39 Hitler, *Mein Kampf*, 403.

40 Hitler, *Mein Kampf*, 403, emphasis in original.

41 Hitler, *Mein Kampf*, 430, emphasis in original.

Hitler concluded that "contamination by Negro blood on the Rhine in the heart of Europe is just as much in keeping with the perverted sadistic thirst for vengeance of this hereditary enemy of our people as is the ice-cold calculation of the Jew." This began the "bastardizing the European continent at its core" which deprived "the white race of the foundations for a sovereign existence through infection with lower humanity."[42] The end result was many of the few blacks that lived in Nazi Germany also suffered persecution.[43] The racial scientists disagreed on exactly which races were inferior, but most all eugenic scientists agreed that "there was never any doubt about…blacks."[44]

ORIENTALS ALSO AN INFERIOR RACE

The Nazi leadership also regarded the Orientals as an inferior race but wanted to retain them as allies until the war was won—then they would decide what to do about the oriental problem. It is for this reason that Hitler taught that the state should determine who can marry based on racial lines so as to prevent producing a "monster halfway between men and apes."[45] Goebbels claimed that "Hitler made fun of the Japanese Minister after an evening party in the Chancellery, and said that [Minister] Matsuoka reminded him of a yellow ape from the primeval jungle."[46]

Once the inferior races (evidently all humans but Aryans) were all exterminated, Hitler believed that future generations would be eternally grateful for the benefits that his race programmes brought to humanity. As a committed Darwinist, Hitler "consciously sought to make the practice of Germany conform to the theory of evolution" in order to benefit all humanity.[47] British evolutionist Arthur Keith added that, if war is the progeny of evolution,

---

42 Hitler, *Mein Kampf*, 624.

43 Firpo Carr, *Germany's Black Holocaust, 1890–1945: The Untold Truth!* (Los Angeles: Scholar Technological Institute, 2003).

44 George L. Mosse, *Toward the Final Solution: A History of European Racism* (New York: Howard Fertig, 1978), 81.

45 Hitler, *Mein Kampf*, 132.

46 Rudolf Semmler, *Goebbels: The Man Next to Hitler* (London: Westhouse, 1947), 26.

47 Arthur Keith, *Evolution and Ethics* (New York: G.P. Putnam's Sons, 1946), 230.

and I am convinced that it is—then evolution has "gone mad," reaching such a height of ferocity as must frustrate its proper role in the world of life—which is the advancement of her competing "units," these being tribes, nations, or races of mankind.[48]

Keith also believed that there is no way of eliminating war "save one, and that is to rid human nature of the sanctions imposed on it by the law of evolution. Can man…render the law of evolution null and void? …I have discovered…. There is no escape from human nature."[49] The problem was "Germany has drunk the vat of evolution to its last dregs, and in her evolutionary debauch[ery] has plunged Europe into a bath of blood."[50] As a committed Darwinist, Keith added that this fact is not proof that the law of evolution is evil because, "A law which brought man out of the jungle and made him king of beasts cannot be altogether bad."[51]

SUMMARY

Of the many factors that produced Hitler's eugenic and genocidal programmes, according to his own writings, one of the more important was Darwin's notion that evolutionary progress occurs primarily as a result of the elimination of the weak in the struggle for survival and allowing the strong to flourish.[52] Although it is no easy task to assess all of the many conflicting motives of Hitler, Darwin-inspired eugenics clearly played a critical role. It both justified and encouraged Hitler's views on eugenics, race, and war. Darwinism also played a major role in the early twentieth century eugenics movement in other nations including America and Canada.[53]

---

48 Keith, *Evolution and Ethics*, 105.

49 Keith, *Evolution and Ethics*, 105.

50 Keith, *Evolution and Ethics*, 105.

51 Keith, *Evolution and Ethics*, 105.

52 Jerry Bergman, "Darwinism as a Factor in the Twentieth-Century Totalitarianism Holocausts," *Creation Research Society Quarterly* 39, Vol. 1:47–53.

53 Edwin Black, *War against the Weak: Eugenics and American's Campaign to Create a Master Race* (New York: Four Walls Eight Windows Press, 2003); Harry Bruinius, *Better for All the World: The Secret History of Forced Sterilization and America's Quest for Racial Purity* (New York: Knopf, 2006).

Hitler not only unabashedly intended to produce a superior race, he also openly relied on Darwinian thought in both his extermination and war policies.[54] The Holocaust was one of the fruits of Hitler's reading literature "on social Darwinism that had formed the basis of Hitler's education."[55] Hitler firmly believed that the world would eventually appreciate his programmes that lifted humans to genetically higher levels as a result of reducing race pollution by preventing superior Aryans from breeding with inferior races:

> Hitler was influenced above all by the theories of the nineteenth-century social Darwinist school, whose conception of man as biological material was bound up with impulses towards a planned society. He was convinced that the race was disintegrating, deteriorating through faulty breeding as a result of a liberally tinged promiscuity that was vitiating the nation's blood. And this led to the establishment of a catalogue of 'positive' curative measures: racial hygiene, eugenic choice of marriage partners, the breeding of human beings by the methods of selection on the one hand and extirpation on the other.[56]

As Rudolf Höss adds, "such a struggle, legitimized by the latest scientific views, justified the racists' conceptions of superior and inferior people and nations and validated the conflict between them."[57] Historian George Victor concluded that the Holocaust was largely Hitler's idea, and "he believed correctly that, if he died before launching it, there would be no Holocaust. The men Hitler had designated as his successors—Hoess and Göring—did not share his genocide intentions" and, Victor claimed, openly opposed dealing with the problem of inferior races by murder.[58] Hitler's leadership was critical in birthing

---

54 E. Jackel, *Hitler's Weltanschauung* (Middletown: Wesleyan University Press, 1972).

55 Joachim C. Fest, *The Face of the Third Reich: Portraits of the Nazi Leadership* (New York: Pantheon, 1970), 273.

56 Fest, *The Face of the Third Reich*, 99

57 Rudolf Höss, *Commandant of Auschwitz: Autobiography of Rudolf Höss* (Cleveland: World Publishing Company, 1959), 110.

58 Victor, *Hitler: The Pathology of Evil*, 187.

the Holocaust, and Darwinism played a central role in Hitler's beliefs about race.[59]

Genetic research indicates the possibility that Hitler had Jewish background, which makes his inferiority concerns somewhat ironic. Jean-Paul Mulders traced Hitler's living relatives in both the Führer's native Austria and the United States. Geneticists identified groups of genes called haplogroups that define populations. Hitler's dominant haplogroup, E1b1b, is relatively rare in Western Europe, but between 50 an 80 per cent of North Africans share Hitler's dominant group, which is especially prevalent among in the Berber tribes of Morocco, Algeria, Tunisia and Somalia. Hitler's second most dominant haplogroup is the most common in Ashkenazi Jews. As Decorte noted, "The findings are fascinating if you look at them in terms of the Nazi worldview, which ascribed such an extreme priority to notions of blood and race. This pure type of 'superman' and the [Nazi] breeding programs to perfect 'purity' were sheer fabrication."[60]

---

59 Richard Weikart, *From Darwin to Hitler* (New York: Palgrave Macmillan, 2004); Paul Weinding, *Health, Race and German Politics between National Unification and Nazism, 1870–1945* (Cambridge: Cambridge University Press, 1989).

60 Cited in Haaretz Service, "DNA tests reveal Hitler's Jewish and African roots," *Jewish World* (August 24, 2010): 1.

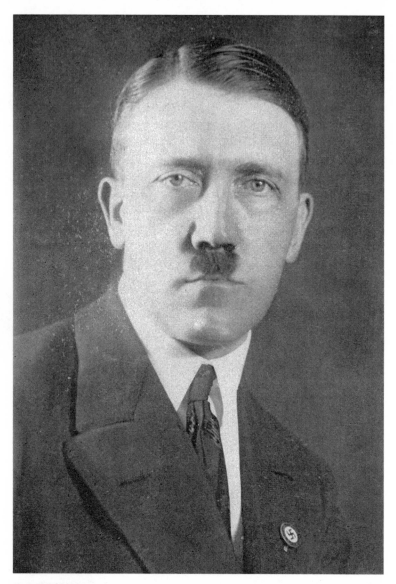

Adolf Hitler

Though his mother was a devout Catholic, his father was agnostic—and it was this worldview that Hitler adopted while very young and held to for his lifetime.

Bundesarchiv, Bild 102-18375 / photographer: unknown, circa 1923/1924

Was Adolf Hitler a Christian?

INTRODUCTION

It is claimed by some, especially by atheists and critics of Christianity, that Adolf Hitler was a Christian because he was baptized as a Catholic, was never excommunicated, was once an altar boy, at times used Christian vocabulary and even talked about the Almighty's blessings on his work.[1] Some then argue against Christianity, asking, "How could Christianity be true when it has such examples as the believing Christian Adolf Hitler (some even adding that he was a devout Christian)?"

Richard Dawkins takes the approach that Hitler may not have been a Catholic or a Christian, but he was not an atheist either. Dawkins further argued that "Hitler's...anti-Semitism owed a lot to his never-renounced Roman Catholicism."[2] Dawkins later wrote that "Hitler was born into a Catholic family, and went to Catholic schools and churches as a child...never formally renounced his Catholicism, and there are

---

1 Kevin Phillips, *Post-Conservative America: People, Politics, and Ideology in a Time of Crisis* (New York: Random House, 1982), 161.

2 Richard Dawkins, *A Devil's Chaplain: Reflections on Hope, Lies, Science, and Love* (Boston: Houghton Mifflin, 2003), 158.

indications throughout his life that he remained religious."[3] Dawkins then quotes a man who was very close to Hitler, Rudolf Hess, who once stated that Hitler was a good Catholic Christian, and German General Gerhard Engel who claimed Hitler told him, "I shall remain a Catholic for ever."[4] Dawkins does not openly state, but implies by these quotes and several like it, that Hitler was at least a theist, if not a Catholic. Some go even farther than Dawkins' modest claim about Hitler. For example, Wayne Paulson writes:

> My overall motivation is to help hasten the day when all religions will become extinct. I view them as being very harmful to society and to individuals. Their irrational nature allows for the justification of any belief and atrocity. After all, if the God of Christianity commits murder, torture, genocide, and advises cannibalism (still practiced today in the Eucharist), what is so terrible about killing a few more thousand people in a god's name? The recent attack on the World Trade Center is but one example of the danger of such beliefs. The Nazi Holocaust is another—a direct consequence of centuries of Christian anti-Judaism and anti-Semitism by Christianity—primarily the Catholic and Lutheran churches. *Hitler, a Roman Catholic Christian*, finally carried it out—in the most Christian country in the world, with the willing support of the public, and with Swastika flags flying proudly in the churches.[5]

This paragraph, although based on certain valid observations, is irresponsible. One atheist website goes so far as to claim that Hitler was not only a Christian but "agreed with the modern 'intelligent design' creationists," and was also "a religious fanatic, a Christian and a creationist."[6] Obviously, whether or not Hitler was a Christian is, at best,

---

3   Richard Dawkins, *The God Delusion* (Boston: Houghton Mifflin, 2006), 273.

4   Dawkins, *The God Delusion*, 273–274.

5   http://waynepaulson.topcities.com/DialogX1.htm; accessed March 12, 2005; emphasis mine.

6   Anonymous, "Hitler's Religion" (http://www.creationtheory.org/Essays/Hitler. xhtml; accessed August 10, 2012); and "Atheist Morality: Was Hitler an Atheist?" (http://www.creationtheory.org/Morality/AtheistMorality-Hitler.xhtml; accessed August 10, 2012).

only indirectly related to Christianity's validity, but the question has come up so often that it is necessary to address in some detail this claim.

HITLER'S ATTITUDES TOWARD CHRISTIANITY AS A YOUTH

Hitler clearly had strong, even vociferous anti-religious feelings as an adult, as did most high-level Nazi party leaders. Hitler's mother was a devout Catholic, but his father was an active agnostic. Hitler eventually rejected his mother's religion and adopted his father's worldview. When very young, Hitler was a "small, pale choirboy...pious believer," but as he got older he leaned more and more toward his father's "free-thinking attitude."[7] Hitler scholar George Victor wrote that Hitler "grew up anti-Christian and a near atheist."[8]

Hitler's closest childhood friend, August Kubizek, wrote that for the entire time he knew Hitler, he (Hitler) not only never attended mass, but refused to go with his mother when she attended. She was very disappointed and begged him to go to mass but, evidently, she eventually came to "terms with the fact that her son wanted to follow another path"—his father's.[9] Hitler was obviously very influenced by so-called free thinkers. He once excitedly told Kubizek about a book he was reading on "the Church witch-hunts" and "on another occasion one about the Inquisition," both of which made him outraged against the church. Hitler made his own religious beliefs very clear as an adult: "I myself am a heathen to the core."[10]

HITLER'S VIEWS ABOUT CHRISTIANITY

The antagonism of Hitler and the Nazis to Judaism is well known. In short, the Nazis drew "on a crude form of Darwinism" in order to define themselves "as a racial group bent on world domination."[11] Although Hitler often claimed Germany's war was about such traditional reasons as the need for more *lebensraum* (living space for the

---

7 August Kubizek, *The Young Hitler I Knew* (London: Greenhill Books, 2006), 94.

8 George Victor, *Hitler: The Pathology of Evil* (Washington: Brassey's, 1998), 21.

9 Kubizek, *The Young Hitler*, 95.

10 Cited in Adolf Hitler, *The Speeches of Adolf Hitler, April 1922–August 1939*, ed. Norman Baynes (New York: Oxford University Press, 1942), 369.

11 Jack R. Fischel and Susan M. Ortmann, *The Holocaust and Its Religious Impact: A Critical Assessment and Annotated Bibliography* (Westport: Praeger, 2004), 43–44.

superior race to expand into), he made it clear that he "hated Christianity" and eventually was going to eradicate it after the war ended.

One reason for Hitler's fervent opposition to Christianity was that he believed that "it had crippled everything noble about humanity."[12] In words reported to be Hitler's, "The heaviest blow that ever struck humanity was the coming of Christianity."[13] Hitler was influenced by one of his idols, Alfred Rosenberg, who taught that the Old Testament was a Jewish book, and for this reason Christianity, which is based on the Hebrew Scriptures, must be eliminated from Germany.[14]

His reasoning was based on his belief that Christianity was an "illegitimate" Jewish child and, as a Jewish child, it was swine like its parent—both needed to be eradicated. Although Hitler singled out the Jesuits for special scorn, all of Christianity was "Jewish Christianity," which was comparable with "Jewish Bolshevism." Hitler considered Christianity the "invention of the Jew Saul."[15] In short "the Aryan race had been conquered by the Semitic spirit in the form of Christianity. Christianity was…a Semitic import, which had weakened the fabric of the Aryan race by virtue of introducing moral commandments, which protected the weak from the strong."[16] Hitler concluded that Judaism and Christianity were both evil, calling them Bolshevists, swine or worse, and for this reason, both had to be destroyed.[17]

This view of Hitler influenced most of the leaders of the Nazi hierarchy. One Nazi official wrote, the reason he resigned from the Christian church was because as a "National Socialist and opponent of Jews, it is impossible for me to continue to belong to present-day Christianity, because it is supported by the Old Testament, which is Jewish and friendly to Jewish things."[18] He stressed that "Christianity

---

12 Cited in Ian Kershaw, *Hitler 1936–45: Nemesis* (New York: W.W. Norton, 2000), 936.

13 Adolf Hitler, *Hitler's Secret Conversations, 1941–1944*, trans. Norman Cameron and R.H. Stevens; intro. H.R. Trevor-Roper, "The Mind of Adolf Hitler" (New York: Farrar, Straus and Young, 1953), 6.

14 Karla Poewe, *New Religions and the Nazis* (New York: Routledge, 2006), 118.

15 Larry Azar, *Twentieth Century in Crisis* (Dubuque: Kendall Hunt, 1990), 154.

16 Fischel and Ortmann, *The Holocaust and Its Religious Impact*, 44.

17 Kershaw, *Hitler 1936–45*, 330, 488.

18 Poewe, *New Religions and the Nazis*, 118.

and Bolshevism" were "two versions of the eternal revolutionary Jewish threat" and that when Germany exterminates these plagues they will have performed a deed for the good of humanity.[19] The Nazis used the state-controlled schools and universities to achieve this goal. Consequently, a

> major priority of Nazi educators was the liberation of the fierce Germanic instincts which more than a thousand years of foreign influence had repressed; and in their estimation, Christianity bore a major responsibility for blunting the expression of that Germanic spirit. The new German schools would help create a militarized society which would both purge the national spirit and promote the high-tension ethos which accepted war as a normal condition in a life of struggle.[20]

Germany's main father of Darwinism, Ernst Haeckel, argued in his *Natural History of Creation* (1868) that "the church with its morality of love and charity is an effete fraud, a perversion of the natural order."[21] This natural order, namely Darwinian natural selection, functions "without the recourse to mercy or compassion in the Judeo-Christian tradition."[22] The Nazis also viewed Darwinism and Christianity as polar opposites because Christianity

> makes no distinction of race or of colour; it seeks to break down all racial barriers. In this respect, the hand of Christianity is against that of Nature, for are not the races of mankind the evolutionary harvest which Nature has toiled through long ages to produce? May we not say, then, that Christianity is anti-evolutionary in its aim?[23]

---

19 Christopher R. Browning, *The Origins of the Final Solution* (Lincoln: University of Nebraska Press, 2004), 370.

20 Gilmer W. Blackburn, "The Portrayal of Christianity in the History Textbooks of Nazi Germany," *Church History* 49, Vol. 4 (December 1980): 433–446.

21 Richard Milner, *The Encyclopedia of Evolution* (New York: Facts on File, 1990), 206.

22 Fischel and Ortmann, *The Holocaust and Its Religious Impact*, 44.

23 Arthur Keith, *Evolution and Ethics* (New York: G.P. Putnam's Sons, 1946), 72.

Hitler was also very influenced by many leading German academics and scientists, especially during the 1930s when a "scientifically credible set of principles" in support of eugenics was widely supported by academia in Germany, America, Sweden and elsewhere.[24] Furthermore, opposition to Christianity was a prominent feature of German science, and later German political theory, for decades. A major reason why Hitler opposed Christianity was that he viewed it and science as diametrically opposed to each other.[25] Hitler concluded that, in the end, science would win and that the Christian church would eventually be destroyed. He believed that Darwinian mechanisms created the superior German race, and his goal was to use Darwinian mechanisms to create a utopia on earth by the elimination of inferior races. Typical claims by German scientists were in a lecture titled "On evolution: Darwin's Theory," by professor Ernst Haeckel who

argued that Darwin was correct…humankind had unquestionably evolved from the animal kingdom. Thus, and here the fatal step was taken in Haeckel's first major exposition of Darwinism in Germany, humankind's social and political existence is governed by the laws of evolution, natural selection, and biology, as clearly shown by Darwin. To argue otherwise was backward superstition. And, of course, it was organized religion which did this and thus stood in the way of scientific and social progress.[26]

Martin Bormann, Hitler's closest associate for years, and one of the most powerful men in Nazi Germany, was equally blunt: the church was opposed to evolution and for this reason the church must be aggressively opposed. He stressed that the Nazis were on the side of science and evolution, not Christianity. Furthermore, Nazism and Christianity are incompatible because Christianity is built on the

---

24 Donald Dietrich, "Racial Eugenics in the Third Reich: The Catholic Response," in Jack R. Fischel and Sanford Pinsker, eds., *The Churches' Response to the Holocaust* (Greenwood: Penkevill Publishing Company, 1986), 88.

25 Azar, *Twentieth Century in Crisis*, 154.

26 George Stein, "Biological Science and the Roots of Nazism," *American Scientist* 76, No. 1 (Jan–Feb 1988): 50–58.

ignorance of men and strive[s] to keep large portions of the people in ignorance.... On the other hand, National Socialism is based on scientific foundations. Christianity's immutable principles, which were laid down almost two thousand years ago, have increasingly stiffened into life-alien dogmas. National Socialism, however, if it wants to fulfil its task further, must always guide itself according to the newest data of scientific researches.[27]

Bormann even claimed that the Christian churches have long been aware that

scientific knowledge poses a threat to their existence. Therefore, by means of such pseudo-sciences as theology, they take great pains to suppress or falsify scientific research. Our National Socialist worldview stands on a much higher level than the concepts of Christianity, which in their essentials were taken over from Judaism. For this reason, too, we can do without Christianity.[28]

That Hitler's opposition to Christianity was based on Darwinism was detailed by Oxford historian Alan Bullock, who wrote that Hitler "showed the sharpest hostility" toward Christianity because, in

Hitler's eyes Christianity was a religion fit only for slaves; he detested its ethics in particular. Its teachings, he declared, was a rebellion against the natural law of selection by struggle and the survival of the fittest. "Taken to its logical extreme, Christianity would mean the systematic cultivation of the human failure."[29]

In fact, much of the opposition to the eugenics movement came from conservative German Christians such as the confessing church.[30]

---

27 George L. Mosse, *Nazi Culture: Intellectual, Cultural, and Social Life in the Third Reich* (Madison: University of Wisconsin Press, 1981), 244.

28 Mosse, *Nazi Culture*, 244.

29 Alan Bullock, *Hitler, A Study in Tyranny* (New York: Harper & Row, 1964), 389.

30 See Eric Metaxas, *Bonhoeffer—Pastor, Martyr, Prophet, Spy: A Righteous Gentile vs. The Third Reich* (Nashville: Thomas Nelson, 2010).

One reason was the confessing church's Christian teaching that we should protect the poor, the weak and the sick, teachings that opposed Nazi eugenic goals.[31] Himmler wrote that to be a Nazi and carry out their "good but dreadful work," one must overcome Christian training.[32] Hitler believed that persons of African descent were "monstrosities halfway between man and ape" and for this reason disapproved of German Christians going to "Central Africa" to establish "Negro missions," resulting in the turning of "healthy...human beings into a rotten brood of bastards."

In a chapter he titled, "Nation and Race," Hitler wrote,

> The stronger must dominate and not blend with the weaker, thus sacrificing his own greatness. Only the born weakling can view this as cruel, but he, after all, is only a weak and limited man; for if this law did not prevail, any conceivable higher development (*Hoherentwicklung*) of organic living beings would be unthinkable.... Those who want to live, let them fight, and those who do not want to fight in this world of eternal struggle do not deserve to live.[33]

NON-NAZI RACIST THEORIES

Admittedly, some people who did not accept Darwinism espoused non-evolutionary theories that accommodated, or even espoused, racism, such as the idea that those of African descent were not the offspring of Adam but of the "beasts of the earth" that the Bible mentioned in Genesis 1:25,30. Nonetheless, these theories were developed mostly in response to justify existing social systems and unexamined biases.

German racism would have had a difficult time existing if the historical creation position void of "Ham" and other curse theories was widely accepted. One of these pseudo-biblical curse theories was the claim that Genesis teaches "two types of men" were originally created:

---

31 Fischel and Pinsker, eds., *The Churches' Response to the Holocaust*.

32 Victor, *Hitler: The Pathology of Evil*, 112.

33 Adolf Hitler, *Mein Kampf* (Cambridge: Houghton Mifflin/The Riverside Press, 1962), 286, 325, 402–403, 285, 289.

the superior race line, Adam and Eve; and the "beasts of the earth," the inferior black race line.[34] Few people, though, accepted this line of argument and almost no one in Germany did.

Most biblical Christians have historically believed that, although blacks were culturally and physically different from whites, they were, nonetheless, fully human with a soul that needed to be saved. Consequently, extensive missionary activity was exerted to seek the conversion of those of African descent. Black tribal African religion almost disappeared as a result of Christian conversions as early as the middle 1800s, and only small remnants of it remained after the 1840s.

For these reasons, early in Nazi rule the Christian church, especially the Catholic Church, was one of the main targets of the Nazi policy of persecution. Specifically, the

SS was given a free hand in a reign of terror against both clergy and laity, as a demonstration that any institution or individual who might become a focal point of national resistance would be destroyed. The clergy, as always, were the chief suspects. Lists were drawn up of Catholics who were "especially hostile to Germany" and who, as such, deserved summary treatment. In November 1939 it was reported from the Polish town of Bromberg (Bydgoszcz) that the eradication of Polish priests was planned, preceded only by the prior extermination of the Jews.[35]

HITLER PLAYS POLITICS

In a talk given by Hitler on April 7, 1933, Hitler made it absolutely clear that in Germany's future there would be "no place" in the German "utopia for the Christian Churches" and "nothing will prevent me from eradicating totally, root and branch, all Christianity in Germany.... A German Church, a German Christianity, it is all rubbish.... One is

---

34 George Hawtin, *The Living Creature: The Origin of the Negro* (self published, 1980); Charles Lee Magne, *The Negro and the World Crisis* (Hollywood: New Christian Crusade Church, 1972).

35 John S. Conway, *The Nazi Persecution of the Churches, 1933–1945* (New York: Basic Books, 1968), 29.

either Christian or German."[36] Soon after Hitler made this statement, he gave a radio talk on the night before the July 23 Protestant church elections urging the people to vote *Deutsche Christen* because they "stood self-aware on the same ground as the National Socialist state."[37]

The *Deutsche Christen* was a pressure group movement within German Protestantism that supported the anti-Semitic and *Führerprinzip* ideological principles of Nazism with the goal of aligning German Protestantism as a whole toward those principles. *Führerprinzip* or "leader principle," was the fundamental basis of political authority in the Third Reich, which is most succinctly understood to mean that the Führer's word is above all written law (i.e., he is a dictator).

Hitler realized that elimination of Christianity was a long-term goal, and he "was prepared to put off long-term ideological goals in favour of short-term advantage."[38] He knew that he had to fight one German battle at a time—and elected to destroy the churches in due time.[39] In 1942, Hitler said, "practical politics demands that, for the time being at least, we must avoid any appearance of a campaign against the church."[40] Bullock wrote, due to political considerations Hitler

> restrained his anti-clericalism, seeing clearly the dangers of strengthening the Church by persecution. For this reason he was more circumspect than some of his followers, like Rosenberg and Bormann, in attacking the Church publicly. But, once the war was over, he promised himself, he would root out and destroy the influence of the Christian Churches. "The evil that is gnawing our vitals," he remarked in February 1942, "is our priests, of both creeds. I can't at present give them the answer they've been asking for but…it's all written down in my big book. The time will come when I'll settle my account with them.… They'll hear from me all right. I shan't let myself be hampered with judicial samples."[41]

---

36 Poewe, *New Religions and the Nazis*, 112.

37 Poewe, *New Religions and the Nazis*, 112.

38 Kershaw, *Hitler 1936–45*, 238.

39 *The Speeches of Adolf Hitler*, 369–370.

40 *The Speeches of Adolf Hitler*, 369

41 Bullock, *Hitler, A Study in Tyranny*, 389.

Although the Christian church would in time be destroyed, for now it was needed to help achieve Nazi goals. Hitler at times even included references to Christianity in his speeches, mostly in his very early speeches, but even here he exploited Christianity to justify his hatred of ethnic Jews. A typical example is in a speech given on April 12, 1922. He noted that one well-known German said being a Christian prevented him from being anti-Semitic, to which Hitler responded that, in contrast, his feelings as a

Christian points me to my Lord and Savior as a fighter...to the man who once in loneliness, surrounded only by a few followers, recognized these Jews for what they were and summoned men to fight against them and who, God's truth! was greatest not as a sufferer but as fighter. In boundless love as a Christian...in His might...seized the scourge to drive out of the Temple the brood of vipers and of adders. How terrific was His fight for the world against the Jewish poison. To-day, after two thousand years, with deepest emotion I recognize more profoundly than ever before the fact that it was for this that He had to shed His blood upon the cross. As a Christian...I have the duty to be a fighter for truth and justice...to see to it that human society does not suffer the same catastrophic collapse as did the civilization of the ancient world...which was driven to its ruin through this same Jewish people.[42]

As a consummate politician, Hitler openly exploited the church by implying he was a Christian.[43] In *Mein Kampf*, Hitler even wrote, "I believe that I am acting in accordance with the will of the Almighty Creator: *by defending myself against the Jew, I am fighting for the work of the Lord.*"[44] In the meantime, "Hitler's henchman continued to cajole the Protestant church into doing their bidding."[45] The Nazis and their Führer were quite capable of deceptively declaring themselves fighters

---

42 *The Speeches of Adolf Hitler*, 19–20.

43 Phillips, *Post-Conservative America*, 161.

44 Hitler, *Mein Kampf*, 65, emphasis in the original.

45 Poewe, *New Religions and the Nazis*, 112.

"on the Lord's side" when it suited their purposes.[46] Only after the war ended would Germany be able to fully implement the "final solution" to the "Christian problem."[47] Until then, "calm should be restored...in relations with the Churches."[48] But it was "'clear,' noted Geobbels, himself numbering among the most aggressive anti-Church radicals, 'that after the war it has to find a general solution.... There is, namely, an insoluble opposition between the Christian and a Germanic-heroic world-view.'"[49]

Although the Nazis made it clear that they intended to "wipe out the Jews—as well as the Negroes, Freemasons, Jehovah's Witnesses, priests of all religious persuasions, and all other 'deviants and people of impure blood,'" they were also both "pathological and pragmatic" liars in claiming they were on the side of Christianity.[50] The church, in turn, often thought the best of the Nazis and turned the other cheek to their evils. The state's conflict with the churches was a source of great bitterness for many church members, but, amazingly,

> Hitler was largely exempted from blame. Despite four years of fierce "Church struggle," the head of the Protestant Church in Bavaria, Bishop Meiser, publicly offered prayers for Hitler, thanking God "for every success which, through your grace, you have so far granted him for the good of our people." The negative features of daily life, most [people] imagined, were not of the Führer's making. They were the fault of his underlings, who frequently kept him in the dark about what was happening.[51]

Many church members wanted to believe that Hitler was on their side, and a few were actually convinced by Hitler's deception that he supported Christianity:

---

46 Gerald Astor, *The Last Nazi: The Life and Times of Joseph Mengele* (New York: Donald Fine, 1985), 22.

47 Kershaw, *Hitler 1936–45*, 516.

48 Kershaw, *Hitler 1936–45*, 39.

49 Kershaw, *Hitler 1936–45*, 449.

50 John Laffin, *Hitler Warned Us* (New York: Barnes & Noble Books, 1998), 17.

51 Kershaw, *Hitler 1936–45*, 28.

Even for those within Germany known to be critical of the regime, Hitler could in a face-to-face meeting create a positive impression. He was good at attuning to the sensitivities of his conversation-partner, could be charming, and often appeared reasonable and accommodating. As always, he was a skilled dissembler. On a one-to-one basis, he could pull the wool over the eyes of hardened critics. After a three-hour meeting with him at the Berghof in early November 1936, the influential Catholic Archbishop of Münich-Freising, Cardinal Faulhaber—a man of sharp acumen, who had often courageously criticized the Nazi attacks on the Catholic Church—went away convinced that Hitler was deeply religious.[52]

University of British Columbia historian John Conway documented that, despite the many good-will gestures

and compliance made by the Churches in the first twelve months of Nazi rule, a basic antagonism and suspicion continued on the Nazi side, with a determination to forestall any clerical opposition by branding it as "political" and by subjecting it to police supervision or suppression. The slogan used to justify this attitude was that "politics do not belong in the church."[53]

The fact that many Christians in Germany then were nominal cultural Christians who were rapidly indoctrinated into the Nazi worldview helps to

explain how the SS troops could perform monstrous acts of cruelty and yet return home for Christmas and attend church and still think of themselves as good Christians. They were not murderers, they were men who were building a race of supermen and helping the inferior people get on with their evolutionary journey.[54]

---

52 Kershaw, *Hitler 1936–45*, 29.

53 Conway, *The Nazi Persecution of the Churches*, 67.

54 Erwin W. Lutzer, *Hitler's Cross: The Revealing Story of How the Cross of Christ Was Used as a Symbol of the Nazi Agenda* (Chicago: Moody Press, 1995), 95.

In 1933, Hitler gave honour to God in one address to a

distinguished assemblage and pledged his emphatic support to the maintenance of Christianity in Germany. [But the]...inaugural ceremony of the Hitler regime in a Protestant church presented the Fuehrer an unparalleled opportunity to begin a policy of studied duplicity which characterized his government's attitude toward religion from the start. By perennially injecting affirmations of religion into his speeches, the Nazi Fuehrer was able to pose as the defender of Christianity against "godless Bolshevism," while behind the scenes craftily planning the utter annihilation of the Christian faith.[55]

Although Hitler fooled many in the church, he did not hide his strong contempt for Christianity from everyone. For example, when Germany invaded Poland, around 200 executions a day occurred—all without trials—which included the "nobility, clerics, and Jews," all of whom were eventually to be exterminated.[56] Furthermore, since the inception of Nazism those Kershaw called "Nazi fanatics" had openly conducted a "campaign against the church."[57] For example, SS commandant Theodor Eicke put great pressure on SS members to "renounce their religions."[58]

The infamous concordant that Hitler signed in 1933 with the Vatican ostensibly designed to guarantee the freedom of the Catholic Church was, in fact, a ruse. Not long after the signatures on the document were dry, the head of the German Catholic Action organization, Dr. Erich Klausner, was murdered by Hitler's minions and, furthermore, to

discredit the Church, monks were brought to trial on immorality charges. In 1935 the Protestant churches were placed under state control. Protesting ministers and priests were sent to concentra-

---

55 Gilmer W. Blackburn, "The Portrayal of Christianity in the History Textbooks of Nazi Germany," *Church History* 49, Vol. 4 (December 1990): 433–446.

56 Kershaw, *Hitler 1936–45*, 243.

57 Kershaw, *Hitler 1936–45*, 702.

58 Victor, *Hitler: The Pathology of Evil*, 111.

tion camps. They had become "supervisees" on a par with the Jews and communists. Pope Pius XI, realizing the anti-Christian nature of Nazism, charged Hitler with "the threatening storm clouds of destructive religious wars...which have no other aim than...that of extermination." But the Nazi shouts of "Kill the Jews" drowned out the warning voice of the Pope and the agonized cries of the tortured in the concentration camps.[59]

HITLER'S END GOAL

It was not hatred of Christianity that was Hitler's first central concern, but rather it was the implementation of social Darwinism that was central to Hitler and his regime. He likened Jews to tuberculosis, which could infect a healthy body, and, therefore, the Jewish germ must be destroyed lest it infect others.[60] Eradicating "'Jewish-Bolshevism' was central, not peripheral, to what had been deliberately designated by Hitler as a 'war of annihilation.'"[61] The Nazi regime's leaders had sealed their fate with Hitler as a result of the

regime's genocide and other untold acts of inhumanity...the regime had only its own collective suicide in an inexorably lost war to contemplate. But like a mortally wounded wild beast at bay, it fought with the ferocity and ruthlessness that came from desperation. And its Leader, losing touch ever more with reality, hoping for miracles, kept tilting at windmills—ready in Wagnerian style in the event of ultimate apocalyptic catastrophe, and in line with his undiluted social-Darwinistic beliefs, to take his people down in flames with him if it proved incapable of producing the victory he had demanded.[62]

Hitler saw Christians and the church as weak, and, as Lutzer noted, he viewed both

59 Max I. Dimont, *Jews, God and History* (New York: New American Library, 1994), 397.

60 Kershaw, *Hitler 1936–45*, 582–583.

61 Kershaw, *Hitler 1936–45*, 461.

62 Kershaw, *Hitler 1936–45*, 615.

Protestants and Catholics with contempt, convinced that all Christians would betray their God when they were forced to choose between the swastika and the Cross: "Do you really believe the masses will be Christian again? Nonsense! Never again. That tale is finished. No one will listen to it again. But we can hasten matters. The parsons will dig their own graves. They will betray their God to us. They will betray anything for the sake of their miserable jobs and incomes."[63]

Hitler was largely proved correct here. The failure of Christianity was not that it produced the Nazi monster, but that it did very little to stop it. The German churches' sin was not in inspiring Hitler to commit his many crimes, but in doing very little to stop him—the same sin that the churches are often guilty of in the West today. However, fortunately, some Christians did speak out against the Nazi crimes. That the church was not *totally* silent was testified to by the great physicist Albert Einstein who said about the Confessing Church that as a

> lover of freedom, when the (Nazi) revolution came in Germany, I looked to the universities to defend it, knowing that they had always boasted of their devotion to the cause of truth; but no, the universities were immediately silenced. Then I looked to the great editors of the newspapers, whose flaming editorials in days gone by had proclaimed their love of freedom; but they, like the universities, were silenced in a few short weeks.... Only the Church stood squarely across the path of Hitler's campaign for suppressing truth. I never had any special interest in the Church before, but now I feel a great affection and admiration [for it] because the Church alone has had the courage and persistence to stand for intellectual and moral freedom. I am forced thus to confess that what I once despised I now praise unreservedly.[64]

Jack Fischel, in a review of the literature, concluded that individual Catholic clergy and lay people managed to save about 800,000

---

63 Lutzer, *Hitler's Cross*, 104.
64 "German Martyrs," *Time Magazine* 36, Vol. 26 (December 23, 1940): 38–41.

Jews.[65] As Nazi Germany became more aggressive in implementing its eugenics programmes, "some group protests were organized notably by church leaders.... Sterilizing and killing people considered unfit also aroused opposition, particularly from the churches."[66] Most other institutions did far *less* to oppose Hitler than the Christian churches.[67] It is important to stress that in

> most of the occupied countries, only the fear of widespread public revolt deterred the Nazis from launching a general onslaught against the whole body of the clergy, particularly against the upper ranks of the hierarchy. The bishops generally escaped imprisonment, but the treatment meted out to a few notable exceptions, especially in Poland and Czechoslovakia, was indicative of the probable fate which awaited the [church] hierarchy when Nazi control was finally established.[68]

Some of the many examples of the onslaught of the Christian clergy Conway cited included:

> The Czech Orthodox Bishop Gorazd was executed. Four bishops, Kozal of Wladislavia, Fulman and his suffragan Goral of Lublin, and Picquet of Clermont-Ferrand, were exiled to concentration camps in Germany. The Bishop of Plock, Nowowiejski, and his suffragan, Wetmanski, both died of their sufferings while imprisoned in Poland. The seventy-nine-year-old Bishop of the Polish Evangelical Church, Juliusz Bursche, was sent into exile in Berlin where he was held in solitary confinement until his death several months later. Other leaders of the Churches, some of whom had rashly expressed enthusiasm for Germany's success, were placed under arrest or isolated from their clergy and parishioners.[69]

---

65 Fischel and Pinsker, eds., *The Churches' Response to the Holocaust*, 19.

66 Victor, *Hitler: The Pathology of Evil*, 83.

67 Eugen Gerstenmaier, "The Church Conspiratorial," in Eric H. Boehm, ed., *We Survived: Fourteen Histories of the Hidden and Hunted in Nazi Germany* (Boulder: Westview Press, 2003), 172–189.

68 Conway, *The Nazi Persecution of the Churches*, 297.

69 Conway, *The Nazi Persecution of the Churches*, 297.

Opposing Hitler carried many risks, but a few brave souls did stand up and resist. During the first few years of his leadership,

> Hitler extended his control over every aspect of German life.... Those few institutions that threatened to defy him, such as the Church, were rigorously controlled. "This is the last time a German court is gong to declare someone innocent whom I have declared guilty," said Hitler, when the Protestant theologian Martin Niemoeller was acquitted of subversion.[70]

HITLER BEGINS HIS WAR AGAINST CHRISTIANITY

Hitler did not wait until the war ended to begin destroying Christianity. Although the resistance efforts by the clergy were sometimes exaggerated,

> after the first few years of Hitler's rule the Gestapo and the Nazi Party singled out the clergy for heavy doses of repression to guarantee their silence and their parishioners' obedience. Thousands of clergymen, both Catholic and Protestant, endured house searches, surveillance, Gestapo interrogations, jail and prison terms, fines, and worse.[71]

Hitler's killing machine murdered about a total of 6 million Jews, and over 5 million Christians, which was a major focus of Hitler's war against religion.[72] Many of the Christians murdered were Polish clergy and intellectuals, or were part of the resistance movement. This little known fact caused Jewish historian Max Dimont to declare that "the world blinded itself to the murder of Christians" by Nazi Germany.[73]

---

70 David Boyle, *World War II: A Photographic History* (The Netherlands: Metro Books, 2001), 22.

71 Eric A. Johnson, *Nazi Terror: The Gestapo, Jews, and Ordinary Germans* (New York: Basic Books, 1999), 224.

72 Richard C. Lukas, *Forgotten Holocaust: The Poles under German Occupation, 1939–1944* (New York: Hippocrene Books, 1997).

73 Dimont, *Jews, God and History*, 391–392.

In Poland alone, 881 Catholic priests were annihilated.[74] In addition, so many priests ended up in concentration camps that, if possible, they were often housed together to avoid converting the other inmates.

Dachau concentration camp held the largest number of Catholic priests—over 2,400—in the Nazi camp system. They came from about 24 nations, and included parish priests and prelates, monks and friars, teachers and missionaries. Over one third of the priests in Dachau alone died.[75] Dachau survivor, Father Johannes Lenz, who documented the martyrdom and the physical and mental agony that Dachau inmates experienced, claimed that the Catholic Church was the only steadfast fighter against the Nazis. Christian clergy and lay persons were murdered by the thousands in Dachau, and those who survived were considered "missionaries in Hell." This conforms to official Nazi writings, which espoused both anti-Semitic and anti-Christian ideas that "had a single purpose. Hitler's aim was to eradicate all religious organizations within the state and to foster a return to paganism."[76]

Hitler was able to act on Catholics with more aggression earlier than other Christians because, especially since 1871, Catholics had already suffered much discrimination in predominately Protestant, specifically Lutheran, Germany—as a minority they were viewed as outsiders.[77] The many documents that prove the Nazis plan to "eliminate Christianity and convert its followers to an Aryan philosophy" are now on the online version of *Rutgers Journal of Law and Religion.*[78] As institutional religion declined, Nazism was seen by Hitler as its rightful replacement.[79]

---

74 Azar, *Twentieth Century in Crisis*, 154.

75 Johannes Lenz, *Untersuchungen über die künstliche Zündung von Lichtbögen unter besonderer Berücksichtigung der Lichtobogen-Stromrichter nach Erwin Marx* (Braunschweig: Hunold, 2004).

76 Dimont, *Jews, God and History*, 397.

77 Donald Dietrich, "Racial Eugenics in the Third Reich: The Catholic Response," in Fischel and Pinsker, eds., *The Churches' Response to the Holocaust*, 87.

78 Sheila Hotchkin, "Rare Documents from Nazi Trial Being Posted on Internet," *The Bryan Times*, Thursday, January 10, 2002, 3.

79 Kershaw, *Hitler 1936–45*, 840.

SUMMARY

It is very clear from the historical evidence that Hitler was not only *not* a Christian, even if the term was broadly defined, but was *openly opposed* to the basic Christian faith, teachings and doctrines. He, at times, represented himself as a Christian, especially early in his political career when he was fighting for his place in the political arena. Those who claim he was a Christian often quote certain words to make it appear he was a Christian, but when evaluating the beliefs of a man one must look beyond a few statements made for political gain.

Alan Bullock said it well when he wrote, the "truth is that, in matters of religion at least, Hitler was a rationalist and a materialist. 'The dogma of Christianity,' [Hitler] declared in one of his wartime conversations, 'gets worn away before the advances of science.... Gradually the [Christian] myths crumble.'"[80] The church did much to fight Hitler, but did far too little too late.

The major exception was the Theological Declaration of Barmen (*Die Barmer Theologische Erklärung*) in 1934, a statement written by the Confessing Church opposing the Nazi-supported "German Christian" movement which was anti-Semitic and extremely nationalistic. The Declaration was written by Reformed theologian Karl Barth and other Confessing Church leaders, including Dietrich Bonhoeffer. Nonetheless, the churches cannot by any stretch of the imagination be held responsible as the cause of Nazism.

In the end, to its great detriment, except the Confessing Church, the church largely stayed out of politics—as many people think the church also should do in North America today. At the time, most mainline German churches had abandoned biblical Christianity, and those that had not were more apt to oppose Hitler and Nazism.[81] As a result of the passiveness of both the German church and people in general, Hitler was able to carry out many of his goals—such as the almost total destruction of the Jewish people in Europe—with relatively little opposition.

---

80 Bullock, *Hitler, A Study in Tyranny*, 389.
81 Metaxas, *Bonhoeffer—Pastor, Martyr, Prophet, Spy.*

Darwinism, Nazi race policies and the Holocaust

INTRODUCTION

O f the many factors that produced the fatal blend that resulted in the Nazi Holocaust and World War II, one of the more important was Darwin's notion that evolutionary progress occurs primarily as a result of the elimination of the weak in the struggle for survival. Although it is no easy task to assess all of the many conflicting motives of Hitler and his supporters, Darwinian-inspired eugenics clearly played a critical role.[1]

Darwinism also both justified and encouraged the Nazi views on race and war.[2] If the Nazi party had fully embraced and consistently

---

1   Adolf Hitler, *Hitler's Secret Conversations, 1941–1944*, trans. Norman Cameron and R.H. Stevens; intro. H.R. Trevor-Roper (New York: Farrar, Straus and Young, 1953).

2   William Bell Riley, *Hitlerism or the Philosophy of Evolution in Action* (Minneapolis: Irene Woods, 1941); W. Rowan, "Charles Darwin" in *Architects of Modern Thought* (Toronto: Canadian Broadcasting Corporation, 1955); Richard Weikart, *From Darwin to Hitler* (New York: Palgrave Macmillan, 2004); Richard Weikart, "The Impact of Social Darwinism on Anti-Semitic Ideology in Germany and Austria, 1860–1945" in Geoffrey Cantor and Marc Swetlitz, eds., *Jewish Tradition and the Challenge of Darwinism* (Chicago: The University of Chicago Press, 2006); Richard Weikart, *Hitler's Ethic: The Nazi Pursuit of Evolutionary Progress* (New York: Palgrave MacMillan, 2009).

acted on the belief that all humans were descendants of Adam and Eve, and equal before God as taught in both the Old and New Testaments (the Hebrew and Greek Scriptures), it is probable that the Holocaust and World War II never would have occurred.

Expunging the Judeo-Christian-Muslim doctrine of human divine origins from mainline German theology and its schools, and replacing it with Darwinism, openly contributed to the acceptance of social Darwinism that culminated in the Holocaust.[3] Darwin's theory, as modified by biologist Ernst Haeckel,[4] combined with the racist theories of Houston Stewart Chamberlain and others, clearly contributed to the death of over 9 million people in the concentration camps, and the approximately 55 million others, in a war whose economic toll for all countries was about $18.75 trillion American dollars (in 2012 dollars).[5] Furthermore, a major reason that Nazism reached the *extent* of the Holocaust was the widespread acceptance of social Darwinism by the scientific and academic community.[6]

The very heart of Darwinism was the belief that evolution proceeds by the differential survival of the fittest individuals. This requires differences among a species that eventually became great enough that those individuals possessing them—the fittest—were more apt to leave more offspring. Although the process of forming new races may

---

3   Allan Chase, *The Legacy of Malthus: The Social Costs of the New Scientific Racism* (New York: Alfred Knopf, 1980).

4   Ernst Haeckel, *The History of Creation: Or the Development of the Earth and Its Inhabitants by the Action of Natural Causes* (New York: Appleton, 1876); Ernst Haeckel, *The Riddle of the Universe* (New York: Harper, 1900); Ernst Haeckel, *The Wonders of Life: A Popular Study of Biological Philosophy* (New York: Harper, 1905); Ernst Haeckel, *Eternity: World War Thoughts on Life and Death, Religion, and the Theory of Evolution* (New York: Truth Seeker, 1916); Ernst Haeckel, *The Evolution of Man* (New York: Appleton, 1920).

5   "The economic cost of the war is estimated at US$1500 billion" [Hermann Kinder and Werner Hilgemann, eds., *The Penguin Atlas of World History*, trans. Ernest A. Menze (Harmondsworth: Penguin Books, 2003)]. In 2012 US dollars, $1.5 trillion converts to $18.75 trillion.

6   Pierre Aycoberry, *The Nazi Question: An Essay on the Interpretations of National Socialism, 1922–1975* (New York: Pantheon, 1981); Alan D. Beyerchen, *Scientists under Hitler: Politics and the Physics Community in the Third Reich* (New Haven: Yale University Press, 1977); George Stein, "Biological Science and the Roots of Nazism," *American Scientist* 76, No. 1 (Jan–Feb 1988): 50–58.

begin with slight differences, differential survival rates eventually produce distinct races, part of a process that evolutionists postulate leads to speciation, meaning the development of a new species.

The egalitarian ideal that all humans are created equal, which now dominates Western ideology, has not historically been universal among nations and cultures.[7] A major force that worked against this view was social Darwinism, especially its crude survival-of-the-fittest worldview.[8] The idea that the quality of the race can be improved by selective breeding is as old as Plato's *Republic* but,

> modern eugenic thought arose only in the nineteenth century. The emergence of interest in eugenics during that century had multiple roots. The most important was the theory of evolution, for Francis Galton's ideas on eugenics—and it was he who created the term "eugenics"—were a direct logical outgrowth of the scientific doctrine elaborated by his cousin, Charles Darwin.[9]

That Nazi governmental policy was openly influenced by Darwinism, the Zeitgeist of both science and educated society of the time, is clear from an examination of extant documents, writings, and artifacts produced by Germany's twentieth-century Nazi movement and its many scientist supporters.[10] The Nazi treatment of Jews and other "races" then believed to be "inferior" was largely a result of their conclusion that Darwinism provided profound insight that could be used to significantly improve humankind.[11] The political philosophy of Germany was built on the belief that critical factors for progress included chiefly

> struggle, selection, and survival of the fittest, all notions and observations arrived at…by Darwin…but already in luxuriant

---

7   Ethel Tobach, John Gianusos, Howard R. Topoff and Charles G. Gross, *The Four Horsemen: Racism, Sexism, Militarism, and Social Darwinism* (New York: Behavioral Publications, 1974).

8   Stein, "Biological Science and the Roots of Nazism."

9   Marc Lappe, "Eugenics," in Kenneth Ludmerer, ed., *The Encyclopedia of Bioethics* (New York: Free Press, 1978), 457.

10   Stein, "Biological Science and the Roots of Nazism."

11   Arthur Keith, *Evolution and Ethics* (New York: G.P. Putnam's Sons, 1946), 230.

bud in the German social philosophy of the nineteenth century.... Thus developed the doctrine of Germany's inherent right to rule the world on the basis of superior strength...of a "hammer and anvil" relationship between the Reich and the weaker nations.[12]

THE IMPORTANCE OF RACE IN DARWINISM

Evolution is based on acquiring new traits through mutations and gene shuffling that enable those possessing the traits to survive better in adverse conditions, and therefore leave more offspring, than those who do not possess them. The source of the raw material for natural selection to select from is primarily genetic mutations. People who inherit a mutation that enables more of them to survive and reproduce compared with those without that trait will be more likely to pass that trait on to the next generation. Superior individuals will be more likely to survive, and as a result, their genetic information will, over a period of several generations, be present in increasing numbers of individuals, while genetic information of the "weaker" individuals eventually will become extinct.

This process, once called *raciation* but now labelled *speciation*, is the source of the putative evolutionary "progress" that can, in theory, continue forever. If every member of a species were fully equal, natural selection would have nothing from which to select. Consequently, survival would be a result of chance, and evolution would cease for that species.

According to Darwinian theory, genetic differences that aid survival gradually produce new races, some of which have a survival advantage. These new groups became the superior (i.e., more evolved) race. When that trait eventually spreads throughout the entire race, because of the survival advantage it confers on those that possess it, a higher, more evolved, human will result. Hitler and the Nazi party claimed that one of their major goals was to apply this orthodox science to improve society. Furthermore, the core idea of Darwinism was not evolution, but selection of the fittest.[13] Hitler stressed that, to produce a better society, the Nazis must understand, and cooperate, with this science.

---

12 Joseph Tenenbaum, *Race and Reich* (New York: Twayne, 1956), 211.
13 Stein, "Biological Science and the Roots of Nazism," 53.

John Jay College historian Daniel Gasman concluded that in "no other country...did the ideas of Darwinism develop as seriously as a total explanation of the world as in Germany" and, as a result, the "literal transfer of the laws of biology" as interpreted by Darwin's theory were applied to the social realm.[14] The inequality doctrine, although an integral part of German philosophy for years, reached its apex under the Hitler regime and obtained its chief intellectual support from Darwinism and Darwin's German disciple, Ernst Haeckel.[15]

Haeckel's belief that "the morphological differences between two generally recognized species—for example sheep and goats—are much less important than those...between a Hottentot and a man of the Teutonic [Aryan] race" soon became German policy.[16] Especially important in Nazi policy was the belief that the Germans had evolved the "furthest from the common form of apelike men [and outstripped]...all others" and it would be this race that must raise humans to a "new period of higher mental development."[17] This was true not only mentally but physically, because Haeckel believed evolution achieves a "symmetry of all parts, and equal development which we call the type of perfect human beauty."[18]

The evolutionary superiority of Aryans, the race superior to all others, gave them not only the right, but the *duty*, to subjugate all other peoples. And race was a major plank of Nazi philosophy. The Nazis incorporated Darwinism

in their political system, with nothing left out.... Their political dictionary was replete with words like space, struggle, selection, and extinction (*Ausmerzen*). The syllogism of their logic was clearly stated: The world is a jungle in which different nations struggle for space. The stronger win, the weaker die or are killed.[19]

14 Daniel Gasman, *The Scientific Origin of National Socialism* (New York: American Elsevier, 1971), xiv.

15 Sheila Faith Weiss, *Race Hygiene and National Efficiency: The Eugenics of Wilhelm Schallmayer* (Berkeley: University of California Press, 1988); Aycoberry, *The Nazi Question.*

16 Haeckel, *The History of Creation*, 434.

17 Haeckel, *The History of Creation*, 332.

18 Haeckel, *The History of Creation*, 321.

19 Tenenbaum, *Race and Reich*, 211–212 .

An important fact is that "biological racism had become entrenched in anti-Semitic discourse and also was becoming mainstream among German anthropologists."[20] The Nazi view of Darwinian evolution and race was a major part of the fatal combination of ideas and events that produced the Holocaust and World War II:

> One of the central planks in Nazi theory and doctrine was, of course, evolutionary theory [and]...that all biology had evolved spontaneously upward, and that inbetween links (less evolved types) should be actively eradicated...that natural selection could and should be actively *aided*, and therefore [the Nazis] instituted political measures to eradicate...Jews, and the blacks, whom they considered [less evolved].[21]

Terms such as "superior race," "lower human types," "pollution of the race," and the term *evolution* itself (*Entwicklung*), were often used by Hitler and other Nazi leaders. Their race views were not fringe science, as is often claimed, but rather were

> straightforward German social Darwinism of a type widely known and accepted throughout Germany and which, more importantly, was considered by most Germans, scientists included, to be scientifically true. More recent scholarship on national socialism and Hitler has begun to realize that...[social Darwinism] was a specific characteristic of Nazism. National socialist "biopolicy," [was] a policy based on a mystical-biological belief in radical inequality, a monistic, antitranscendent moral nihilism based on the eternal struggle for existence and the survival of the fittest as the law of nature, and the consequent use of state power for a public policy of natural selection.[22]

The philosophy that humans can control and even use Darwinian theory

---

20 Weikart, "The Impact of Social Darwinism," 110.

21 Beate Wilder-Smith, *The Day Nazi Germany Died: An Eyewitness Account of the Russian and Allied Invasion of Germany* (San Diego: Master Books, 1982), 27.

22 Stein, "Biological Science and the Roots of Nazism," 51.

to produce a more highly evolved human is repeatedly mentioned in the writings and speeches of prominent Nazis.[23] Accomplishing the Darwinian goal for society required ruthlessly eliminating the less fit by openly barbarian behaviour. Miami University professor George Stein noted that the core of German social Darwinism was developed by Haeckel and his colleagues. Specifically, the Darwinists argued on scientific grounds that humankind was

> merely a part of nature with no special transcendent qualities or special humanness. On the other hand, the Germans were members of a biologically superior community…politics was merely the straightforward application of the laws of biology. In essence, Haeckel and his fellow social Darwinists advanced the ideas that were to become the core assumptions of national socialism…. The business of the corporate state was eugenics or artificial selection.[24]

Prior to 1933, German scientists published thirteen scientific journals devoted primarily to racial hygiene and established over 30 different institutions, many connected with universities or research centres devoted to "racial science."[25] In the Nazi era, close to 150 scientific journals, many of which are still highly respected today, covered racial hygiene and allied fields.[26] Enormous data files were kept on the races, most of which were analyzed and used for research papers published in various German and other scientific journals. The Kaiser Wilhelm Institute for Anthropology, Human Heredity, and Eugenics was established in 1927 to study eugenics and related areas, including venereal disease and alcohol.

The various eugenic institutes also researched the "persistence" of various "primitive racial traits" in certain races inside and outside of

---

23 Eberhard Jäckel, *Hitler's Weltanschauung* (Middletown: Wesleyan University Press, 1972).

24 Stein, "Biological Science and the Roots of Nazism," 56.

25 Robert N. Proctor, *Racial Hygiene: Medicine under the Nazis* (Cambridge: Harvard University Press, 1988), 291.

26 Paul Weindling, *Health, Race and German Politics Between National Unification and Nazism, 1870–1945* (Cambridge: Cambridge University Press, 1989).

Germany. Eugenicists soon claimed that they found an abundance of evidence for the Cro-magnon racial type in inferior races, and also Neanderthal racial traits. Like their American and British counterparts, German racial hygiene institutes and researchers at various universities began to discover genetic evidence for virtually every human malady from criminality to hernias, even divorce and "loving to sail on water." They saw their work as a noble effort to continue "Darwin's attempts to elucidate the origin of species."[27]

The central concept of the *survival of the fittest* philosophy, the observation that all animals and plants contain a tremendous amount of genetic variety and that some of these differences may have a survival advantage in certain environments, has been well documented. The best example is artificial selection in which breeders select males and females with the maximum amount of the trait they are concerned with, and then again select from their offspring those animals that display the maximum of that trait. As a result, a wide variety of modified plants and animals have been bred. Of course, artificial selection is not natural selection, a problem with which Darwin never fully dealt.

Breeding for certain traits, though, invariably is a trade off that usually results in the loss of other desirable characteristics. Because producing a plant or animal with certain traits usually results in the loss of other traits, cows are bred either as dairy cows or for meat, but not both. The Nazi's theory inadequately considered this data and the implications of the tremendous amount of biological diversity that we now know exists.

The racist theories closely followed the spread of Darwinian evolutionary theory, which had a wide following in Germany almost immediately after the publication of the German edition of *On the Origin of Species*.[28] As Harvard Professor Stephen Jay Gould concluded, "Biological arguments for racism...increased by orders of magnitude following

---

27 Proctor, *Racial Hygiene: Medicine under the Nazis*, 291.

28 Karl A. Schleunes, *The Twisted Road to Auschwitz: Nazi Policy toward German Jews, 1933–1939* (Urbana: University of Illinois Press, 1970); Norman Cohn, *Warrant for Genocide: The Myth of the Jewish World Conspiracy and the Protocols of the Elders of Zion* (New York: Scholow Press, 1981).

the acceptance of evolutionary theory" by scientists in most nations.[29]

Also used for the support of racism were comparisons of various cultures that were assumed to be the product of racial superiority. The Nazis concluded that inferior races usually produced inferior cultures, but only superior races could produce superior cultures.[30] Hence, historian Dr. Karl Schleunes notes that racism came into scientific repute through its solid link with what he calls the third great synthesis of the nineteenth-century, the Darwinian theory of evolution and the survival-of-the-fittest worldview.[31]

AMERICAN AND BRITISH SUPPORT

Darwinists' views about race existed not only in Nazi Germany but also in America, as is apparent from surveys of textbooks published from 1880 to around 1950. For example, Princeton biologist Edwin Conklin stated in his college text that comparisons

of any modern race with the Neanderthal or Heidelberg types shows that...Negroid races more closely resemble the original stock than the white or yellow races. Every consideration should lead those who believe in the superiority of the white race to strive to preserve its purity and to establish and maintain the segregation of the races.[32]

German eugenicists relied heavily on work completed in Britain and America, especially that research related to sterilization policies.[33] For example, the national compulsory sterilization laws were quite literally based on the "model eugenical sterilization law drawn up by the supervisor and the eugenics record office of Cold Spring Harbor,

---

29 Stephen Jay Gould, *Ontogeny and Phylogeny* (Cambridge: Harvard University Press, 1977), 127.

30 Earnest Albert Hooton, *Why Men Behave Like Apes and Vice Versa; or, Body and Behavior* (Princeton: Princeton University Press, 1941).

31 Schleunes, *The Twisted Road to Auschwitz.*

32 Edwin G. Conklin, *The Direction of Human Evolution* (New York: Scribner's, 1921), 34, 53.

33 Harry Bruinius, *Better for All the World: The Secret History of Forced Sterilization and America's Quest for Racial Purity* (New York: Knopf, 2006).

New York."[34] Franz Bumm, the President of the Reich Health Office, noted that "the value of eugenics research had been convincingly demonstrated in the United States, where anthropological statistics had been gathered from 2 million men recruited for the American armed forces."[35]

Soon after the American Supreme Court ruled that sterilization of minorities for eugenic purposes was constitutional, Adolf Hitler's cabinet passed a eugenic sterilization law using the American ruling as an example.[36] The 1933 German law was compulsory for all people, "institutionalized or not, who suffered from allegedly hereditary disabilities including feeblemindedness, schizophrenia, epilepsy, blindness, severe drug or alcohol addiction and physical deformities that seriously interfered with locomotion or were grossly offensive."[37]

The German laws were then used to inspire even harsher laws in the United States—in Virginia, Dr. Joseph DeJarnette argued that the progressive and scientific-minded Americans should be shamed by the "enlightened" progressive German legislation, and that *Americans* should be taking the lead in this area instead of Germany.[38] As a whole, the Germans and Americans shared information and ideas and influenced each other to develop eugenics programmes.

The next step in Germany was for the government to provide "loans" to couples that it concluded were "racially and biologically desirable" and therefore should have more children. The birth of each child reduced the "loan" indebtedness by 25 per cent. Later came sterilization laws and then, in 1939, euthanasia of certain mentally handicapped or diseased persons.

Ultimately, euthanasia was extended to include physically disabled persons, some with minor disabilities. These policies motivated American and British eugenicists to endorse the German programme

---

34 Chase, *The Legacy of Malthus*, 343.

35 Proctor, *Racial Hygiene: Medicine under the Nazis*, 40.

36 Edwin Black, *War against the Weak: Eugenics and American's Campaign to Create a Master Race* (New York: Four Walls Eight Windows Press, 2003).

37 Daniel J. Kevles, *In the Name of Eugenics: Genetics and the Uses of Human Heredity* (New York: Knopf, 1985), 116.

38 Stefan Kühl, *The Nazi Connection: Eugenics, American Racism, and German National Socialism* (New York: Oxford University Press, 2002).

as a model because it was "without [the] nefarious racial content" of American programmes.[39]

Conversely, German eugenicists repeatedly acknowledged their debt to the American and British researchers and periodically honoured eugenicists from British and American universities with various awards. Furthermore, many of the American eugenicists argued that the Nazis were outdoing them and were able to convince American courts (including the Supreme Court) of the validity of even some of the most outrageous eugenic claims.[40] Some of these eugenic-based ideas became part of American law and practice until after World War II when the full horror of the German eugenics programmes became widely known.

JEWS IN GERMANY AND DARWINISM

The early German eugenic leadership moderated their anti-Semitic rhetoric in an attempt to attract Jews to the eugenics movement.[41] Many early German eugenicists believed that German Jews were Aryans and, consequently the eugenic movement was supported by many Jewish professors and doctors both in Germany and abroad. The Jews were only gradually incorporated into the German eugenic theory, and later its laws.

The views of Darwinian racists only *gradually* entered into spheres of German society that they previously had not affected.[42] The Pan-German League (*Alldeutscher Verband*), dedicated to "maintaining German racial purity," was originally not overtly anti-Semitic, and assimilated Jews were allowed full membership. Many German eugenicists believed that, although blacks or Gypsies were racially inferior, their racial theories did not fit Jews, since many Jews had achieved significant success in Germany. By 1903, the influence of race ideas permeated the League's programme to the degree that, by

39 Kevles, *In the Name of Eugenics*, 118.

40 Kühl, *The Nazi Connection*; William Stanton, *The Leopard's Spots: Scientific Attitudes toward Race in America, 1815–1859* (Chicago: University of Chicago Press, 1960).

41 Weikart, "The Impact of Social Darwinism"; Ruth Lewin Sime, *Lise Meitner: A Life in Physics* (Berkeley: University of California Press, 1996)

42 Beyerchen, *Scientists under Hitler*.

1912, the League declared itself based on "racial principles" and soon excluded Jews from membership.[43]

In spite of the scientific support for these racial views, not until World War II did they have a major effect on most Jews. Most German Jews were proud of being Germans and considered themselves Germans first and Jews second. Many Jews modified the German *intelligentsia's* racial views by including themselves in it. Their assimilation into German life was so complete that most Jews felt the anti-Semitism of the eugenists did not represent a serious threat to their security.

Most Jews were also convinced that Germany was now a safe harbour for them.[44] In fact, during World War II, an estimated 150,000 *Mischlinge* (part Jewish) men served in the German Army, many with distinction—and hundreds served at the rank of major or even higher as colonels or generals.[45] It was later revealed that the "ideal" German soldier, whose picture was plastered everywhere, for Nazi propaganda purposes was half Jewish.[46]

Many German Gentiles still firmly held to the Genesis creation model and rejected the views on which racism was based, including Darwinism. What happened in Germany later was obviously not well received by Jewish geneticists, even non-Jewish eugenicists and certain other groups. As Greta Jones notes, the world

> eugenics movement felt a mixture of apprehension and admiration at the progress of eugenics in Germany…[but] the actual details of the eugenics measure which emerged after Hitler's rise to power were not unequivocally welcomed. Eugenicists pointed to the USA as a place where strict laws controlled marriage but where a strong tradition of political freedom existed.[47]

---

43 Schleunes, *The Twisted Road to Auschwitz.*

44 Schleunes, *The Twisted Road to Auschwitz*, 33.

45 Bryan Mark Rigg, *Hitler's Jewish Soldiers: The Untold Story of Nazi Racial Laws and Men of Jewish Descent in the German Military* (Lawrence: University of Kansas, 2002).

46 Rigg, *Hitler's Jewish Soldiers*, 78.

47 Greta Jones, *Social Darwinism and English Thought: The Interaction between Biological and Social Theory* (Atlantic Highlands: The Humanities Press, 1980), 168.

While ethnic Jewish persons were still held as an example of educational and professional achievement in much of American and British eugenic literature, German eugenicists began classifying Jews as evolutionarily inferior. Although intelligent, they were often seen as using their intelligence in crafty and underhanded ways for selfish gain, partly because they were seen as hereditarily immoral. Furthermore, although many American and British eugenicists objected to Germans judging certain groups as inferior, such as many Eastern Europeans, many American eugenicists also classified these groups as inferior.[48]

EVOLUTION USED TO JUSTIFY EXISTING GERMAN RACISM

Dr. Karl Schleunes noted, rather poignantly, that the publication of Darwin's 1859 book, *On the Origin of Species,* had an immediate impact in Germany's Jewish policy. Once the social Darwinists raised the struggle from the biological to the social plane, "Darwin's notion of struggle for survival…legitimized by the latest scientific views, justified the racist's conception of superior and inferior peoples…and validated the conflict between them."[49]

The anti-Semitic attitudes of the German people were only partly to blame for causing the Holocaust—only when Darwinism was added to the preexisting mix of attitudes did a lethal combination result. The Darwinian revolution and the writings of its chief German spokesman and most eminent scientist, Professor Haeckel, gave the racists what they were confident was powerful verification of their race views.[50] The support of the scientific establishment resulted in racist thought having a much wider circulation than had been possible up to this time, and enormous satisfaction "that one's prejudices were actually expressions of scientific truth."[51]

And what greater authority than science could racists have for their views? Nobel laureate Konrad Lorenz, a dedicated Nazi, one of the

---

48 Black, *War against the Weak.*

49 Schleunes, *The Twisted Road to Auschwitz,* 31–32.

50 Leon Poliakov, *The Aryan Myth* (New York: Barnes & Noble, 1996).

51 Schleunes, *The Twisted Road to Auschwitz,* 32.

most eminent animal behaviour scientists at that time, and often credited as being the founder of his field, stated,

> Just as in cancer the best treatment is to eradicate the parasitic growth as quickly as possible, the eugenic defense against the dysgenic social effects of afflicted subpopulations is of necessity limited to equally drastic measures.... When these inferior elements are not effectively eliminated from a [healthy] population, then—just as when the cells of a malignant tumor are allowed to proliferate throughout the human body—they destroy the host body as well as themselves.[52]

Lorenz's works were important in developing the Nazi programme designed to eradicate the "parasitic growth" of inferior races. The government's programmes to ensure the "German Volk" maintained their superiority made racism almost unassailable. Although some scholars, such as biologist James King, claim that the Holocaust pretended "to have a scientific genetic basis,"[53] the position of Darwinism within the government and the university elite of the time was so entrenched that few contemporary scientists seriously questioned the direct application of social Darwinism to governmental policy.[54]

EUGENICS BECOMES MORE EXTREME

Most of the early American, Canadian and British eugenicists stressed volunteerism should be relied on for implementation of eugenic programmes. Francis Galton, though, concluded the problem of inferior races contaminating the gene pool "was so clear-cut, and so dire, as to warrant state intervention of a coercive nature in human reproduction."[55] Later, eugenicists increasingly supported directed government action in applying eugenic laws—natural selection may produce the most fit

---

52 Cited in Chase, *The Legacy of Malthus*, 349.

53 James King, *The Biology of Race* (Berkeley: University of California Press, 1981), 156.

54 John S. Haller, Jr., *Outcasts from Evolution: Scientific Attitudes of Racial Inferiority, 1859–1900* (Urbana: University of Illinois Press, 1971).

55 Cited in Kevles, *In the Name of Eugenics*, 91.

race but only artificial selection enforced by the government could ensure that the eugenically superior dominated.

Many social workers, psychiatrists and other mental health workers in Britain, the United States and Germany were convinced of genetic origin of social deficiencies, and they increasingly felt compelled to force the government to intervene.[56] Discouraged by the lack of effectiveness of their science in influencing governmental policy, and fully convinced that eugenics had been empirically demonstrated by the brilliant scientific work of Charles Darwin, Karl Pearson, Francis Galton, and many others, Western eugenic proponents felt envy that only Germany was able to fully implement the programmes that many scientists in America and Europe were then strongly advocating.[57]

Nazi Germany, though, was not alone in applying science to government policy. In the United States during the early 1900s, "it came to be a hallmark of good reform government to shape policy with the aid of scientific experts…[and soon eugenic] experts aplenty were to be found in the biology, psychology, and sociology departments of universities or colleges."[58] Significantly, the German eugenics programmes elicited little opposition from the West. The United States policies also worked against saving the lives of those that Germany decided were racially inferior. The implications of its eugenic immigration acts, especially the American Johannson Quota Act of 1924, which was not repealed until 1941, had enormous consequences for human lives:

> At least nine million human beings of what Galton and Pearson called degenerative stock, two-thirds of them the Jews…continued to be denied sanctuary at our gates. They were all ultimately herded into Nordic *Rassenhygiene* camps, where the race biologists in charge made certain that they ceased to multiply. And ceased to be.[59]

---

56 Nancy L. Gallagher, *Breeding Better Vermonters: The Eugenics Project in the Green Mountain State* (Hanover: University of New England Press, 1999).

57 Chase, *The Legacy of Malthus.*

58 Kevles, *In the Name of Eugenics*, 101.

59 Kevles, *In the Name of Eugenics*, 360.

The first step in a eugenic programme was to determine which groups were genetically superior, a judgement that was heavily influenced by culture. Many Germans did not accept the American and British conclusions as to which races were inferior, and for this reason the Germans instituted their own programme. This meant that they must first determine what traits were superior. The ideal traits were

a human type whose appearance had been described by the race theorist Hans F.K. Günther as "blond, tall, long-skulled, with narrow faces, pronounced chins, narrow noses with a bridge, soft hair, widely spaced pale-coloured eyes, pinky-white skin-colour."[60]

Although superficial observation enabled most people to make a broad classification of race, as the Nazis soon learned when they explored it in depth, race status is by no means easy to determine. Many of the groups that they felt were inferior, such as Slavic peoples (mostly the Poles, Russians and Ukrainians), Jews, Gypsies and others, were not easily distinguishable from the pure "Aryan" race. In grouping people into races to select the "best," the Nazis measured a wide variety of physical traits including brain case sizes.

The Nazis relied heavily upon the work of Hans F.K. Günther, professor of "racial science" at the University of Jena. Although Günther's "personal relationships with the party were stormy at times," his racial ideas received wide support throughout the German government and were an important influence in German policy.[61] Günther recognized that, although "a race may not be pure, its members share certain dominant characteristics," thus paving the way for stereotyping.[62]

Günther concluded that all Aryans share an ideal Nordic face that contrasted with the Jews, whom he concluded were a mixture of races. Günther stressed that a person's genealogical lineage, anthropological

60 Joachim C. Fest, *The Face of the Third Reich: Portraits of the Nazi Leadership* (New York: Pantheon, 1970), 99–100.

61 George L. Mosse, *Nazi Culture: Intellectual, Cultural, and Social Life in the Third Reich* (Madison: University of Wisconsin Press, 1981), 57.

62 Mosse, *Nazi Culture*, 57.

measurements of his skull, and evaluations of physical appearance were all important. Even though physical appearance was stressed, the Nazis believed, "the body is the showplace of the soul" and "the soul is primary."[63]

Females with the traits—such as IQ—that eugenicists judged as superior Aryan race qualities, were even placed in special homes and kept pregnant as long as they remained in a programme called *Lebensborn*. Nonetheless, research on the offspring of the experiment have concluded that, as is now known, IQ regresses toward the population mean and the IQs of the offspring were generally lower than that of the high IQ parents.[64]

THE BAD BLOOD THEORY

Darwinism was a major influence on the Nazi party's conclusion that not only were certain races and ethnic groups inferior, but mental patients were also genetically inferior. Part of the reason was because it was then believed that heredity had a major controlling influence on mental illness (or that the mentally ill may have non-Aryan blood in them) and, consequently, those persons with "bad blood" had to be destroyed. Jewish historian Leon Poliakov notes that many intellectuals in the early 1900s accepted *telegony*, the idea that "bad blood" would *contaminate a race line forever*, or that "bad blood drives out good [blood], just as bad money displaces good money."[65] Only extermination would permanently eliminate these inferior genetic lines, thereby furthering evolution. Darwin even compiled a long list of cases where bad blood polluted a white gene line, causing it, he concluded, to produce impure progeny forever.

Numerous respected biologists, including Ernst Rüdin, a professor at the Kaiser Wilhelm Institute in Munich and also headed the Max Planck Institute for Brain Research, and many of his colleagues— including Erwin Baur, Eugen Fischer, Fritz Lenz, Francis Galton and

63 Mosse, *Nazi Culture*, 58.

64 Stephen Murdoch, *IQ: A Smart History of a Failed Idea* (New York: Wiley, 2007), 119–138; Marc Hillel and Clarissa Henry, *Of Pure Blood* (New York: McGraw-Hill, 1976).

65 Poliakov, *The Aryan Myth*, 282.

Eugene Kahn, later a professor of psychiatry at Yale—actively advocated this hereditary argument. These scientists either directly or
indirectly influenced the German compulsory sterilization laws
designed to prevent those with defective or "inferior" genes from
contaminating the Aryan gene pool.

Later, when the "genetically inferior" were also judged as "useless
eaters," massive killings became justified. The groups judged inferior
were gradually expanded to include a wide variety of races and national
groups. Later, it even included less healthy older people, epileptics,
persons with both severe and mild mentally defects, deaf-mutes, and
even persons with certain terminal illnesses.[66]

The list of groups judged "inferior" was later expanded to include
persons who had Negroid or monogoloid *features*, Gypsies, and those
who did not pass a set of ingeniously designed overtly racist tests now
known to be worthless. After Jesse Owen won several gold medals at
the 1936 Berlin Olympics, Hitler reportedly chastised the Americans
for permitting blacks to enter the contests.[67] How the weak were to be
"selected" for elimination was not consistent nor were the criteria used
to determine "weak."[68]

The justification of these programmes was that "leading biologists
and professors" advocated them. According to psychiatrist and author
Frederic Wertham, Dr. Karl Brandt reasoned that since the learned
professors were in support, the programme must be valid and "who
could there be who was better qualified [to judge the programme]
than they?"[69]

EVOLUTION AND WAR IN NAZI GERMANY

Darwinism not only offered the Germans a meaningful interpretation
of their recent military past, but also justification for future aggression: "German military success in the Bismarckian wars fit neatly into
Darwinist categories [and in]…the struggle for survival, the fitness of

---

66 Frederic Wertham, *A Sign for Cain: An Exploration of Human Violence* (New York:
Macmillan, 1966); Chase, *The Legacy of Malthus*.

67 Stanton, *The Leopard's Spots*.

68 Weindling, *Health, Race and German Politics*.

69 Wertham, *A Sign for Cain*, 160.

Germans had been clearly demonstrated."[70] In other words, war was a positive force not only because it eliminated the weaker races, but also because it weeded out the weaker members of the superior races. Hitler not only unabashedly intended to produce a superior race, but he openly relied on Darwinian thought in both his extermination and war policies.[71]

Partly for this reason, Nazi Germany openly glorified war because it was an important means of eliminating the less fit of the highest race, a step necessary to "upgrade the race." Clark concludes, quoting extensively from *Mein Kampf*, that

> Hitler's attitude to the League of Nations and to peace and war were based upon the same principles. "A world court without a world police would be a joke...the whole world of Nature is a mighty struggle between strength and weakness—an eternal victory of the strong over the weak. There would be nothing but decay in the whole of nature if this were not so. States which [violate]...this elementary law would fall into decay.... He who would live must fight. He who does not wish to fight in this world where permanent struggle is the law of life, has not the right to exist." To think otherwise is to "insult" nature. "Distress, misery and disease are her rejoinders."[72]

German greatness, Hitler stressed, came about primarily because Germans were jingoists, and had been eliminating their weaker members for centuries.[73] Although Germans were no strangers to war, this new justification gave powerful support to their policies. The view that eradication of the weaker races was a major source of evolution was well expressed by Wiggam when he said the human race

> had scarcely more brains than his anthropoid cousins, the apes. But, by kicking, biting, fighting, outmaneuvering and outwitting

---

70 Schleunes, *The Twisted Road to Auschwitz*, 31.

71 Jäckel, *Hitler's Weltanschauung*.

72 Robert Clark, *Darwin: Before and After* (Grand Rapids: Grand Rapids International Press, 1958), 115–116.

73 Norman Rich, *Hitler's War Aims* (New York: W.W. Norton & Co., 1973).

his enemies, and by the fact that the ones who had not sense and strength enough to do this were killed off, man's brain became enormous and he waxed both in wisdom and agility if not in size and morals.[74]

In other words, war is positive in the long run because only by lethal conflicts can humans evolve. Hitler even claimed as truth the contradiction that human civilization as we know it would not exist if it were not for constant war. Furthermore, many of the leading scientists of his day openly advocated this view:

> Haeckel was especially fond of praising the ancient Spartans whom he saw as a successful and superior people as a consequence of their socially approved biological selection. By killing all but the "perfectly healthy and strong children" the Spartans were "continually in excellent strength and vigor." Germany should follow this Spartan custom, as infanticide of the deformed and sickly was "a practice of advantage to both the infants destroyed and to the community." It was, after all, only "traditional dogma" and hardly scientific truth that all lives were of equal worth or should be preserved.[75]

The common assumption that European civilization evolved far more than others, primarily because of its constant warmongering in contrast to other nations, is false. War is actually typical of virtually all peoples except certain small island groups who have abundant food, or peoples in very cold areas.[76] Historically, many tribes in Africa were continually involved in wars, as were most peoples in Asia and America.

Ironically, Hitler, as well as Haeckel, Ploetz and others, recognized that war also killed the strong and most fit simply because those unfit for military service were not drafted and consequently were less likely

---

74 Albert Edward Wiggam, *The New Dialogue of Science* (Garden City: Garden City Publishing Co, 1922), 102.

75 Stein, "Biological Science and the Roots of Nazism," 56.

76 Gerald L. Posner and John Ware, *Mengele: The Complete Story* (New York: McGraw Hill, 1986).

to die in combat and more likely to have families.[77] This was only one of many contradictions in the Nazi movement.

NAZISM IS APPLIED EVOLUTION

From our modern perspective, many people have concluded that World War II and its results ensued from the ideology of an evil madman, and his equally evil administration. Hitler, though, did not see himself as evil, but as humanity's benefactor. Richard Weikart concluded that Hitler was inspired by Darwinism to pursue a utopian project of biologically improving the human race, and this evolutionary ethic influenced most every major feature of Nazi policy including eugenics, racism, offensive warfare, racial extermination and even population expansion.[78] Putting members of these inferior races in concentration camps was not so much an effort to punish but, as his apologists repeatedly claimed, was a protective safeguard similar to quarantining sick people to prevent contamination of the rest of the community.[79]

The Nazis believed that eliminating Jews and other "inferior races" was a scientific and rational way of serving an objectively greater good.[80] Hitler felt that the world would eventually be grateful to him and his programmes that lifted the human race to genetically higher levels of evolution as a result of reducing race pollution by preventing marriages of Aryans with inferior races:

Hitler was influenced above all by the theories of the nineteenth-century social Darwinist school, whose conception of man as biological material was bound up with impulses towards a planned society. He was convinced that the race was disintegrating, deteriorating through faulty breeding as a result of a liberally tinged promiscuity that was vitiating the nation's blood. And this led to the establishment of a catalogue of "positive" curative

77 Paul Crook, *Darwinism, War and History* (New York: Cambridge University Press, 1994).

78 Weikart, *Hitler's Ethic.*

79 Ellis Washington, "Nuremberg Project: Social Darwinism in Nazi Family and Inheritance Law," *Rutgers Journal of Law and Religion* (Fall 2011).

80 Peter J. Haas, "Nineteenth Century Science and the Formation of the Nazi Policy." *Journal of Theology* 99 (1995): 6–30.

measures: racial hygiene, eugenic choice of marriage partners, the breeding of human beings by the methods of selection on the one hand and extirpation on the other.[81]

As Höss adds, "such a struggle, legitimized by the latest scientific views, justifies the racists' conceptions of superior and inferior people and nations and validated the conflict between them."[82]

Many in Germany, early on, recognized the harm of Darwinism, and the Prussian Minister of Education for a time in 1875 forbade the "schoolmasters in the country to have anything to do with Darwinism…with a view of protecting schoolchildren from the dangers of the new doctrines."[83] A significant question is this: Would the Nazi Holocaust have occurred if this ban had remained in effect? At the entrance of this struggle was Haeckel who garnered much support from free thinkers and others who

> gathered around him in spite of his many delusions, when such measure as the school regulations mentioned above were adopted…. All the more so as the outcome proved Haeckel's justification; Darwinism might be prohibited in the schools, but the idea of evolution and its method penetrated everywhere…. And to this result, Haeckel has undeniably contributed more than most; everything of value in his utterances has become permanent, while his blunders have been forgotten, as they deserve.[84]

Many biologists today, writing the above, would drop "as they deserve" because Haeckel is regarded by his critics as an unscrupulous forger who played no small role in the horrible events that occurred in the 1930s and 1940s.

The well-documented influence of Darwinism on the Holocaust has been greatly downplayed by the mass media. Many current writers

---

81 Fest, *The Face of the Third Reich*, 99.

82 Höss, *Commandant of Auschwitz*, 110.

83 Erik Nordenskjöld, *The History of Biology*, trans. Leonard Bucknell Eyre (New York: Tudor Publishing Company, 1935), 522.

84 Nordenskjöld, *The History of Biology*, 522.

gloss over, totally ignore or even distort the close connection between Darwinism and Nazi racism and the policies it produced. But, as Stein admonishes, little doubt exists that the

history of ethnocentrism, racism, nationalism, and xenophobia has been also a history of the use of science and the actions of scientists in support of these ideas and social movements. In many cases it is clear that science was used merely as raw material or evidence by ideologically interested political actors as proof of preconceived notions.[85]

He adds that there is also little doubt that this self-protecting attitude is based on a willful misreading of history. He concludes that support for ethnocentrism and racism included many well-respected scientists who were very "active in using their own authority as scientists to advance and support racist and xenophobic political and social doctrines in the name of science."[86] He adds that the scientists of the day could not deny that they used science to advance racism, and it is historical whitewash to attempt to claim that the past abuse of science was not respected science but merely pseudoscience.

THE CLAIM THAT CHARLES DARWIN WAS JUST REFLECTING HIS CULTURE

Significantly, Charles Darwin was not just responding to his culture: "we have all heard, time and time again, that the reason Darwin's theory was so…sexist, and racist is that Darwin's society exhibited these same characteristics." Professor David Hull answers this charge by noting that Darwin was not "so callow that he simply read the characteristics of his society into nature."[87] Clearly, Darwin played a major role in creating the society that scientists today claim was at fault for adversely influencing Darwin, excusing him for his contribution.

---

85 Stein, "Biological Science and the Roots of Nazism," 50.
86 Stein, "Biological Science and the Roots of Nazism," 50.
87 David Hull, "Uncle Sam Wants You. A review from the book *Mystery of Mysteries: Is Evolution a Social Construction?* by Michael Ruse," *Science* 284 (1999): 1131–1132.

Relatively few scientific studies exist that directly deal with Darwinism and Nazism, partly because many evolutionists avoid the subject for the reason that evolution is inescapably selectionist. One of the most well-documented studies supporting this, using primary sources, is that of historian Richard Weikart.[88] One of the best reviews of Darwinian and Nazi documents concludes the Nazis felt confident that their extermination programmes were firmly based on science.[89]

Recently, a number of popular articles have published surprisingly candid accounts of this topic.[90] The source of the worst of Nazism was Darwinism, and we must first understand history to prevent its repetition because "those who ignore the lessons of history are condemned to repeat it."[91]

After an extensive study of the "natural selection" homicides committed in German institutions, Dr. Frederic Wertham concluded that the psychiatric and medical professions were among the most enthusiastic supporters of Nazi race programmes.[92] They not only willingly implemented Nazi policy, but often went well beyond what the law required. He relates the activities of numerous eminent psychiatrists and physicians from leading German universities. Many of these scientists who not only supported the Nazi policy of "artificial evolution" but eagerly implemented these policies and are still quoted today in the literature as experts.[93] Highly respected scientific works published in Nazi Germany and elsewhere openly advocated elimination of those judged, not only a "foreign body in human [meaning Aryan] society" but people who were "below the level of beasts."

Although the justification for extermination programmes included a desire to eliminate "hereditary diseases" that were a "drain on the German people," most of those murdered did not have hereditary

---

88 Weikart, *From Darwin to Hitler.*

89 Benno Müller-Hill, *Murderous Science: Elimination by Scientific Selection of Jews, Gypsies, and Others, Germany, 1933–1945* (Oxford: Oxford University Press, 1988).

90 For example, see Paul Gray, "Cursed by Eugenics," *Time* (January 11, 1999): 84–85.

91 Jones, *Social Darwinism and English Thought.*

92 Wertham, *A Sign for Cain.*

93 Quirin Schiermeier, "Dispute Erupts over Nazi Research Claims," *Nature,* Vol. 398, No. 6725 (March 25, 1999): 274.

conditions.[94] Nazism believed the state had a duty to provide "redemption from evil" in the form of a quick and painless drug to eliminate useless eaters.[95]

LACK OF OPPOSITION TO NAZI RACISM

Even though Germany had been the leader in the Protestant Reformation, the so-called Enlightenment and Darwinian ideas rapidly replaced the Christian worldview. German society rapidly adopted a thoroughly secular worldview that relied on science and materialistic philosophy for values and morals. Nazis rationalized that forcing Jews and other "inferior races" into concentration camps was not cruel or even punishment, but similar to quarantining the sick to prevent them from spreading their disease to the healthy. Conditions in the camps later deteriorated but, certain Nazis claimed, the main concern at first was to quarantine inferior races so as to prevent race contamination of the Aryan gene pool. Actually, the largest number of Jews were exterminated before camp conditions had deteriorated.

These ideas were not opposed by most scientists then, but rather "most members of the scientific and academic communities" not only "did very little to oppose the rise of Hitler and national socialism" but in many cases they

lent their considerable prestige as scientists to the support of the ideas of the national socialist movement [The Nazis]. It is simply true historically that German academics and scientists did, in fact, contribute to the development and eventually success of national socialism, both directly through their efforts as scientists and indirectly through the popularization or vulgarization of their scientific work.[96]

Dr. Wertham, himself a German psychiatrist, notes that psychiatrists became so carried away with their Darwinism that they later actually

---

94 Stein, "Biological Science and the Roots of Nazism," 50–58; Wertham, *A Sign for Cain*, 158.

95 Haeckel, *The Wonders of Life*, 118–119.

96 Stein, "Biological Science and the Roots of Nazism," 159.

reached into the outside community looking for victims for their death camps! They first convinced the parents or guardian that "such people [should] be placed under [their] guardianship and sent to an institution" and from there "they were quickly put into the gas chambers."[97]

Wertham concluded that the whole procedure of determining those deemed "unfit" for mating (and even living) was characterized by an almost complete absence of compassion, mercy or pity for the victims. He judged that the most reliable estimate of the number of "psychiatric" and other patients killed in German institutions as part of the euthanasia programme was at least 275,000.[98]

One institution alone, Hadamar, celebrated in 1941 the "cremation of the ten thousandth mental patient...[p]sychiatrists, nurses, attendants, and secretaries all participated. Everybody received a bottle of beer for the occasion."[99] Dr. Wertham even claimed that the entire population of every institution in German-controlled territory would likely have been eliminated if the Allies had not defeated Germany. In many cases, the total population of many institutions—even large ones—was eradicated, and the institutions closed.[100]

Because certain church leaders and humanitarians protested these eugenic killings, Hitler himself finally intervened. While on leave, many soldiers learned that a mentally ill brother, grandparent, aged relative or a friend injured in the war had "disappeared."[101] The knowledge that their countrymen at home were being murdered by the hundreds of thousands was demoralizing. Wertham claims that the Nazi government realized that many soldiers became fearful that they may well end up in the gas chambers if they were wounded in the war.[102]

Hitler recognized that the expansion of the race "purification" programme to those who were not "economically able to contribute," such as the war injured, hindered Germans' motivation to fight for their fatherland. Wertham concluded that this latest expansion of killing

97 Wertham, *A Sign for Cain*, 159.

98 Wertham, *A Sign for Cain*, 158.

99 Wertham, *A Sign for Cain*, 157.

100 Wertham, *A Sign for Cain*.

101 Bruno Bettelheim, *The Informed Heart: Autonomy in a Mass Age* (New York: Free Press, 1960).

102 Wertham, *A Sign for Cain*, 187.

"officially stopped" but in reality continued, though less blatantly and more hidden than before.

Nazism is often used as a example of the danger of "religious" zeal, yet only occasionally does popular literature mention the key role of the eugenics of Francis Galton, whose theories were based on the theory of natural selection espoused by his cousin, Charles Darwin. Firmly convinced that Darwinian evolution was true, Hitler saw himself as a benefactor of all humankind. By breeding a superior race, he thought he would, in the end, gain the world's admiration as the man who pulled humanity up to a higher level of evolutionary development. What Hitler attempted to do must be ranked alongside the most heinous crimes of history, and Darwin as the father of one of the most destructive philosophies in history.

SUMMARY

The writings of leading Nazis and early twentieth-century German biologists reveal that Darwin's theory had a major influence on Nazi race policies. Hitler believed that the human gene pool could be improved by using selective breeding similar to how farmers breed for superior cattle. In formulating its racial policies, Hitler's government relied heavily on Darwinism, especially the elaborations by biologist Ernst Haeckel.

As a result, a central policy of Hitler's administration was the development and implementation of policies designed to produce a "superior race." This required, at the very least, preventing the "inferior races" from mixing with those judged superior in order to reduce contamination of the latter's gene pool.[103] The "superior race" belief was based on the theory of racial inequality, a major presumption and requirement of Darwin's original survival of the fittest theory. This philosophy culminated in the Final Solution, the extermination of approximately 6 million Jews and over 5 million other people who belonged to what German scientists judged were "inferior races."[104]

---

103 Richard Milner, *The Encyclopedia of Evolution* (New York: Facts on File, 1990).

104 Gerald Astor, *The Last Nazi: The Life and Times of Joseph Mengele* (New York: Donald Fine, 1985); Jerry Bergman,"Darwinism as a Factor in the Twentieth-Century Totalitarianism Holocausts," *Creation Research Society Quarterly* , 39, No. 1 (2002): 47–53.

05

Hitler's leading
Darwinian scientists

INTRODUCTION

The writings of leading early twentieth-century German biologists reveal that many of them actively supported Nazi race policies. They believed that the human gene pool could be improved by using selective breeding similar to the manner that farmers used to breed cattle. In formulating their racial policies, Hitler's government relied heavily on the works of Darwinists and prominent Darwinian spokesmen such as Haeckel. Consequently, the development and implementation of government policies designed to evolve a "superior race" had widespread support from the scientific community. This philosophy culminated in the extermination of approximately 6 million Jews and over 5 million other people who belonged to what German scientists labelled as "inferior races."

GERMANY, THE LEADER IN SCIENCE

In the first part of the twentieth century, Germany was the science Mecca of the world, and German scientists were the most accomplished in their respective fields.[1] They won the lion's share of Nobel

---

1   Philip Campbell, "Germany Rising," *Nature* (September 30, 2010), 467: 499–500.

Laureates and honours until the end of World War II, and most supported, or at least were sympathetic to, the Nazi racial genocide. The importance of German science is illustrated by the fact that researchers the world over until the Second World War had to learn German to read the major scientific literature.[2] The critical effect of the replacement of the Judeo-Christian-Muslim creationist worldview by Darwinism on Nazi race policies has been well documented.[3] Protestant minister William Bell Riley even called Hitler's Nazism "the philosophy of evolution in action."[4]

It is also well documented that Nazi leaders were profoundly influenced by Darwinism, but it is somewhat less well known that the Nazis enjoyed widespread support from most of the German scientific community, especially biologists.[5] The now classic work by German Jewish historian Max Weinreich constitutes a "formidable indictment against the German intellectual elite."[6]

Importantly, German scholars and intellectuals, most university trained and many university professors "provided the ideas and techniques which led to and justified" the unparalleled slaughter of the Jews and other "inferior" races.[7] Weinreich notes that the physical anthropologists, biologists and all branches of the social sciences, and humanities in particular, supported and often actively contributed to the Holocaust machine.

Nazi beliefs about race also were widely shared by the worldwide scientific community, especially biologists. Darwin's major influence

---

2   Philip Campbell, "Germany Rising," 499.

3   Richard Weikart, *From Darwin to Hitler* (New York: Palgrave Macmillan, 2004); E. Michael Jones, "Darwin and the Vampire: Evolution's Contribution to the Holocaust," *Culture Wars* 17 (November 1988): 18–29; Ian Kershaw, *Hitler 1936–45: Nemesis* (New York: W.W. Norton, 2000).

4   William Bell Riley, *Hitlerism: or The Philosophy of Evolution in Action* (Minneapolis, 1941), 3, cited in Ronald L. Numbers, "*Creationism in 20th-Century America*," *Science* 218 (November 5, 1982): 538–544.

5   Ute Deichmann, *Biologists under Hitler*, trans. Thomas Dunlap (Cambridge: Harvard University Press, 1996).

6   Martin Gilbert, "Foreword," in Max Weinreich, *Hitler's Professors*, 1946 ed. (Reprint, New Haven: Yale University Press, 1999), v.

7   Weinreich, *Hitler's Professors*, 6.

on Nazi policy can be evaluated by an examination of the writings of leading early twentieth-century German biologists. Arthur Keith concluded that the Nazi treatment of Jews and other "races," then believed to be "inferior," was largely a result of the widespread belief among biologists that Darwinism provided profound insight that could be used to significantly improve humankind.[8] In short, Nazism was

> based on Charles Darwin's doctrine of the survival of the fittest …which Herbert Spencer argued that those better adapted to the conditions of life prevailed not only in nature but in human society as well. Thus, from Darwin's doctrine, the [Nazi] racists concluded that the strong and victorious were also in the right.[9]

The goal of the Nazis eventually was the totally extermination of all people that they judged "inferior," especially Jews "in all lands," so that "no [inferior] germ-cell would remain" in the world and, consequently, they could never again pollute the pure Aryan race.[10] As noted, the core philosophy driving the Nazi Holocaust was that just as breeders could raise superior strains of horses and dogs so too it is possible to enhance the quality of humans by controlling their breeding. According to Nazi ideology

> race was the factor that governed men's lives. It was because of their race that they acted for good or bad and tended toward survival or extinction. When citizens were corrupted by the rule of an inferior race, government was corrupted. When they were governed by a positive and lofty race—endowed with the right, the will, and the ability to rule—they enhanced humankind, its society, and its culture. Hence, the reform of government was possible only by improving the race.[11]

---

8 Arthur Keith, *Evolution and Ethics* (New York: G.P. Putnam's Sons, 1946), 230.

9 Leni Yahil, *The Holocaust: The Fate of the European Jewry, 1932–1945* (New York: Oxford University Press, 1990), 37.

10 Daniel Jonah Goldhagen, *Hitler's Willing Executioners: Ordinary Germans and the Holocaust* (New York: Knopf, 1996), 414.

11 Yahil, *The Holocaust: The Fate of the European Jewry*, 37.

As Professors Weikart and Stein show, this view was widely shared by Darwinists of the time.[12]

The first language into which Darwin's *On the Origin of Species* was translated—only a year after it was published in English—was German.[13] Although Darwinism was championed in many nations, it had more influence on German state policy than in any other country in the world.[14] So important was evolution that the Nazi goal was

> absolute control over the evolutionary process, over the biological human future. Making widespread use of the Darwinian term "selection," the Nazis sought to take over the functions of nature (natural selection)…in orchestrating their own "selections," their own version of human evolution. In these visions the Nazis embraced … a newer…claim to "scientific racism."[15]

The result was putative Jewish characteristics judged harmful, such as greed

> could be linked with alleged data of scientific disciplines, so that a "mainstream of racism" formed from "the fusion of anthropology, eugenics, and social thought." The resulting "racial and social biology" could make vicious forms of anti-Semitism seem intellectually respectable to learned men and women.[16]

So pervasive was biological evolution in the Nazi ideology that Professor Robert Lifton suggested the Nazi state could be called a "biocracy," rule by biology, which has as its goal the

> purification and revitalization of the Aryan race…. Just as in a theocracy, the state itself is no more than a vehicle for the divine

---

12 Weikart, *From Darwin to Hitler*; George Stein, "Biological Science and the Roots of Nazism," *American Scientist* 76, No. 1 (Jan–Feb 1988): 50–58.

13 Joseph Tenenbaum, *Race and Reich* (New York: Twayne, 1956).

14 Robert Jay Lifton, *The Nazi Doctors: Medical Killing and the Psychology of Genocide* (New York: Basic Books, 1986).

15 Lifton, *The Nazi Doctors*, 17.

16 Lifton, *The Nazi Doctors*, 17.

purpose, so in the Nazi biocracy was the state no more than a...
means to achieve "*a mission of the German people on earth*": that
of "*assembling and preserving the most valuable stocks of basic racial
elements in this* [Aryan] *people.*"[17]

A major effect that Darwinian evolution had on German society was
a complete "destructiveness of cosmic purpose." No longer could the
universe be seen as created and existing according to a Divine plan,
but rather as a result of random events that implied neither finality
nor purpose exists in nature.[18] Although Adolf Hitler and his associates,
and not the biological theorists, were the Nazi rulers, in Lifton's opinion the difference was "far from absolute" because among

the biological authorities called forth to articulate and implement
"scientific racism"—including physical anthropologists, geneticists, and racial theorists of every variety—doctors inevitably
found a unique place. It is they who work at the border of life and
death, who are most associated with the awesome, death-defying,
and sometimes death-dealing aura of the primitive shaman and
medicine man. As bearers of this shamanistic legacy and contemporary practitioners of mysterious healing arts, it is they who are
likely to be called upon to become biological activists.[19]

Hitler had broad support from, not only biologists, but even from
physical scientists. One of the first scientists to proudly become a
disciple of Hitler was the famous Nobel Laureate physicist Philipp
Lenard.[20] In 1924, Dr. Lenard published an "ecstatic statement in favor
of Hitler and the Nazi Party...co-signed by another famous physicist,
Nobel Laureate Johannes Stark. Not long after Lenard was honoured
by Hitler, most German scientists lent their support to both Hitler
and Lenard."[21]

---

17 Lifton, *The Nazi Doctors*, 17. Emphasis in original. Quotation is from Adolf Hitler,
Mein Kampf (Cambridge: Houghton Mifflin/The Riverside Press, 1962), 397–398.

18 Jones, "Darwin and the Vampire: Evolution's Contribution to the Holocaust."

19 Lifton, *The Nazi Doctors*, 17

20 Weinreich, *Hitler's Professors*, 11.

21 Weinreich, *Hitler's Professors*, 13

The inequality doctrine, the idea that some humans races are superior to others, was an integral part of German philosophy for years but reached its apex only under Hitler's regime. It obtained its chief intellectual support from Darwinism, especially from Darwin's major disciple, Ernst Haeckel.[22]

ERNST HAECKEL

Ernest Haeckel, a highly respected zoology professor at the University of Jena, was one of Darwin's leading proponents in Germany. He was reared as a Christian and creationist, but his worldview radically changed when he was exposed to evolution, materialism and the anti-Christian ideas of his professors. In time, he came to "detest" organized religion and adopted "quasi-mystical" naturalistic beliefs.[23] Haeckel was trained as a physician at Würzberg University and graduated in 1859, shortly before the publication of Darwin's *On the Origin of Species*. Darwin's *Origins* book

> dramatically changed his life. Here, he thought, was the answer to everything he had been seeking in science, philosophy, ethics, religion, politics—a unified, or monist, view of the world. His own fanaticized version of evolution became an obsession and guiding passion, with Darwin his greatest hero.[24]

Haeckel first forcefully presented his new Darwinian views at the 1863 Congress of German Naturalists in a speech that commenced his four-decade-long role as "Darwin's chief apostle."[25] Haeckel soon became a pivotal scientist who helped shape German biological research along Darwinian lines, expanding its range into every area of biology including

---

22 Sheila Faith Weiss, *Race Hygiene and National Efficiency: The Eugenics of Wilhelm Schallmayer* (Berkeley: University of California Press, 1988).

23 John Simmons, *The Giant Book of Scientists: A Ranking of the 100 Greatest Scientists Past and Present* (Australia: The Book Company, 1997), 424.

24 Richard Milner, *The Encyclopedia of Evolution* (New York: Facts on File, 1990), 205.

25 Stein, "Biological Science and the Roots of Nazism," 54.

embryology, morphology, and cell theory. He also raised and discussed many issues which are still alive today and coined the term *ecology*, which he defined as the scientific investigation of the relationship between organism and environment. Stephen Jay Gould has recently documented his extensive historical significance, and some years ago Erik Nordenskjöld could write that "there are not many personalities who have so powerfully influenced the development of human culture–and that, too, in many different spheres—as Haeckel.[26]

Haeckel's ideas of racial superiority soon began to resemble the racism of the infamous Arthur de Gobineau. Haeckel was especially active and successful in promoting the application of social Darwinism to social policy. His central focus was on the idea that social Darwinism explained why some civilizations advanced while others remained primitive.[27] Haeckel made important contributions in several areas of science such as invertebrate zoology, but his

greatest influence was, ultimately, in another, tragic direction— national socialism [Nazism]. His evolutionary racism; his call to the German people for racial purity and unflinching devotion to...his belief that harsh, inexorable laws of evolution ruled human civilization and nature alike, conferring upon favored races the right to dominate others.... His brave words about objective science—all contributed to the rise of Nazism. The Monist League that he had founded and led...made a comfortable transition to active support for Hitler.[28]

Ernst Haeckel was so important to the German Darwinism move-

26 Simmons, *The Giant Book of Scientists*, 424–422.

27 Ernst Haeckel, *The Riddle of the Universe* (New York: Harper, 1900); Ernst Haeckel, *Eternity: World War Thoughts on Life and Death, Religion, and the Theory of Evolution* (New York: Truth Seeker, 1916); Ernst Haeckel, *The Evolution of Man* (New York: Appleton, 1920).

28 Stephen Jay Gould, *Ontogeny and Phylogeny* (Cambridge: Harvard University Press, 1977), 77–78.

ment that he is referred to as the father of German evolution.[29] It was Haeckel who eventually convinced his influential countrymen that

> they must accept their evolutionary destiny as a "master race" and "outcompete" inferior peoples, since it was right and natural that only the "fittest" should survive. His version of Darwinism was incorporated in Adolf Hitler's *Mein Kampf* (1925), which means "My Struggle," taken from Haeckel's translation of Darwin's phrase, "the struggle for existence."[30]

Haeckel's conclusions about the evolution of the different races soon became German policy. He successfully convinced most German scientists and leading Nazis that "the morphological differences between two generally recognized species—for example sheep and goats—are much less important than those...between a Hottentot and a man of the Teutonic race."[31]

Especially important in Nazi policy was the belief that the Germans had evolved the "furthest from the common form of apelike men [and outstripped]...all others" and would be the race to raise humankind up to a "new period of higher mental development." Haeckel's conclusions expanded on a widely held nineteenth-century theme found in the writings of various Darwinists

> that each of the major races of humanity can be considered a separate species. Haeckel believed that varied races of mankind are endowed with differing hereditary characteristics not only of color but, more important, of intelligence, and that external physical characteristics are a sign of innate intellectual and moral capacity.[32]

---

29 Erik Nordenskjöld, *The History of Biology*, trans. Leonard Bucknell Eyre (New York: Tudor Publishing Company, 1935), 27.

30 Milner, *The Encyclopedia of Evolution*, 207.

31 Ernst Haeckel, *The History of Creation: Or the Development of the Earth and Its Inhabitants by the Action of Natural Causes* (New York: Appleton, 1876), 434.

32 Lifton, *The Nazi Doctors*, 441–442.

As an example Haeckel taught that what he called the

"wooly-haired" Negroes to be "incapable of a true inner culture and of a higher mental development." And the "difference between the reason of a Goethe, a Kant, a Lamarck, or a Darwin, and that of the lowest savage…is much greater than the graduated difference between the reason of the latter and that of the most 'rational' mammals, the anthropoid apes." Haeckel went so far as to say, concerning these "lower races," that since they are "psychologically nearer to the mammals (apes and dogs) than to civilized Europeans, we must, therefore, *assign a totally different value to their lives*" (italics added). The Auschwitz [influenced] self could feel a certain national-scientific tradition behind its harsh, apocalyptic, deadly rationality.[33]

He also taught that the superiority of civilized Europeans was true not only mentally, but also physically, because evolution achieves a "symmetry of all parts, and equal development which we call the type of perfect human beauty…no woolly-haired nation has ever had an important history."[34] The races that he believed were inferior included "the lower races–such as the Veddahs or Australian Negroes."[35]

Ernst Haeckel also concluded that the most evolved "race" was "the Indo-Germanic race, which has far surpassed all the other races of men in mental development." He deduced from his research that this race separated at a very early period in evolution into "two diverging branches," that were very different in their level of evolutionary development.[36]

Haeckel's conclusions were *not* a minority or extreme view in Germany then and much of the world; rather he was viewed as a mainline highly "respected scientist."[37] The views of some of his fol-

---

33 Lifton, *The Nazi Doctors*, 441–442.

34 Haeckel, *The History of Creation*, 10, 321.

35 Ernst Haeckel, *The Wonders of Life: A Popular Study of Biological Philosophy* (New York: Harper, 1905), 390.

36 Haeckel, *The Evolution of Man*, 431.

37 Stein, "Biological Science and the Roots of Nazism," 56.

lowers, however, often were even more extreme.[38] Haeckel fought hard to convince the world that a belief he once held, namely the Jewish (and Christian) creation story, was wrong. One major reason why he rejected the Genesis account of creation was that creationism taught that all races came from one original human couple, Adam and Eve, and therefore all races were equal. Haeckel wrote, the

> five races of men, according to the Jewish legend of creation, are said to have been descended from "a single pair"—Adam and Eve—and in accordance with this are said to be varieties of one kind or species. If, however, we compare them without prejudice, *there can be no doubt that the differences of these five races are as great and even greater than the "specific differences" by which zoologists and botanists distinguish recognized "good" animal and vegetable species....* The excellent paleontologist Quenstedt is right in maintaining that, "*if Negroes and Caucasians were snails, zoologists would universally agree that they represented two very distinct species, which could never have originated from one pair by gradual divergence.*"[39]

After his conversion to Darwinism, Haeckel ardently advocated romantic nationalism, racial regeneration, and anti-Semitism.[40] Haeckel became the major spokesman of Darwinism in Germany, and his name became synonymous with materialism and naturalism. Simmons claimed that Haeckel's last years were not happy and that he was especially upset by World War I, the war between his country, Germany and England, the home of his hero, Charles Darwin.[41]

HOUSTON STEWART CHAMBERLAIN

Another influential academic who was responsible for spreading racism in Germany was Houston Stewart Chamberlain (1855–1927), the son of a British admiral and a German woman. Chamberlain was

---

38 Stein, "Biological Science and the Roots of Nazism," 56.
39 Haeckel, *The Evolution of Man*, 412–413. Emphasis added.
40 Lifton, *The Nazi Doctors*, 424.
41 Simmons, *The Giant Book of Scientists*, 424.

Houston Stewart Chamberlain (1855–1927)
Chamberlain popularized the notion of the superiority of the Aryan race.

influenced by his father-in-law, the composer Richard Wagner (1813–1883). Wagner and Chamberlain both exerted a powerful influence on Hitler.

Chamberlain was one of several popular German writers to argue that the Aryans were innately biologically superior to all other races and peoples, including the Persians, Greeks, and especially the "parasitic Semites" whom he branded as a "race of inferior peoples." In 1899 he published a book titled, *The Foundations of the 19th Century*, in which he concluded that Darwinism had demonstrated that the Aryan race was superior to all other races.[42] Aryans were so superior to all other races that they were the *very foundation of advanced civilization*.[43]

Chamberlain believed Aryans were the "foundation" of modern industrial society because, among other achievements, they led in the industrial revolution and the Enlightenment. Although Chamberlain openly disagreed with some of Darwin's conclusions, he agreed with Darwin about the importance of the racial struggle for existence. Darwin interpreted the evolutionary success of *homo sapiens* as being principally the result of its evolutionary superior brain, as shown by the much larger brain case typical of higher primates (and especially by the apex of brain evolution in humans). He ignored facts, such as Neanderthals had an even larger brain than modern humans.

Chamberlain seized on this idea and concluded that human racial differences were reflected not only in skull variations (primarily shape and size variations), but also in all of those traits that historically have been used to identify human races (skin colour, nose, lip and eye shape, among others). Chamberlain taught that the brain is of far more importance than any other body structure in measuring human evolutionary advance.

It was widely believed at the time that the larger the brain, the higher the intelligence. He utilized as evidence for his theory not only the findings and assumptions of physical anthropologists, but also the then-fashionable "science" of cephalic indexes, the measurement of

---

42 Paul Weindling, *Health, Race and German Politics between National Unification and Nazism, 1870–1945* (Cambridge: Cambridge University Press, 1989).

43 John Cornwell, *Hitler's Scientists: Science, War, and the Devil's Pact* (New York: Viking, 2003), 78.

brain size and traits, supposedly a measure of evolutionary advancement level.

Cephalic indexes were based on the idea that brain configuration and other physical traits could be used both to distinguish humans from monkeys and to rank the human races from less to more advanced. This idea received widespread support from the German academic and scientific communities and helped to

> prepare the way for national socialist [Nazi] biopolicies.... Beginning in the 1890s with the work of Otto Ammon on cephalic indexes and other such scientific proof of Aryan superiority, much German anthropology, especially the most scientific branch, physical anthropology...[concluded] If humankind evolved through natural selection...then it was obvious that the races of humankind must be arranged hierarchically along the ladder of evolution. ...there is little doubt that the anthropologists who discovered all the measurable divergent physical, psychological, and mental characteristics of the various races thought they were scientific. And so did the general public.[44]

Chamberlain's work is still very influential today, primarily among white power and various racist groups as a "racial explanation for human history."[45] Furthermore "most of the isms which have profoundly influenced the twentieth century [such as communism, fascism and Marxism] have their genesis in these decades."[46]

EARLY SUPPORT FOR NAZI POLICIES

The academic foundation for Nazi policies existed before Hitler, and even before the Nazi party was formed. As early as 1917, the president of Stanford University, biologist Dr. Vernon Kellogg, concluded that Darwinism was used as part of the justification for war and German supremacy advanced by high-level German officers, "many of whom

---

44 Stein, "Biological Science and the Roots of Nazism," 57.

45 Karl A. Schleunes, *The Twisted Road to Auschwitz: Nazi Policy toward German Jews, 1933–1939* (Urbana: University of Illinois Press, 1970), 30

46 Schleunes, *The Twisted Road to Auschwitz*, 30

had been university professors before the war."[47] They not only proposed an evolutionary rationale, but advocated a particularly crude
form of natural selection that inexorably involved bloody battles where
the "weak" were more likely to die.[48] Kellogg, in his report on the
beliefs of top-level German generals, noted that:

> Professor von Flussen is Neo-Darwinian, as are most German
> biologists and natural philosophers. The creed of the *Allmacht*
> ["all might"] of a natural selection based on violent and fatal
> competitive struggle is the gospel of the German intellectuals;
> all else is illusion and anathema.... This struggle not only must
> go on, for that is the natural law, but it should go on, so that this
> natural law may work out in its cruel, inevitable way the salvation
> of the human species. By its salvation is meant its desirable natu-
> ral evolution.[49]

Kellogg concluded that the German professors and generals believed
the most evolutionarily advanced race "should win in the struggle for
existence." Furthermore,

> this struggle should occur precisely that the various [racial] types
> may be tested, and the best not only preserved, but put into posi-
> tion to impose its kind of social organization—its *Kultur*—on the
> others, or, alternatively, to destroy and replace them. This is the
> disheartening kind of argument that I faced at [the German]
> Headquarters.... Add...the additional assumption that the Ger-
> mans are the chosen race, and German social and political orga-
> nization the chosen type of human community life, and you have
> a wall of logic and conviction that you can break your head
> against but can never shatter.[50]

---

47 Vernon Kellogg, *Headquarters Nights: A Record of Conversations and Experiences
at the Headquarters of the German Army in France and Belgium* (Boston: Atlantic Monthly
Press, 1917), 28–30.

48 Stephen Jay Gould, *Bully for Brontosaurus: Reflections in Natural History* (New
York: Norton, 1991), 424.

49 Kellogg, *Headquarters Nights*, 28–30.

50 Kellogg, *Headquarters Nights*, 28–30.

One reason why popular support was so high for Nazism was because the public schools also taught evolution as critically important in social policy. German historian Richard Grunberger noted that since

Nazi ideology leaned heavily on Darwinist notions, the Party's educational pioneers—like Baldur von Schirach or Robert Ley— liked to talk of the Adolf Hitler Schools institutionalizing the principle of continuous selection. Having been pre-selected during their second year in the *Jungvolk*, potential Adolf Hitler pupils were racially examined and sent to a fort-night's youth camp for a final sifting. A main criterion of selection was physical appearance; after acceptance, Adolf Hitler scholars were largely evaluated according to qualities of leadership.[51]

ACADEMIC JOURNALS SUPPORT NAZI PROGRAMMES
German scientists took their science, which became known as "racial hygiene," very seriously. As noted, prior to 1933, German scientists published thirteen scientific journals devoted primarily to racial hygiene and related fields, and also established over thirty institutions, many of which were connected with major universities or research centres devoted to "racial science."[52] During the Nazi era, close to 150 scientific journals, many of which still are highly respected today, covered racial hygiene and allied fields.[53] Enormous data files were kept on the races, many of which were analyzed and used for research papers published in various German and other scientific journals. The Kaiser Wilhelm Institute for Anthropology, Human Heredity, and Eugenics was established in 1927 and is still active today under a new name—minus the word eugenics.

The various eugenic institutes also researched the "persistence" of various "primitive racial traits" in certain races in and outside of

51 Richard Grunberger, *The 12-Year Reich: A Social History Of Nazi Germany, 1933–1945* (New York: Holt, Rinehart and Winston, 1971), 298.

52 Robert N. Proctor, *Racial Hygiene: Medicine under the Nazis* (Cambridge: Harvard University Press, 1988), 39.

53 Weindling, *Health, Race and German Politics between National Unification and Nazism.*

Germany. Eugenicists soon found much evidence for the "Cro-magnon racial type in certain races, and presumably also [for the] Neanderthal" type, even though they had a larger brain on the average than modern man.[54] Like their American and British counterparts, the researchers at various German racial hygiene institutes and universities discovered genetic evidence for virtually every human trait from criminality to hernias, including even divorce and "loving to sail on water." The scientists saw their work as a noble effort to continue "Darwin's attempts to elucidate the origin of species."[55]

DARWINISM INFLUENCED NAZI LEADERS

Many of Hitler's top aides, including Martin Bormann, Heinrich Himmler and Rudolf Höss,[56] held similar Darwinian-based racist beliefs. Höss was raised a Catholic but renounced his Catholic membership in 1922, at the age of 22, just after completing his education and just before joining the National Socialist Party. He read extensively about racial theories, heredity and ethnology. His racial views guided his policy in the concentration camps that he administered, including Auschwitz.[57] The result was that he converted this former forced-labour camp into an evolution laboratory where inmates were no longer persons but "simply goods to be processed in the gigantic death-factory he had organized."[58]

Heinrich Himmler, the head of the SS and the architect of the Final Solution, believed (in harmony with Darwinism) that history has consisted of "a constant, merciless struggle among races for survival" and that as a result of this struggle German and Nordic races were "above all others."[59]

---

54 Proctor, *Racial Hygiene*, 291.

55 Proctor, *Racial Hygiene*, 291.

56 Not to be confused with Rudolf Hess, Hitler's Deputy.

57 Rudolf Höss, *Commandant of Auschwitz: Autobiography of Rudolf Höss* (Cleveland: World Publishing Company, 1959).

58 Raymond Rudorff, *Monsters: Studies in Ferocity* (New York: The Citadel Press, 1969), 240.

59 Richard Breitman, *The Architect of Genocide: Himmler and the Final Solution* (New York: Alfred Knopf, 1991), 35.

Caring for the weak, sick, lame, old or poor ran counter to the chief driving force of evolution—the survival of the fittest and non-survival of the less fit. This meant that the weak must be eradicated for the benefit of the race as a whole. The Nazi regime did not view these policies as wrong, or even inhumane, but instead openly prided itself on its advanced scientific ideology and modern view of the world.[60] Given the Nazis' wholesale acceptance of Darwinism, their race and deterministic ideas may well have been inescapable.[61]

Among the leading internationally respected scientists that supported Darwinism as a means of promoting racist eugenics include professors Fritz Lenz and Eugen Fischer who, with Erwin Baur, wrote a major, widely circulated (even translated into English) genetics textbook.[62] This textbook contained wild over-generalizations such as that a Negro lacks foresight and is

not inclined to work hard in the present in order to provide for wellbeing in a distant future...[and is] not particularly intelligent...and above all [he is] devoid of the power of mental creation, is poor in imagination, so that he has not developed any original art and has no elaborate folk sagas or folk myths.[63]

The Nazis reasoned that race pollution reduces the calibre of the potential leaders, and should thus be condemned. Many anthropologists, including those in America, supported this conclusion in writing. Examples include Dr. Earnest Hooton of Harvard, one of the first physical anthropologists in America. He, in turn, trained virtually every physical anthropologist in America for generations. Another was Carlton Coon, a prolific and best-selling author whose books openly advocated a polygenetic evolution, the belief that the races evolved

---

60 Daniel Gasman, *The Scientific Origin of National Socialism* (New York: American Elsevier, 1971).

61 Jacques Barzun, *Darwin, Marx, Wagner: Critique of a Heritage* (New York: Doubleday Anchor Books, 1958), xx.

62 Weikart, *From Darwin to Hitler*.

63 Erwin Baur, Eugen Fischer and Fritz Lenz, *Human Heredity* (New York: MacMillan, 1931), 628–629.

separately.[64] The polygenetic view concluded that the races are not equal, and that some are more primitive than others. Consequently, interbreeding has the potential of "mixing races" to the detriment of their offspring.[65]

The justification for the Nazi racist programmes, including their goal of exterminating the Jews, was based on the research conclusions of the "leading biologists and professors" not only in Germany but in America and elsewhere. According to Frederic Wertham, Dr. Karl Brandt felt that since these programmes had the support of the leading professors, the programme must be valid, and who "could there be who was better qualified [to judge it] than they?"[66] Dr. Brandt headed the administration of the Nazi euthanasia programme from 1939 onward and was appointed Adolf Hitler's personal physician in August 1934.

SUPPORT FOR DARWINISM BY MEDICAL PROFESSORS

The negative influence of Darwinism on German physicians also is well documented.[67] One German doctor, from a medical family traceable back to the early seventeenth century, was interested in biology from a young age. As he grew older, he began to read

Bölsche and Haeckel. Ernst Haeckel, a towering figure in German biology and an early Darwinian, was also a racist, a believer in a mystical *Volk*, and a strong advocate of eugenics who "can be claimed as direct ancestor" of the Nazi "euthanasia" project. Wilhelm Bölsche was a literary critic who became a disciple and biographer of Haeckel and was known to have provided Hitler with "direct access to major ideas of Haeckelian social Darwinism."[68]

---

64 Milford Wolpoff and Rachel Caspari, *Race and Human Evolution: A Fatal Attraction* (New York: Simon and Schuster, 1997); Earnest Albert Hooton, *Why Men Behave Like Apes and Vice Versa; or, Body and Behavior* (Princeton: Princeton University Press, 1941).

65 Daniel J. Kevles, *In the Name of Eugenics: Genetics and the Uses of Human Heredity* (New York: Knopf, 1985).

66 Frederic Wertham, *A Sign for Cain: An Exploration of Human Violence* (New York: Macmillan, 1966), 160.

67 Kershaw, *Hitler 1936–45*; Thomas Röder, Volker Kubillus and Anthony Burwell, *Psychiatrists: The Men behind Hitler* (Los Angeles: Freedom Publishing, 1995).

68 Lifton, *The Nazi Doctors*, 125.

After an extensive study of the "artificial selection" murders committed in German institutions, Wertham concluded that the psychiatric and medical professions were among the most enthusiastic supporters of Nazi race programmes.[69] They not only willingly implemented Nazi policy, but also often went far beyond what the law required.[70] Wertham also related the activities of numerous eminent psychiatrists and physicians who were teaching in leading German universities, many of which are still being quoted as experts in scientific literature today. These men not only supported the Nazi policy of "artificial evolution," but eagerly put it into effect. Highly respected scientific works published in Nazi Germany and elsewhere openly advocated elimination of those persons judged "below the level of beasts" who were a "foreign body in human [meaning Aryan] society."

Hans F.K. Günther, a professor of "race science" at the University of Jena, argued in favour of killing persons "whose death is urgently necessary [namely]...those who are below the level of beasts [such as Jews and Negroes]." Karl Binding and L. Alfred Hoche, authors of a book titled, *The Release of the Destruction of Life Devoid of Value,* advocated the same policy.[71] These articles and books advocating killing were generally favourably reviewed by biologists and university professors.[72] This scholarly material on racism espoused various policies that were later adopted by the Nazis.

Although the justification for extermination programmes included a desire to eliminate "hereditary diseases" that were a drain on German resources, most of those murdered did not have hereditary conditions.[73] The Nazis believed that the state had a duty to provide "redemp-

---

69 Wertham, *A Sign for Cain.*

70 Dieter Kunz and Susan D. Bachrach, eds., *Deadly Medicine: Creating the Master Race* (Chapel Hill: The University of North Carolina Press, 2006).

71 Karl Binding and L. Alfred Hoche, *The Release of the Destruction of Life Devoid of Value: It's* [sic.] *Measure and It's* [sic.] *Form* (1920), trans. Robert L. Sassone (Santa Ana: privately published, 1975).

72 Philipp Gassert and Daniel S. Mattern, *The Hitler Library: A Bibliography* (Westport: Greenwood Press, 2001); Nancy L. Gallagher, *Breeding Better Vermonters: The Eugenics Project in the Green Mountain State* (Hanover: University of New England Press, 1999).

73 Stein, "Biological Science and the Roots of Nazism," 56.

tion from evil" in the form of giving a quick and painless death to those persons judged inferior, an idea that they borrowed from Haeckel and other evolutionists.[74] These ideas were not only unopposed by the scientists, but rather

> most members of the scientific and academic communities...did very little to oppose the rise of Hitler and national socialism, and in many cases lent their considerable prestige as scientists to the support of the ideas of the national socialist movement.... German academics and scientists did, in fact, contribute to the development and eventual success of national socialism, both directly through their efforts as scientists and indirectly through the popularization or vulgarization of their scientific work.[75]

The support of the medical doctors was critical in allowing the atrocities in the camps to the extent that, in Auschwitz alone,

> Nazi doctors presided over the murder of most of the one million victims of that camp. Doctors performed selections—both on the ramp among arriving transports of prisoners and later in the camps and on the medical blocks. Doctors supervised the killing in the gas chambers and decided when the victims were dead. Doctors conducted a murderous epidemiology, sending to the gas chamber groups of people with contagious diseases and sometimes including everyone else who might be on the medical block. Doctors ordered and supervised, and at times carried out, direct killing of debilitated patients on the medical blocks by means of phenol injections into the bloodstream or the heart.[76]

Lifton added that doctors were actively consulted about how best to carry out the process of various tasks in the camps, such as

---

74 Haeckel, *The Wonders of Life*, 118–119.
75 Stein, "Biological Science and the Roots of Nazism," 57.
76 Lifton, *The Nazi Doctors*, 18.

how to burn the enormous numbers of bodies that strained the facilities of the crematoria. In sum, we may say that doctors were given much of the responsibility for the murderous ecology of Auschwitz—the choosing of victims, the carrying through of the physical and psychological mechanics of killing, and the balancing of killing and work functions in the camp.... As one survivor who closely observed the process put the matter, "Auschwitz was like a medical operation," and "the killing program was led by doctors from beginning to end."[77]

In the late 1970s, Lifton interviewed a German doctor who was a fierce anti-Semite during the Nazi era. In the interview, the doctor used Darwinism to explain both the failure of Nazi beliefs about Jews and the enormous success of Jews in the West. The doctor, upon learning that Lifton was Jewish, declared unctuously,

"The Jewish question became our tragedy and your tragedy"... initiated "by the flood [of Jews] from the East, and by Darwinian principles enabling Jews to become especially able "through such a hard selection during these two thousand years" to take so many medical positions that German doctors were excluded from.... "Nowadays we know that all of us, Jews and Germans, belong to the same cultural community" and must stand together against the "adverse cultural community".... Except for rearranging his cast of characters, Dr. S. had not changed much. Racially, he practiced what he preached, and had an enormous family: "I have always believed that those who are fit should have as many children as possible, and those who are unfit should have as few ...as possible."[78]

SUMMARY

Even though Germany had been the leader in both the Protestant Reformation and the Enlightenment, Darwinian ideas advocated by its leading scientists rapidly replaced the Christian worldview, begin-

---

77 Lifton, *The Nazi Doctors*, 18.
78 Lifton, *The Nazi Doctors*, 131.

ning only a few years after Darwin published *On the Origin of Species* in 1859.[79] German society rapidly adopted a thoroughly secular worldview, relying on science and materialistic philosophy for its values and morals. Ironically, the churches, Dietrich Bonhoeffer wrote, "lost their heads and their entire Bible," including Genesis, and even

> before Hitler came to power, as his ascendancy became increasingly probable, the editors of...[many] Christian papers brought their already virulently antisemitic rhetoric into closer concord with that of the Nazis. They did so unbidden, entirely voluntarily, and with unmistakable passion and alacrity.[80]

Some have tried to justify or rationalize the concentration camps by claiming that forcing Jews and other "inferior races" into them was not cruel punishment, or even punishment, but was similar to quarantining the sick to prevent them from spreading their disease to the healthy. This justification claims that conditions in the camps later deteriorated, but the main concern at first was simply to quarantine inferiors in order to prevent them from contaminating the Aryan gene pool. The goal, as became clear in time, was to eliminate a group of people believed to be, not just inferior, but unworthy of life and, in Hitler's words, harmful like bacilli that must be eradicated.[81]

Relatively few academic studies deal directly with Darwinism and Nazism—and many evolutionists today try to avoid the subject because they realize evolution is inescapably selectionist. The best reviews of Darwinism and Nazism documents supporting the fact that the Nazi extermination programmes were based firmly on science were completed by historians of German nationality.[82] Recently, several popular science and news magazines have published surprisingly candid and honest accounts of this topic.[83]

---

79 Kershaw, *Hitler 1936–45*.

80 Goldhagen, *Hitler's Willing Executioners*, 108.

81 Kunz and Bachrach, eds., *Deadly Medicine*; Kershaw, *Hitler 1936–45*.

82 Benno Müller-Hill, *Murderous Science: Elimination by Scientific Selection of Jews, Gypsies, and Others, Germany, 1933–1945* (Oxford: Oxford University Press, 1988).

83 Heather Pringle, "Confronting Anatomy's Nazi Past," *Science* (July 16, 2010): 274–275; Paul Gray, "Cursed by Eugenics," *Time* (Jan. 11, 1999): 84–85.

Some of the most scholarly academic studies that focusing on Darwinism's influence on Nazi Germany are those of Professor Richard Weikart. Weikart and others have documented that there can be no doubt that a major source of the worst of Nazism was Darwinism. To prevent a repeat performance, we must understand history because, as has often been observed, those who ignore the lessons of history are condemned to repeat them.[84]

Firmly convinced that Darwinian evolution was true, the German Darwinian scientists saw themselves as modern saviours of humankind, believing society someday would acknowledge that their work was responsible for bringing humanity to a higher level of evolutionary development. If negative eugenics is the means of race improvement as the racial hygienists proposed, the Nazis are our saviour and, as a result of their destruction, the human race will suffer grievously.

If social Darwinism is not true, what the Nazis attempted to do must be ranked among the most heinous crimes ever committed, and Darwinism must be considered the source of one of the most destructive philosophies ever foisted on humankind.[85] While Germany was going down in flames, Hitler was "ready in Wagnerian style in the event of ultimate apocalyptic catastrophe, and in line with his undiluted social-Darwinistic beliefs, to take his people down…with him if it [social-Darwinism] proved incapable of producing the victory he had demanded."[86]

Furthermore, some of the leading Nazi scientists, such as Professor Konrad Lorenz, have been highly rewarded since the fall of Nazi Germany. This is an important fact because no scientists "were forced to do things against their will. Whoever participated did so voluntarily. More than 50 percent of the biologists employed by the imperial institutions joined the Nazi party."[87] Zoologist Konrad Lorenz, who joined the Nazi Party in 1938, wrote in 1938 that his "whole scientific work is devoted to the ideas of the National Socialists." Goede writes in

---

84 George Santayana, *Persons and Places* (New York: Charles Scribner's, 1944).

85 Jerry Bergman, "Darwinism and the Nazi Race Holocaust," *Creation ex nihilo Technical Journal* 13 (November 1999), No. 2: 101–111.

86 Kershaw, *Hitler 1936–45*, 615.

87 Wolfgang Goede, "Science under the Swastika," *The Pantaneto Forum*, Issue 32 (October 2008): 8.

summary that Konrad Lorenz

in 1973 was honored with the Nobel Prize—so much for the memory, conscience and investigative competence of the international science community.... Dr. Susanne Heim, who headed the historical commission summarized her Max Planck study in a single sentence: "Scientists are highly vulnerable to intellectual and moral corruption—opportunities will be used if they promise more influence and success."[88]

---

88 Goede, "Science under the Swastika," 8.

Hitler's academics and doctors

INTRODUCTION

The German Führer, Adolf Hitler, and the Nazi movement as a whole, had strong support from almost the entire German scientific and academic community, especially during the early years of his dictatorship. Their support extended to his eugenic policies, including the extermination of the Jews and others whom the racial hygiene "experts" judged as racially inferior.

Among Darwin's most important disciples, and a major supporter of Hitler, was the scientific and academic establishment. During the twentieth century, Germany's scientific community was the most advanced in the world. Cambridge University historian John Cornwell wrote that during the first three decades of the last century Germany held the premier position for scientific achievement compared with all other nations of the world. German scientists were then among the most accomplished and honoured in most fields, as demonstrated by the fact that they were awarded the lion's share of Nobel prizes, as noted in the previous chapter.

Academics, including doctors, biologists, anthropologists and "all branches of the social sciences and the humanities," provided the necessary scholarship and technical support that enabled the Holocaust to occur.[1] Rudolf Ramm wrote in 1943 that the fact is, "biology and genetics are the roots from which the National Socialist worldview has grown."[2] An important point is that "many intellectuals cooperated fully in Nazi racial programmes, and many of the social and intellectual foundations for these programmes were laid long before the rise of Hitler to power."[3] Snyder included only one academic, musicology professor Kurt Huber, in his study of those who opposed Hitler.[4] Huber's concern about Hitler may have been partly because he (Huber) was physically handicapped and a candidate for the extermination camps.

Professor Wolf was able to document only three professors who "raised their voices in protest against the dismissal of their colleagues or against the burning of the books."[5] The 1914 Nobelist Max von Laue was one of the few scientists to openly defy the Nazis, and his opposition was typically symbolic, such as going to the funeral of the Jewish scientist Otto Hahn.[6]

Another example of the strong support of academia for Nazi policies was when Pastor Dietrich Bonhoeffer openly opposed how the Jews were treated and then opposed Hitler, the result was

Bonhoeffer's right to teach at Berlin University was officially revoked. He had given a lecture there on February 14, which turned out to be his last. His long relationship with the world of academia ended forever. He would protest and appeal, but there was no way to rescind the judgment. And yet, in the topsy-turvydom of Hitler's Germany in which academia was closed to Jews, it can hardly have been entirely disheartening. His [Jewish] brother-in-law Gerhard Leibholz was forced to "retire" that April.[7]

---

1   Max Weinreich, *Hitler's Professors*, 1946 ed. (Reprint, New Haven: Yale University Press, 1999), 7.

2   Cited in Robert N. Proctor, *Racial Hygiene: Medicine under the Nazis* (Cambridge: Harvard University Press, 1988), 6.

3   Proctor, *Racial Hygiene*, 10.

4   Louis L. Snyder, *Hitler's German Enemies: Portraits of Heroes Who Fought the Nazis* (New York: Hippocrene Books, 1990).

5   Abraham Wolf, *Higher Education in Nazi Germany* (London: Methuen, 1944), 30.

6   Marcus Chown, *The Magic Furnace: The Search for the Origins of Atoms* (New York: Oxford University Press, 2001), 11.

7   Eric Metaxas, *Bonhoeffer—Pastor, Martyr, Prophet, Spy: A Righteous Gentile vs. The*

Dietrich Bonhoeffer (1906-1945)

Bonhoeffer was one of the few religious academics in Germany who openly opposed Hitler's treatment of the Jews. He was imprisoned by the Nazis in the Flossenbürg concentration camp and hanged on April 9, 1945.

Wolf documented close to 300 professors who "signed a declaration in praise of Hitler," and students at dozens of major German universities boycotted Jewish professors.[8] He was able to locate only three professors that "raised their voices in protest against the dismissal of their colleagues or against the burning of the books, and one of the three was a Swiss (Professor Karl Barth)" who was forced to resign from his chair in the University of Bonn and return to his home country, Switzerland.[9] Dr. Karl Barth was a theologian who became well known for his courageous and almost unheard of action protesting the Nazis. Many professors went beyond signing declarations. In fact, medical "doctors played a crucial role in the science of organized cruelty that we call the Holocaust."[10] Furthermore, Hitler's support involved impressive numbers of academics and scholars that

> were to a large extent people of long and high standing, university professors and academy members, some of them world famous, authors with familiar names and guest lecturers abroad, the kind of people Allied scholars used to meet and fraternize with at international congresses.[11]

The claim of the harm of so-called

> racial mixing was incorporated into academic anthropology by Eugen Fischer, professor at the University of Freiburg. As a young scholar, Fischer...traveled to German Southwest Africa to investigate miscegenation firsthand. His book, *The Rehoboth Bastards and the Bastardization Problem among Humans* (1913), examined a community of descendants of European men and African women.[12]

---

8   Wolf, *Higher Education in Nazi Germany*, 30.

9   Wolf, *Higher Education in Nazi Germany*, 30.

10   Elie Wiesel, "Without Conscience," foreword to Vivien Spitz, *Doctors from Hell: The Horrific Account Of Nazi Experiments on Humans* (Boulder: Sentient Publications, 2005), xvii.

11   Weinreich, *Hitler's Professors*, 7.

12   Richard Weikart, *Hitler's Ethic: The Nazi Pursuit of Evolutionary Progress* (New York: Palgrave MacMillan, 2009), 141.

Professor Fischer concluded from his research that miscegenation usually resulted in progeny that were about midway between the two parental races, causing the average offspring to degenerate compared with the race of the "higher" evolved parent. It was for this reason that "he opposed racial mixture and supported racial segregation in German colonies. Fischer's work was important in giving a scientific patina to opposition to miscegenation."[13] Fischer's two-volume work, *Foundations of Human Hereditary Teaching and Racial Hygiene*, co-written with Erwin Baur and Fritz Lenz, was a major scientific basis for Nazi racist policy.[14]

Although we have no firm evidence that Hitler read any of Fischer's books, many anthropologists and racial thinkers promoted the same or similar ideas, and Hitler likely learned his racial conclusions from a number of sources.[15] We do know that Hitler learned many of his racist conclusions from biology and medical professors who

> played an important role in the debate over racial policy. According to the official Nazi commentary on the Nuremberg Laws, the law was framed in such a way that it would eventually lead to the elimination of the mixed race. Hitler...knew about the significance of Mendelian genetics for racial mixture at least by 1928, for he mentioned in his Second Book that because of Mendelian genetics some offspring in a racially mixed marriage would favor one race, while some siblings might favor the other.... Cornelia Essner claims that a speech Hitler gave in late September 1935 showed "surprisingly good racial-biological knowledge."[16]

Hitler relied on Mendelian laws to support his conclusion that, even four to six generations after racial mixture occurred, a "pure Jew" could result which would "constitute a great danger" for Germany's

---

13 Weikart, *Hitler's Ethic*, 141.

14 Edwin Black, *War against the Weak: Eugenics and American's Campaign to Create a Master Race* (New York: Four Walls Eight Windows Press, 2003), 269–275.

15 Weikart, *Hitler's Ethic*, 141.

16 Weikart, *Hitler's Ethic*, 144.

racial purity goals. To support his contention, Hitler provided an example of one man who had the physical characteristics of Jews

> even though his last Jewish ancestor had been born in 1616. This confirms, Hitler reported, that "in the course of generations a racially pure Jew can emerge by Mendelian laws." This proved to Hitler that *Mischlinge* should not be accorded equal status.[17]

As a result, debates were common within Nazi circles over how to classify persons who were half- or quarter-Jews, the so-called *Mischlinge*. The solution was to turn to biological science, a solution that illustrates the importance of biology

> in framing Nazi racial laws. One of the key disagreements among Nazi racial experts was about how to apply Mendelian genetics to interracial marriage and sexual relations. On September 25, 1935, one of the leading race experts of the Interior Ministry, Arthur Gütt, wrote a brief synopsis [that]...supported allowing quarter-Jews to marry Germans, and he thought that half-Jews should be sorted by anthropologists to determine their racial fitness.[18]

If the *Mischlinge* were deemed by the eugenic experts to have sufficient Germanic physical traits then they were permitted to marry Germans, but not marry other *Mischlinge*. Karl Astel, a Nazi and prominent University of Jena scientist disagreed with Gütt and "submitted a rebuttal to Himmler, arguing that because of Mendelian genetics, no *Mischlinge* should be allowed to reproduce with Germans. Otherwise Jewish hereditary traits could resurface in subsequent generations, even if they were latent presently."[19]

At the start of World War II, another important factor was the entire cultural life of German scientists and academics that had for decades been

---

17 Weikart, *Hitler's Ethic*, 144.
18 Weikart, *Hitler's Ethic*, 143.
19 Weikart, *Hitler's Ethic*, 143.

more or less under the influence of biological thinking, as it was begun particularly around the middle of the last century, by the teachings of Darwin.... Though it took decades before the courage was found, on the basis of the initial findings of the natural sciences, to carry on a systematic study of heredity, the progress of the teaching and its application to man could not be delayed any more.[20]

Professor Cornwell concluded that, although most scientists merely acquiesced to Hitler, some arguing that science lies outside of politics and morality, no small number of scientists enthusiastically collaborated with the Nazis. Nonetheless, by the end of World War II, very few German scientists remained untainted by a regime bent on eugenics and genocide.[21]

SUPPORT BY ACADEMICS AND SCIENTISTS

Although well documented, it is not widely known that Germany's medical doctors were among Hitler's strongest and earliest supporters. In a study of doctors under Hitler, professor Michael Kater determined that "German physicians...were overrepresented in the Nazi party as well as its adjunct organizations as early as 1933" a claim that has been documented with "graphic clarity."[22]

German psychiatrist Fredric Wertham observed that German doctors "without coercion, acted not figuratively but literally in line with the slogan of one of the most notorious concentration-camp commanders." That slogan was "There are no sick people in my camp. They are either well or dead."[23] Weikart wrote that the Nazis "had no difficulty finding physicians willing and enthusiastic to participate in killing the disabled, for quite a few leading physicians already had

---

20 Weinreich, *Hitler's Professors*, 33.

21 John Cornwell, *Hitler's Scientists: Science, War, and the Devil's Pact* (New York: Viking, 2003).

22 Michael H. Kater, *Doctors under Hitler* (Chapel Hill: The University of North Carolina Press, 1989), 54.

23 Frederic Wertham, *A Sign for Cain: An Exploration of Human Violence* (New York: Macmillan, 1966), 155.

jettisoned the idea that the disabled had a right to live."[24] Hitler's conclusions about the loss of

> biological vitality and evolutionary progress of the German people was a common theme in eugenics literature in the early twentieth century. In a book written shortly before World War I, the famous professor of hygiene and avid eugenics advocate, Max von Gruber, warned about biological degeneration that would occur if German [Aryan] birthrates continued to decline. He voiced the same concern in a 1918 article in Germany's *Awakening Renewal* that Hitler may well have read. Many other eugenicists, including Ploetz, agreed with Gruber that limitation of births would result in biological degeneration.[25]

Hitler's eugenic programmes were supported by numerous scholarly writings, such as a book by Dr. Hans Hoff, a professor at the University of Vienna, titled in English, *Euthanasia and Destruction of Life Devoid of Value*. Germany's racial cleansing campaign that led to their euthanasia programmes and the Nazi death camps were manned, or largely supported by, medical doctors and scientists. Fredric Wertham, in a study of Nazi eugenic programmes concluded that doctors "were directly responsible" for the "unprecedented occurrence of mass violence [and] the deliberate killing of large numbers of mental patients."[26]

So many academics and scientists supported the Holocaust that the Nuremberg war crimes held a separate trial for those involved in torture and murder.[27] Furthermore, with devastating consequences, Hitler's scientists developed both conventional and high-tech weapons that enabled Nazi Germany to continue waging war far longer than they otherwise could have.

In the end, though, organizational weakness and chaos undermined any technological advantages that Germany possessed.[28] The Nazi era's

---

24 Weikart, *Hitler's Ethic*, 187.

25 Weikart, *Hitler's Ethic*, 127.

26 Wertham, *A Sign for Cain*, 153.

27 Spitz, *Doctors from Hell*.

28 Alan Steinweis, *Kristallnacht 1938* (Cambridge: Harvard University Press, 2009).

final sordid chapter involved what turned out to be development of futile "wonder weapons"; brutal, inhumane and often worthless concentration camp experiments; the use of slave labour; and the technologies that allowed unsurpassed cruelty and mass murder, all supported in various ways by a large number of prominent scientists. The extent of the influence of German and other scientists is indicated by the fact that some early twentieth-century eugenicists actually argued that polygamy would be a way to

advance human evolution. The philosopher Christian von Ehrenfels and the chemist and anti-Semitic publicist Willibald Hentschel were the most prominent advocates of replacing monogamy with polygamy. Other eugenicists, such as August Forel and some feminist eugenicists, pressed for freer sexual relations to replace strict monogamy. This debate among eugenicists over marriage reform was reflected in discussions among Nazi leaders about marriage and sexual relations.[29]

The Nazis also had the local police locate all homeless people, a social class that the

Nazis considered biologically inferior. In 1938 the Gestapo put over ten thousand vagrants and beggars in concentration camps, since by that time everyone chronically unemployed was labeled work-shy and "asocial." Not only vagrants and the unemployed, but also alcoholics, prostitutes, and "habitual criminals" were often labeled "asocial" by the Nazis.[30]

The source of these ideas was German biologists and professors. Weikart wrote that "many biologists and eugenicists before and during the Nazi period" believed that "asocial" traits were hereditary. This is exemplified in the partnership of Siegfried Koller, medical statistician, and Heinrich Wilhelm Kranz, director of the University of Giessen Institute for Genetics and Racial Hygiene, authors of a major study of

---

29 Weikart, *Hitler's Ethic*, 129.
30 Weikart, *Hitler's Ethic*, 118.

"asocials" published around 1940.[31] They concluded that "to move toward a biological solution of the antisocial problem, it is absolutely imperative to deem antisocials from antisocial families as the biologically most unhealthy and most dangerous" of all families.[32] As a result of this conclusion, the Nazi government

advocated compulsory sterilization, forced labour, marriage prohibitions, and annulment of existing marriages for those deemed "asocial." Koller's work was well-received by Nazi authorities, who appointed him to the Biostatistical Institute of the University of Berlin in March 1941.[33]

The Nazis also asked Professor Koller to oversee the planning to "solve" the problem of "asocials." Some of the other prominent professors who actively supported Hitler's eugenic programmes included Dr. Emil Kraepelin, a graduate of Leipzig University. He taught clinical psychiatry at the Kaiser Wilhelm Institute in Munich and researched the hereditary factors involved in mental illness.[34]

Another prominent professor was Dr. Ernst Röder, a medical doctor who taught at University of Munich Medical School and was the director of the psychiatry branch of the Kaiser Wilhelm Institute until the war ended. He then attempted to flee the country, but was arrested in 1945.[35] In 1943, Röder wrote an article in the periodical *Rassen-und Gesellschaftsbiologie* (*Racial and Social Biology*) that revealed his loyalty to Hitler. In it he said,

It is the unfailing historical merit of Adolf Hitler and his true followers that they dared to take the first decisive step past the purely scientific discoveries to open the way for the ingenious racial hygienic work in and on the German people. It was impor-

---

31 Weikart, *Hitler's Ethic*, 118.

32 Weikart, *Hitler's Ethic*, 118.

33 Weikart, *Hitler's Ethic*, 118.

34 Thomas Röder, Volker Kubillus and Anthony Burwell, *Psychiatrists: The Men behind Hitler* (Los Angeles: Freedom Publishing, 1995), 234.

35 Röder, Kubillus and Burwell, *Psychiatrists: The Men behind Hitler*, 235.

tant to him to…keep pure the German race, to fight the parasitic races of foreign blood such as the Jews and the Gypsies, and to further increase the population according to quantity and quality and prevent the propagation of the hereditarily ill and inferior… the Nuremberg Laws, the State Citizen Law and the Law for the Protection of German Blood made because of a build-up of Jewish influence, particularly prevented the further infiltration of Jewish blood into the German gene pool.[36]

The Nuremberg Laws classified a German as Aryan if all four of their grandparents were of "German or kindred blood," and "Jews" if they descended from three or four Jewish grandparents. A German with two or just one Jewish grandparent was classified as a *Mischling*, or crossbreed of "mixed blood." The Nuremberg Laws also deprived German Jews of citizenship and prohibited marriage between Jews and other Germans. These laws were actually the beginning of the Holocaust, and scientists played a central role in the development and implementation of them. Professor Grabowski concluded that the

…Nuremberg Laws were implemented by the top scientists at the leading research centers in Germany. One of the most active in this area was professor Otmar von Verschuer of the University of Frankfurt, arguably the most renowned racial scientist of the day. Von Verschuer, who praised Hitler for being the first statesman "to recognize hereditary biological and race hygiene," helped establish the Institute for Heredity, Biology, and Racial Purity at the University of Frankfurt.[37]

Components of the expression "hereditary biological and race hygiene" were euphemisms for programmes that justified actions against a variety of people and included everything from discrimination, to sterilization, to genocide.

---

36 Cited in Röder, Kubillus and Burwell, *Psychiatrists: The Men behind Hitler*, 235–236.

37 John Grabowski, *Josef Mengele* (Farmington Hills: Lucent Books, 2004), 27.

THE GENOCIDE BEGINS

Under Hitler, the German medical community was accustomed to receiving questionnaires to be completed for racial hygiene bureaucrats; so it was not unusual when the "Committee for the Scientific Treatment of Severe Genetically Determined Illness" wrote to doctors and midwives in 1939 to compile

> details of any children under three years of age exhibiting Down's syndrome, spina bifida, missing or malformed limbs, spasticism and a range of similar conditions. The registration forms were sent to Berlin, where a panel of doctors sifted through them writing either a plus or minus sign on each. In October, those children whose files had been marked with a plus were collected from their parents and taken to special paediatric clinics. There they were put to death.[38]

The methods used to kill those with so-called "genetic illnesses" (many of which were not genetic) at first varied, and later much more effective methods were developed:

> Some clinics used cyanide gas, others administered an overdose of morphine. In one clinic where, presumably, the doctors were anxious about the legality of what they were being asked to do, the children were simply left to starve to death. The physicians need not have been so concerned about themselves: the Führer signed a secret order exempting participating medical staff from prosecution and backdated it to September so that even the pioneers of child-murder would be covered.[39]

The next step was to send a set of forms asking about children in the next age bracket, a process that was "repeated until the state had identified, abducted and murdered all handicapped children up to the age of seventeen."[40] Last, the adult "handicapped" and mentally defi-

---

38 Dennis Sewell, *The Political Gene: How Darwin's Ideas Changed Politics* (London: Picadon, 2009), 138–139.

39 Sewell, *The Political Gene*, 438–439.

40 Sewell, *The Political Gene*, 139.

cient were targeted, resulting in killing many thousands of persons, many of which were not afflicted with a genetic disease, and some that had very minor "handicaps" such as hare lip. The whole process was carried out by, or under the supervision of, medical doctors. In January 1940, Dr. Karl Brandt visited a Brandenburg psychiatric hospital to witness new and more effective killing methods:

> A prototype gas chamber had been constructed, disguised as a communal shower room. Approximately twenty inmates of the asylum were led naked into the room. After the door was closed, a doctor then turned on a supply of carbon-monoxide gas, which dispersed into the room through small holes in what otherwise looked like water pipes. Six minutes later, the room was cleared of gas and a team of SS men took the bodies to the hospital crematorium. Karl Brandt expressed his satisfaction and ordered that, as in this case, qualified doctors must carry out all future exterminations.[41]

The claim that these professionals were *forced* to participate in these crimes is, in the case of doctors and academics, false. Dr. Hans Hefelman, a high-level euthanasia programme bureaucrat, testified, "No doctor was ever ordered to participate in the euthanasia programme; they came of their own volition."[42] Himmler, in a written statement to a high-level judge, noted that operations undertaken in psychiatric hospitals were ordered and administered solely by medical doctors.[43] Proctor wrote that "Doctors were never ordered to murder psychiatric patients and handicapped children," rather they

were *empowered* to do so, and fulfilled their task without protest, often on their own initiative. Hitler's original memo of October 1939 was not an order (*Befehl*), but an empowerment (*Vollmacht*), granting physicians permission to act.[44]

---

41 Sewell, *The Political Gene*, 139.
42 Wertham, *A Sign for Cain*, 167.
43 Wertham, *A Sign for Cain*, 167.
44 Proctor, *Racial Hygiene*, 193.

As German zoologist and geneticist Dr. Ludwig Plate wrote, "progress in evolution goes forward over millions of dead bodies" of "inferior" humans, and the "key elements of the worldview had been constructed and repeatedly reaffirmed by linguists, racial anthropologists, evolutionary scientists and geneticists."[45]

SUPPORT FROM PHYSICISTS

It was not just biologists and medical doctors who supported Hitler in large numbers, but also physicists. Nobel laureate Philipp Lenard and Professor Johannes Stark opposed not only Jews but even what they called "Jewish physics," the research conclusions of Jewish scientists, such as the work produced by Albert Einstein.[46] Lenard, Stark and others argued the work of Aryan physicists was superior to that of "Jewish science." Part of their opposition to Jews was "Einstein's avowed pacifism, internationalism, and support of Zionism."[47]

Lenard's loyalty to Nazism was revealed in an "ecstatic statement in favor of Hitler and the Nazi party" that he had published early in the history of the Nazi movement.[48] Although strident anti-Semitism by physicists such as by Lenard was not the norm, "a milder version was widespread." Bernstein concluded that

> Von Laue was almost the only German physicist who publicly continued to lecture on relativity, attributing the theory to Einstein, and he courageously opposed Nazi physicists at every step in their efforts to gain control of German physics.[49]

It was not only Jews that the Aryan scientists opposed, but also those few who spoke out on behalf of Jews, such as Max Planck who opposed the appointment of anti-Semite mathematician Theodor Vahlen to the German Academy. Even "Planck's retirement did not

---

45 Cited in Christopher Hutton, *Race and the Third Reich* (Cambridge: Polity, 2005).

46 Alan D. Beyerchen, *Scientists under Hitler: Politics and the Physics Community in the Third Reich* (New Haven: Yale University Press, 1977).

47 Beyerchen, *Scientists under Hitler*, 4.

48 Weinreich, *Hitler's Professors*, 11.

49 Jeremy Bernstein, *Hitler's Uranium Club: The Secret Recordings at Farm Hall*, 2nd ed. (New York: Copernicus Books, 2001), 994.

free him from the attacks of the Aryan physicists" that resulted from his stand against anti-Semitic scientists.[50] Planck was merciously ridiculed by Aryan scientists as "no physicist," and his work was condemned as nothing but "mathematical reworking stumbling after experimental results."[51]

Hitler achieved strong support not only from many scientists, but also the entire academic community including philosophers and historians. Elie Wiesel wrote that one of the major shocks of his adult life came the day he

> discovered that many of the officers of the *Einsatzgruppen*—the death commandos in Eastern Europe—had received degrees from Germany's best universities. Some held doctorates in literature, others in philosophy, theology, or history. They had spent many years studying, learning the lessons of past generations, yet nothing kept them from killing Jewish children at Babi Yar, in Minsk, Ponar. Their education provided them with no shield, no shelter from the temptation and seduction of cruelty that people may carry within.[52]

WAR CRIMES OF NAZI PROFESSORS AND ACADEMICS

The "final solution" to the "Jewish problem" was decided at the infamous Wannsee Conference held in the exclusive Berlin suburb of Wannsee on January 20, 1942. Of the fifteen high-level Nazis in attendance, eight held a doctorate degree and several were lawyers.[53] The "final solution" they unanimously agreed on was to exterminate all Jews (a definition they had a difficult time deciding on) in Europe, mostly by use of gas chambers or to work them to death.

So many university professors and academics took part in the Holocaust that a separate war crimes trial called the "Doctors' Trial" was

---

50 J.L. Heilbron, *Dilemmas of an Upright Man: Max Planck and the Fortunes of German Science* (Cambridge: Harvard University Press, 1986), 173.

51 Heilbron, *Dilemmas of an Upright Man*, 174.

52 Wiesel, "Without Conscience," foreword to Spitz, *Doctors from Hell*, xvx.

53 Christopher R. Browning, *The Origin of the Final Solution: The Evolution of Nazi Jewish Policy* (London: William Heinemann, 2004), 411.

held for them in 1946. Of the twenty-three on trial, out of an estimated 400 doctors that "committed medical infractions in concentration camps and 'euthanasia' stations," only a mere twenty physicians were in the end charged with having initiated, directed, and organized crimes against prisoners.[54] These were the worst of the 400 and those against whom clear evidence existed, which could be used at the trial. The trial lasted from December 9, 1946 to July 3, 1947, and sixteen doctors were found guilty and sentenced to death or long prison terms.[55] A witness at the trial wrote:

> There was not one scintilla of remorse shown by any of these defendants. I was stunned at the evil, expressionless, hard faces of these doctors and assistants during the trial. They often expressed resentment when testifying, spewing defensive justifications and denying responsibility.[56]

STUDENT SUPPORT OF NAZISM PRIOR TO 1946

As expected, given their professors' support, college and university

> students were one of the most vocal forces of National Socialists policy at the universities. On April 13, the German Students Association announced its campaign "Against the Un-German Spirit," which would climax in public book burnings on May 10 [1933].[57]

The students rationalized their anti-Semitism by concluding that a

> Jew could only think Jewish, and when he wrote German he was lying; students should view Jews as aliens, and Jewish works should appear in Hebrew, or at least be designated as translations if they were printed in German; students and professors should be selected "according to their guarantee of thinking in the German spirit."[58]

---

54 Kater, *Doctors under Hitler*, 222.

55 Spitz, *Doctors from Hell*, 264–265.

56 Spitz, *Doctors from Hell*, 266.

57 Beyerchen, *Scientists under Hitler*, 16.

58 Beyerchen, *Scientists under Hitler*, 16.

The Nazi government reworded the students' activism by the Prussian minister of education restoring

> student self-government, which had been taken away under the Weimar ministry, and restricted membership in student organizations to Aryans only. Quotas for non-Aryans in the German schools soon followed. Also on the thirteenth, the first dismissals [of Jews] under the Civil Service Law were announced at half a dozen universities.[59]

OPPOSITION TO NAZISM BY PHYSICIANS

As noted, Hitler had enormous support from physicians, both those in academia and those working in hospitals. When Hitler and Himmler made it known to the leaders of the medical profession that their goal was to murder Jews and others, "few in the German medical profession believed it…[was a good idea] to refuse" to be involved in murdering those determined to be "useless eaters."[60] One of the few physicians who openly opposed the Nazis even before they came to power was a Jewish doctor named Julius Moses. Moses was concerned about articles written by the leader of the National Socialist Welfare Organization calling for the killing of disabled persons.

Dr. Moses wrote in 1932 that the Nazi eugenic programmes had to enlist physicians to do the dirty work, writing that "it is the physician who must carry out this extermination…he is to be the executioner."[61] Dr. Erich Hilgengeldt was even more open than the Nazi Welfare Organization in supporting the Nazis' eugenic goals, proclaiming, "the unfit must be ruthlessly exterminated." The "unfit" later included Dr. Moses himself, who died in a concentration camp in the 1940s.[62]

AFTER GERMANY LOST THE WAR

After the war ended, "despite Jewish professor Lise Meitner's powerful criticisms, Hitler's scientists showed little remorse" for their role in

59 Beyerchen, *Scientists under Hitler*, 16.
60 Wiesel, "Without Conscience," foreword to Spitz, *Doctors from Hell*, xviii.
61 Weikart, *Hitler's Ethic*, 186.
62 Weikart, *Hitler's Ethic*, 186.

Nazism's many crimes against humanity, not the least of which was the Holocaust.[63] After the war, "with rare exceptions criminal doctors calmly returned home to resume normal practices and ordinary life" in post Nazi Germany.[64] Science in West Germany simply accommodated itself to the changed situation and moved forward.

Professor Konrad Lorenz, an active Nazi, went back to his scientific work after the war and, as noted above, was later awarded a Nobel Prize in 1973 "for discoveries in individual and social behavior patterns." Lorenz, an Austrian zoologist and ornithologist, is regarded as the founder of the field called *ethology*, the scientific study of animal behaviour, and a sub-field of zoology. He was a committed evolutionist to the extent that he refused even to discuss the merits of the theory because he considered the question closed.

Lorenz also vociferously rejected Christianity and concluded that evolution provided a superior goal—the higher evolution of humanity—to Christianity. Lorenz fervently believed that evolutionary theory reinforced Nazi racial doctrines, including racial inequality and racial solidarity.[65] He also argued in harmony with Nazism that the race is foremost and the individual clearly secondary.

One professional group that did not become active supporters of Hitler, at least after the persecution against them began, were Jewish professors. Professor Kater concluded that, because of expelling Jews, "Germany may have lost as many as 40 percent of its medical faculty to racist fanaticism; the harm to science and education [in Germany] was unfathomable."[66]

The level of support by doctors in Nazi Germany was so strong that "there were so many doctors and scientists involved in the Nazi crimes that to weed them all out would have left post-war Germany with hardly any at all, an intolerable situation in a nation reeling from starvation and decimation."[67] Medawar and Pyke, in documenting the

63 Cornwell, *Hitler's Scientists*, 412.

64 Wiesel, "Without Conscience," foreword to Spitz, *Doctors from Hell*, xx.

65 Konrad Lorenz, "Nochmals: Systematik und Entwicklungsgedanke im Unterricht," *Der Biologe* 9 (1940): 24–36.

66 Kater, *Doctors under Hitler*, 142.

67 Arthur Caplan, "Deadly Medicine: Creating the Master Race," *The Lancet* 363, No. 9422 (May 22, 2004): 1741–1742.

Konrad Lorenz (1903-1989)

Lorenz was just one of the many Nazis who went back to scientific work after the war ended, even being awarded a Nobel Prize in 1973.

many scientists expelled from Germany, mostly Jewish—which ended Germany's fifty-year record of world supremacy in science—as Hitler's gift to America.[68]

Recognizing their central role in the Holocaust, "Professors Astel, de Crinis, Hirt, Kranz and Dr. Gross committed suicide, and so, later, did Professors Clauberg, Heyde and Schneider, when charges [of genocide] were brought against them."[69]

THE SCIENTISTS CONVERT ITALY TO EUGENICS

Italy's Benito Mussolini agreed with Hitler on many issues, but one belief with which he disagreed passionately was Hitler's anti-Semitism and racism.[70] Mussolini even appointed some Jews to high-level posts in Italy. Some of the reasons for this include the beliefs of Hitler and the Nazi elite about the racial "superiority of the Germanic race compared to the Mediterranean peoples" as well as the Czechs, among other peoples.[71] The problem was solved by leading scientists who declared that, "Italians belonged to the Nordic race and are completely Aryan, while the Jews are not of the same race as the Italians."[72]

This ruling by the elite scientists led to race laws, the first one published on July 14, 1938, that began the persecution of Jews in Italy—albeit in Italy it was "superficial and amateurish compared to the brutality Hitler was known for."[73] The result was that the large numbers of Jews that Italy had invited to migrate from Germany "in droves" were forced to return to Germany, many dying in concentration camps.

---

68 Jean Medawar and David Pyke, *Hitler's Gift: The True Story of the Scientists Expelled by the Nazi Regime* (New York: Arcade Publishing, 2001).

69 Benno Müller-Hill, *Murderous Science: Elimination by Scientific Selection of Jews, Gypsies, and Others, Germany, 1933–1945* (Oxford: Oxford University Press, 1988), 82.

70 Santi Corvaja, *Hitler and Mussolini: The Secret Meetings*, trans. Robert L. Miller (New York: Enigma Books, 2008), 17.

71 Corvaja, *Hitler and Mussolini*, 46, 85.

72 Corvaja, *Hitler and Mussolini*, 83

73 Corvaja, *Hitler and Mussolini*, 83–84.

SUMMARY

The well-documented fact is "scientists played a significant role in the formulation of Nazi racial ideology."[74] German academics provided the scholarship, the putative scientific support, and the "techniques that led to and justified...unparalled slaughter" of Jews, Catholic Poles and other groups that the Nazis deemed biologically inferior, a conclusion well documented by numerous scholars, such as Weinreich.[75] Both "Nazi medicine and science...were integral" to the Holocaust and "the monstrous crimes committed in occupied Europe out of hatred for... so-called inferior races and groups."[76] The fact is that

> biomedical scientists played an active, even leading role in the initiation, administration, and execution of Nazi racial programs...scientists actively designed and administered central aspects of National Socialist [Nazi] racial policy.[77]

Arthur Caplan opines that a major reason for the "innocuous rise of eugenics in Weimar Germany" was because the Germans saw eugenics as

> an adjunct to efforts at public health reform. Germans eager for a rebirth after the disaster of the First World War eagerly seized on the hope extended by physicians, geneticists, psychiatrists, and anthropologists that using social Darwinism to guide public health was the vehicle for German regeneration.[78]

The importance of Darwin and his disciples' writings is illustrated by Viktor Frankl, a Jewish doctor who survived the horrors of Auschwitz. Dr. Frankl astutely evaluated the influence of modern scientists and academics in helping to prepare the way for the Nazi atrocities by concluding that the

---

74 Aaron Gillette, *Racial Theories in Fascist Italy* (New York: Routledge, 2002), 185.

75 Weinreich, *Hitler's Professors*, 6.

76 Wiesel, "Without Conscience," foreword to Spitz, *Doctors from Hell*, xx.

77 Proctor, *Racial Hygiene*, 6

78 Caplan, "Deadly Medicine: Creating the Master Race," 1742.

gas chambers of Auschwitz were the ultimate consequence of the theory that man is nothing but the product of heredity and environment—or, as the Nazis liked to say, of "Blood and Soil." I am absolutely convinced that the gas chambers of Auschwitz, Treblinka, and Maidanek were ultimately prepared not in some Ministry…in Berlin, but rather at the desks and in the lecture halls of nihilistic scientists and philosophers.[79]

Dr. Frankl accurately summarized the case against academia and the scientists in Nazi Germany.

---

79 Viktor E. Frankl, *The Doctor and the Soul: From Psychotherapy to Logotherapy*, 3rd ed. (New York: Vintage Books, 1986), xxxii.

07

Dr. Josef Mengele: Darwin's angel of death

INTRODUCTION

Dr. Josef Mengele (March 16, 1911 – February 7, 1979) symbolizes the worst of Nazi Germany's criminals for his grossly barbaric and often lethal medical experiments on prisoners. He is a leading example of where the logical implications of evolution can lead. Today, he symbolizes Nazi brutality and the Nazi Party's goal of producing a superior race by means of directing evolution and applying Darwinism to society by government decree.

Mengele not only committed acts of unspeakable barbarism on young, weak, sick and often innocent humans in the name of science, but totally escaped formal punishment for his hideous crimes.[1] Reared in a devout Catholic family, the former altar boy and model child proved to be an excellent student, earning both M.D. and Ph.D. degrees at leading German universities.[2] As a student he developed an early interest in Darwinism that ruled his life and work.

---

1 Linda Schmittroth and Mary Kay Rosteck, *People of the Holocaust*, Vol. 1: A-J (Detroit: Gale, 1998), 311.

2 Lucette Matalon Lagnado and Sheila Cohn Dekel, *Children of the Flames: Dr. Josef Mengele and the Untold Story of the Twins of Auschwitz* (New York: William Morrow, 1991), 34.

MENGELE BECOMES A DARWINIST

As a young college student, the charming and articulate Mengele abandoned his religion due to his secular studies. He also became more and more receptive to Hitler's goals of a "new Germany" and producing a superior race.[3] At the University of Munich, Mengele studied under Darwinist professor Ernst Rüdin, "who taught his students that some lives were not worth living and doctors had a responsibility to destroy such lives for the good of society as a whole."[4] Professor Rüdin

> was one of the leading proponents of a theory that called for the extermination of people he deemed inferior. He believed that the lives of those afflicted with particular disabilities served no purpose and should be eliminated for the betterment of the race. He went so far as to suggest that doctors had a responsibility to destroy such life. Mengele's acceptance of this philosophy would help explain his ability in future years to experiment on concentration camp inmates without showing the slightest bit of remorse.[5]

Rüdin and other leading members of the medical community were the chief architects of Hitler's compulsory sterilization laws and other similar legislation that formed the basis of the Holocaust. When Mengele embraced these evolutionary and eugenic ideas he became

> even more serious about his studies. He decided that his real interest lay in evolution rather than in medicine. Mengele took to his work with renewed vigor and ambition. He was determined to make a success of himself in his chosen field and to work for the betterment of his beloved homeland.[6]

The extent of the open racism in German academia was so pervasive that

---

3   John Grabowski, *Josef Mengele* (Farmington Hills: Lucent Books, 2004), 19.

4   Claire Welch, *Rise & Fall of the Nazis* (London: Magpie Books, 2008), 310.

5   Grabowski, *Josef Mengele*, 22.

6   Grabowski, *Josef Mengele*, 22.

Race purity and the contaminant threat of Jews became gospel in lower and higher education. When Mengele began his college studies at the University of Munich, anti-Semitism had already sprouted in the sciences, along with the more standard atomic tables and Newton's laws of motion. The impressionable young man...soaked up writings like those of a German oriental scholar, Paul de Lagarde, who despised "those who out of humanity defend these Jews, or who are too cowardly to trample these usurious vermin to death."[7]

Darwinism and German anti-Semitism even infected the non-academic culture. Richard Wagner, "whose operas so entranced Mengele" (and Hitler) openly proclaimed his disdain for Jews.[8] In Mengele's freshman year, Hitler electrified the nation with his speeches, and the

center piece of Hitler's speeches was a call for "racial purity," an idea that was to become the driving force of Mengele's existence. The future dictator beguiled his audiences with his dream—a country populated by blond, blue-eyed supermen and super-women, a vision that would be achieved through...the elimination of all "inferior" races, especially the Jews[9]

In medical school Mengele completed courses in anthropology and paleontology, as well as medicine.[10] Medicine in German universities was then taught in accordance with the "guidelines of the social Darwinists' theories that Hitler and a growing number of German academics found" very appealing, an orientation that closely matched Mengele's real interest—evolution.[11]

Mengele's chosen fields of anthropology and genetics were especially influenced by the racist theories of Nazi dogma. While some

7 Gerald L. Posner and John Ware, *Mengele: The Complete Story* (New York: McGraw Hill, 1986), 9–10.

8 Posner and Ware, *Mengele: The Complete Story*, 9–10.

9 Lagnado and Dekel, *Children of the Flames*, 41.

10 Posner and Ware, *Mengele: The Complete Story*, 9.

11 Posner and Ware, *Mengele: The Complete Story*, 9.

were using violence to achieve their Nazi goal of a superior race, "genetic scientists were hard at work inside their laboratories," buttressing the Nazi theory of Jewish "racial inferiority" with the 'science' of eugenics.[12] Mengele's consummate ambition in life was to "succeed in this fashionable new field of evolutionary research."[13] As a result of his enthusiasm for Darwinism, by early 1934 Mengele was increasingly consumed by his studies. He was not regarded as a gifted student but rather

> distinguished himself more by hard work than anything else. "He was essentially more industrious and ambitious than others," said a fellow student and friend, Dr. Kurt Lambertz. "The more he became involved with the study of anthropology, genetics, heredity and such things, the more his interests grew."[14]

His research was supported by a leading academic, Professor Theodor Mollison, of the University of Munich, whose "expertise in the field of heredity and 'racial hygiene' led Mollinson to claim that he could tell if a person had Jewish forebears simply by looking at a photograph."[15] Mengele earned a Ph.D. for a thesis awarded in 1935 "proving" that a person's "race" could be determined by examining their jawbone. His thesis, titled, "Racial Morphological Research on the Lower Jaw Section of Four Racial Groups" was described as a

> dry but meticulously illustrated dissertation, and concluded that it was possible to detect different racial groups by studying the jaw. In contrast to Mollinson's unscientific assertions, Mengele's report was cogently argued and contained no anti-Semitic or racist overtones.[16]

For his second doctorate he did another thesis on eugenics, this one titled, "Genealogical Studies in the Cases of Cleft Lip-Jaw-Palate."

---

12 Lagnado and Dekel, *Children of the Flames*, 41

13 Posner and Ware, *Mengele: The Complete Story*, 9.

14 Posner and Ware, *Mengele: The Complete Story*, 10.

15 Posner and Ware, *Mengele: The Complete Story*, 10.

16 Posner and Ware, *Mengele: The Complete Story*, 10.

Mengele then served as an intern at the University Hospital in Leibzig before returning to do research under Professor von Vershuer at the *Institut für Erbbiologie und Rassenhygiene* (Institute for Heredity and Eugenics) at the University of Frankfurt.[17] In 1937, Mengele was appointed as a research assistant at The Third Reich Institute for Heredity, Biology and Racial Purity.[18]

Dr. Mengele was now fully convinced that the human race could be improved by deliberately selecting those persons whom he judged were more fit, and then encouraging them to reproduce. A second part of his plan was eliminating those who were judged as less fit. His end goal was to produce a superior race, and he was determined to use Darwinian theory to achieve it.

By 1938, Mengele had joined the infamous SS as part of the physician's group. Assigned to the combat division of the Waffen SS, Mengele was injured as a result of rescuing two German soldiers trapped under a burning tank. For his heroism, he was awarded Germany's highest award for bravery, the Iron Cross First Class.

Mengele's wounds prevented him from returning to the front line and, consequently, as a doctor he was assigned to the infamous Auschwitz concentration camp. At Auschwitz, his main research project was to devise methods of eradicating inferior genes in order to learn how to direct the evolution of Hitler's "perfect race." Mengele also took turns with the other SS doctors to determine who would survive as slave labourers, and who would be sent immediately to the gas chambers. Many of the SS doctors claimed to have disliked this task, but Mengele reportedly performed it with relish.[19]

Only days after his arrival, Mengele sent close to a thousand dark-haired, dark-skinned people believed to have originally migrated from India, known as Gypsies, directly to the gas chambers, purportedly to prevent the spread of typhus bacteria. In his entire tenure at Auschwitz, Mengele personally sent as many as 400,000 inmates to their deaths.[20]

---

17 Gerald Astor, *The Last Nazi: The Life and Times of Dr. Joseph Mengele* (New York: Donald I. Fine, 1985).

18 Schmittroth and Rosteck, *People of the Holocaust*, 1:313.

19 Welch, *Rise & Fall of the Nazis*, 301.

20 Grabowski, *Josef Mengele*, 10.

An evil trio – July 1944: (from left) Richard Baer, Commandant of Auschwitz, Dr. Josef Mengele and Rudolf Höss (the previous Commandant of Auschwitz).

In the Auschwitz camp, the new prisoners were divided into four groups. The first were those who were judged unable to do heavy work, which included about three quarters of all the inmates, including all children, most woman with children, the elderly and those judged physically unfit—not uncommonly for minor reasons such as a limp.[21] The second group included the men who appeared healthy enough for hard labour. The third group consisted of women who were put to work on various tasks, such as sorting the inmates' belongings so they could be sent to Germans in need.

The fourth group were those that Mengele wanted to use for his race research, including twins, dwarfs and others. During his twenty-one months at Auschwitz, Mengele was able to experiment on 3,000 twins alone.[22] This group often suffered greatly from excruciating pain as a result of Mengele's experiments.[23] Ironically, Mengele was also known for the kindness he expressed to those he experimented on, and for this reason was known as "the angel of death"—he exhibited a bizarre combination of elegance, politeness and evil.[24] One reason for the kindness was he did not want his experimental subjects beaten or mistreated because such treatment could affect his research results.

Much of his twin research was directed toward producing "a master race of blond, blue-eyed Aryans."[25] He injected them with a variety of chemicals to determine if different races reacted differently. He also researched the physical and psychological effects of sickness and starvation to determine if racial differences existed in response to the treatment he administered.[26]

OTHER MEDICAL RESEARCH

Yet another experiment was designed to understand the effects of high-altitude flight on pilots, specifically to determine the limits tolerable by humans. Nazi research scientist Dr. Rascher proposed using

21 Richard J. Evans, *The Third Reich at War* (New York: Allen Lane, 2008), 610.

22 Lagnado and Dekel, *Children of the Flames*, 7.

23 Welch, *Rise & Fall of the Nazis*, 256.

24 Robert Jay Lifton, *The Nazi Doctors: Medical Killing and the Psychology of Genocide* (New York: Basic Books, 1986), 17.

25 Lagnado and Dekel, *Children of the Flames*, 9.

26 Evans, *The Third Reich at War*.

camp inmates to determine these limits. A witness described the tests he devised:

> I have personally seen through the observation window of the decompression chamber when a prisoner inside would stand a vacuum until his lungs ruptured.... They would go mad and pull out their hair in an effort to relieve the pressure. They would tear their heads and face with their fingers and nails in an attempt to maim themselves in their madness. They would beat the walls with their hands and head and scream in an effort to relieve pressure on their eardrums. These cases usually ended in the death of the subject.[27]

Of the close to 200 inmates who were subjected to these "experiments," about half died, and those who survived usually were murdered. Dr. Rascher was highly praised by the academic community for the information he gained from this research and soon had completed another research proposal—to study the limits of the extremely low temperatures that aviators experienced. One Nuremberg trial account explains the research protocol:

> A prisoner was placed naked on a stretcher outside the barracks in the evening. He was covered with a sheet and every hour a bucket of cold water was poured over him. The test person lay out in the open like this into the morning. Their temperatures were taken. Later Dr. Rascher said it was a mistake to cover the subject with a sheet and to drench him with water.... In the future the test person must not be covered.[28]

Rascher hoped to use Auschwitz, not Dachau to do these experiments because it was colder there, and the larger grounds created less outrage in the camp when the test persons screamed as they froze to death. Although Dr. Rascher was forced to do the research at Dachau,

---

27 Eric Metaxas, *Bonhoeffer—Pastor, Martyr, Prophet, Spy: A Righteous Gentile vs. The Third Reich* (Nashville: Thomas Nelson, 2010), 510.

28 Metaxas, *Bonhoeffer—Pastor, Martyr, Prophet, Spy*, 511.

several bouts of intensely cold weather allowed him to achieve his research goals. Some subjects were forced to remain nude for 14 hours at 21 degrees Fahrenheit, lowering their interior temperature to 77 degrees and causing severe peripheral frostbite.[29]

Other research methods involved putting subjects into tanks of icy cold water. As the victims froze to death, their temperature, heartbeats, and respiration were regularly recorded. At first Dr. Rascher did not allow use of anesthesia on his subjects but they screamed so loudly that it was impossible to continue the research without it.

In the end, Dr. Rascher conducted close to 400 "freezing" experiments on 300 prisoners. A third froze to death, the rest were gassed or shot afterward. Rascher thought that the experiments he had conducted were "fully justified by the great value of the scientific results obtained," and he

saw nothing wrong in exposing a couple of dozen people to intense cold, in water or air, and then attempting their resuscitation. He was in fact very proud of having discovered a technique which he said would save the lives of thousands who would otherwise have died from exposure.[30]

The extreme cold experiments designed to determine how long it took the average subject to die found that it required, on average, 70 minutes for cold levels typical in the North Sea to produce the level of hypothermia required to kill an experimental subject. Ironically, Dr. Rascher himself ended up as a camp inmate, evidently because he had attempted to publish the results of his research in a Swiss medical journal that could benefit British seamen who, after they were rescued from the sea when their ships were torpedoed, frequently died without ever recovering consciousness.

Other "experiments" included research on treating phosphorous burns caused by incendiary bombs. The SS doctors smeared phosphorous on the arms of inmates then set their arms aflame. Survivors of this barbaric experiment testified that the pain was extremely excru-

---

29 Metaxas, *Bonhoeffer—Pastor, Martyr, Prophet, Spy*, 511.
30 Metaxas, *Bonhoeffer—Pastor, Martyr, Prophet, Spy*, 514.

ciating.[31] The doctors then experimented with various ointments and nostrums. Evidently all of these experiments proved to be of little or no benefit.

An example of the many experiments performed by the Nazi scientists included injecting substances in healthy victims to determine which one was most effective to kill him or her. After much data was collected they determined that gasoline was among the most efficacious. Other research included decompression and oxygen reduction.

Mengele's activities and those of the other professors were actively supported by the German academic establishment: "The notion that some lives were not worth living, soon to become academically respectable, may explain why Mengele experimented on concentration camp inmates as though they were laboratory rats."[32] His experiments were part of his Habilitation degree, required of all German academics for a university professorship.[33] Lagnado and Dekel concluded that many of Germany's most eminent

scientists and research centers joined forces with the Nazis and actively helped to implement the Nuremberg Laws. But none did so with more fervor than the University of Frankfurt's Professor Otmar von Verschuer, possibly the most acclaimed racial scientist of his day. Since the early 1930s, Verschuer had been receiving generous financial support from the Nazis to build his lavish new Institute for Heredity, Biology and Racial Purity, which specialized in racial studies.[34]

Mengele and the other Nazi doctors who completed research, such as the so-called terminal experiments that killed the subjects, published their research in peer-reviewed scientific journals. Mengele and other Darwinists believed this research would demonstrate scientifically that his racist goals were scientifically valid. The camp held regular research seminars with his assistants, including medically qualified

31 Evans, *The Third Reich at War*, 607.
32 Posner and Ware, *Mengele: The Complete Story*, 9.
33 Evans, *The Third Reich at War*, 609.
34 Lagnado and Dekel, *Children of the Flames*, 43.

inmates, to discuss their research, individual cases, and treatment strategies.

The Nazi doctors presented the results of their gruesome, often lethal, research to various scientific conferences and rarely did the august audience of German scientists raise any objections.[35] The Nazi government strongly supported science to the degree that, during the height of the Nazi regime, Germany ranked second in the world in science productivity behind only the United States.[36] All this changed when America entered the conflict and Germany began losing the war.

THE SLIPPERY SLOPE

The work of the German academic and medical establishment, of which Mengele was a prominent part, began with a programme of racial purification by focusing on health issues. Although the Nazi doctors may have began with good intentions, they ended up producing one of the worst genocides in history:

> The Law for the Protection of Hereditary Health established the mental and physical conditions that qualified for compulsory sterilization: feeblemindedness, schizophrenia, manic depression, epilepsy, hereditary blindness, deafness, physical deformities, Huntington's disease, and alcoholism.[37]

The leading German eugenic racial scientists had very strong support from the German scientific establishment, which was confident that their genocide programmes would

> improve the "quality" of the German race. In fact, they were the start of a series of escalating genocidal programs: first, euthanasia or "mercy" killing for the incurably insane; then the mass killings of people the Nazis judged to be biologically inferior, such as Gypsies, Slavs, and Jews; finally *Die Endlösung*, the Final

---

35 Evans, *The Third Reich at War*, 611–612.

36 Robert Millikan, *The Autobiography of Robert A. Millikan* (New York: Prentice-Hall, 1950).

37 Posner and Ware, *Mengele: The Complete Story*, 9–10.

Solution, Hitler's cover name for his plan to exterminate all the Jews in Europe.[38]

The scientific underpinnings used to justify the debasement of Jews was supplied by leading German scientists and academicians, such as agricultural expert Walter Darre, whose book *Blood and Soil* was published by the Nazi Party and "extrapolated barnyard eugenics to humans. Not surprisingly his ideas captivated the former chicken breeder, Heinrich Himmler, who chose Darre to operate the SS's Race and Settlement Office."[39]

Mengele also tried to prove that certain diseases now known to be contagious were caused by racial inferiority. Therefore, the Darwinists reasoned, as one does not negotiate with trichinae and bacilli, nor can trichinae and bacilli be educated. Likewise, the inferior races cannot be effectively educated, but rather must be "exterminated as quickly and thoroughly as possible."[40] Use of the "metaphor of Jews as diseased organisms was of inestimable value for the purveyors of mass murder, particularly physicians intent upon justifying their actions to outsiders and to themselves."[41]

Mengele was "absolutely convinced he was doing the right thing" and, as a result, had no qualms, "not with his conscience, not with anybody, not with anything" about implementing his killing programme for the sake of applying what they believed was the proven science of Darwinism.[42] They concluded because Darwinism was an empirical fact, applying it to benefit humanity was both a moral and laudable goal.

Germany was not alone in its support of anti-Semitism. In the United States, polls taken between 1938 and 1942 indicated that 10 to 15 percent of Americans supported anti-Semitic statutes but "only in Germany did it rally significant political groups" in support.[43] The Nazi

---

38 Posner and Ware, *Mengele: The Complete Story*, 10.

39 Astor, *The Last Nazi*, 21.

40 Astor, *The Last Nazi*, 21

41 Astor, *The Last Nazi*, 21.

42 Lifton, *The Nazi Doctors*, 344.

43 Posner and Ware, *Mengele: The Complete Story*, 9–10.

Party's end goal was to take "absolute control of the evolutionary process…in orchestrating their own 'selections,' their own version of human evolution."[44]

THE WAR ENDS

After the war, Josef Mengele hoped to be able to resume his Darwinian racist "research" in Germany, but he soon realized that this was no longer possible. Since the Nazis were no longer in power, he managed to flee to Argentina on an Italian ship. The former leading evolutionary scientist spent the next thirty years in hiding, sheltered by various neo-Nazi networks in Argentina, Paraguay and Brazil.[45] Mengele died in 1979, a lonely and bitter man, his dream of creating a more perfect race of humans in Germany shattered.

SUMMARY

Mengele's young mind was corrupted by a combination of the political climate in Nazi Germany and the fact that his strong

> interest in genetics and evolution happened to coincide with the developing concept that some human beings afflicted by disorders were unfit to reproduce, even to live. Perhaps the real catalyst in this lethal brew was that Mengele, first at Munich and later at Frankfurt, studied under the leading exponents of this "unworthy life" theory. His consummate ambition was to succeed in this fashionable new field of evolutionary research.[46]

Unfortunately, he succeeded all too well, but in ways that the world now regards as one of the worst tragedies in human history. And the evolutionary ideas that Mengele so enthusiastically absorbed at his university

> were precisely the ones that would propel him down the road to Auschwitz. His apprenticeship as a mass murderer formally

---

44 Lifton, *The Nazi Doctors*, 17.
45 Welch, *Rise & Fall of the Nazis*, 310.
46 Posner and Ware, *Mengele: The Complete Story*, 9.

began not on the selection lines of the concentration camp but in the classrooms of the University of Munich.[47]

Jewish historian Robert Lifton, in his extensive study of Nazi doctors, wrote that he "began and ended" his study of Nazi crimes with Mengele. Indeed, very few men are as closely associated with the Holocaust in the public's mind as Professor Josef Mengele, M.D., Ph.D.

---

47 Lagnado and Dekel, *Children of the Flames*, 42.

Martin Bormann (1900-1945)

Bormann's enormous influence on Hitler, combined with his vitriolic hatred of Jews, Slavs, Christians and non-Aryans, propelled their systematic murder, imprisonment and persecution throughout the war.

Bundesarchiv, Bild 183-R14128A / photographer: unknown, 1934

Martin Bormann:
Hitler's right-hand man

~~~~~~

INTRODUCTION

Martin Bormann (June 7, 1900 – May 2, 1945) joined the Nazi party in 1927 and rose steadily in the Nazi hierarchy. He first held the post of Party Treasurer and, after Adolf Hitler came to power in 1933, was appointed the National Party Organizer. In 1942, Bormann became Hitler's secretary and was appointed deputy Führer. He soon gained Hitler's full trust and achieved immense power within the Third Reich by controlling access to the Führer and even filtering the documents that Hitler saw.

As a result of his position, Bormann had an enormous influence on government policy. He turned out to be "one of the most powerful men in the Reich."[1] Bormann's power was so great that he sometimes even blocked Hitler's closest associates, including Joseph Goebbels, Hermann Göring, Heinrich Himmler and Albert Speer, from seeing Hitler. Many historians have suggested Bormann held so much power that he became Germany's actual co-leader during the war. This is illustrated by a collection of transcripts edited by Bormann

---

1   Mark Mazower, *Hitler's Empire: How the Nazis Ruled Europe* (New York: The Penguin Press, 2008), 28.

during the war and which appeared in print in 1951 as *Hitler's Table Talk 1941–1944.*

MARTIN BORMANN'S BACKGROUND

Bormann was born in Halberstadt, Germany, dropped out of college and joined the German Army during the last few months of the First World War. After the war, he joined a radical political group called *Rossbach Freikorps*. As a result of his involvement, he and future Nazi leader Rudolf Höss were found guilty of murdering and torturing Walter Kadow, who had been accused of betraying saboteur Albert Leo Schlageter. Bormann spent only a year in prison for his part in the murder. Soon Hitler became Bormann's "God," and he determined that "rather than believe in Jesus Christ, the Germans were to worship Adolf Hitler."[2]

EVOLUTION AND EUGENICS

Bormann's eugenic evolutionary racist ideas were clearly reflected in his policies. Bormann is said to have hated the Slavic peoples more than Hitler or even Himmler. Although Hitler claimed he was making war on "the Bolshevist center in Moscow," in fact, he "chose instead to make war on the Russian people" as a racial group.[3]

The importance of racism in Nazi military aggression was illustrated by the fact that Moscow widely distributed photographs showing Nazis hanging or shooting Russian civilians as evidence that the Nazis really were "waging a war of extermination against the Russian people."[4] Evidence supporting this conclusion is, in contrast to the Western policy, "The German army, as a matter of official policy, did not feed Russian civilians or prisoners of war."[5] A top-secret German document uncovered after the war and dated February 1942

---

2 Jochen Von Lang, *The Secretary: Martin Bormann, the Man Who Manipulated Hitler*, trans. Christa Armstrong and Peter White (New York: Random House, 1979).

3 Mazower, *Hitler's Empire*, 150–151, 213.

4 Borris Shub and Bernard Quint, *Since Stalin: A Photo History of Our Time* (New York: Swen Publications Company, 1951), 98.

5 Shub and Quint, *Since Stalin*, 98–99.

revealed that of 3,600,000 Soviet prisoners of war, "only several hundred thousand are still able to work.... A large part has starved or died...in the majority of cases, the camp commanders have forbidden the civilian population to put food at the disposal of prisoners."[6]

The "limitless abuse of Slavic humanity" by the Nazis even extended to genocide, openly murdering millions of Slavic Russians.[7] The reason for this horrible abuse of power was that "the Nazi leaders were absolute racists; they believed utterly in the superiority of their so-called Aryan (non-Jewish Germans and Scandinavians) race. They had no doubt that they were the pinnacle of racial evolution, that eugenically they were the best."[8] Furthermore, the Eastern Europeans were regarded by the Nazis as

sub-human...a dreadful creature...only an imitation of man with man-resembling features, but inferior...as regards intellect and soul...so science proved, they thought. And therefore no inferior group could be allowed to pollute their racial strain.[9]

Bormann was concerned that Ukrainian "children will become Ukrainian adults, with their vulgar, inexpressive faces," a problem that he was determined to solve by drastic measures including murder. He added that he was also very much struck by the fact that in the Ukraine he

saw so many children and so few men. Such prolific breeding may one day give us a knotty problem to solve, for as a race they are much hardier than we.... If these people are allowed, under German supervision—that is, under greatly improved conditions—to multiply too quickly, it will be against our interests, for

---

6   Shub and Quint, *Since Stalin*, 99.

7   Shub and Quint, *Since Stalin*, 96.

8   Rudolph J. Rummel, *Death by Government* (New Brunswick: Transaction Publishers, 2008), 118.

9   Rummel, *Death by Government*, 118–119.

the racial pressures which these damned Ukrainians will exercise will constitute a real danger. Our interests demand just the reverse—namely, that these territories, hitherto Russian, should in time be populated by a larger number of German colonists than local inhabitants.[10]

Bormann added that the "Slavs are to work for us. Insofar as we don't need them, they may die." For this reason, vaccination and German health services were unnecessary for the Slavic peoples. Furthermore, the high

fertility of the Slavs is undesirable. They may use contraceptives and practice abortion, the more the better. Education is danger-ous. It is sufficient if they can count up to a hundred. At best an education is admissible which produces useful servants for us. Every educated person is a future enemy. As to food, they are not to get more than necessary. We are the masters, we come first.[11]

As to the treatment of the Slavs, "Hitler agreed with Bormann and set off on a rambling monologue concerning the manner in which he felt that the Slavs should be handled. Bormann, ...sent a summary... to Rosenberg as a policy directive from the Führer's Headquarters."[12]

The extent of Bormann's cruelty was such that he sent a missive to the Armed Forces High Command claiming that its treatment of Rus-sian prisoners of war "was not severe enough" and some prison guards "had even developed attitudes of being the protectors of the captives. This was intolerable."[13] Bormann's solution was to remove the prison-ers from Army supervision and turn them over to SS who would treat them much more severely and without compassion.

Bormann's spouse, Gerda Bormann, was a very loyal Nazi wife who produced ten Aryan children and was so imbued "with the Nazi doc-

10 Cited in James McGovern, *Martin Bormann* (New York: William Morrow, 1968), 79.

11 Cited in McGovern, *Martin Bormann*, 79.

12 Cited in McGovern, *Martin Bormann*, 79.

13 Cited in McGovern, *Martin Bormann*, 79.

trine of producing large numbers of suitably Aryan children," that she proposed her husband make a *Volksnotehe* (National Emergency Marriage) contract with his mistress to prevent his illegitimate children from having an inferior status. This scheme conjured up by Frau Bormann amounted to legalizing bigamy partly because she believed it was used during the Thirty Years' War to respond to the enormous war manpower losses.[14]

His wife Gerda also "agreed with her husband that the Jews were responsible for most of the troubles of the world."[15] Gerda was so supportive of the goal to eliminate all Jews that she once wrote to her husband that the "power of Jewry was horrible" and

> not even the war would weaken this race, which fought its battles with money rather than blood. "Neither disease nor filth will ever eradicate this vermin," Gerda wailed. "How on earth can we get rid of them wholesale?" Her husband knew, but her question indicates that he had not taken her into his confidence. Nor did he ever give the slightest hint in any of his letters. In matters of secrecy, too, he was his Führer's ideal henchman.[16]

What was the source of Bormann's hatred of Jews? Professor Steinberg wrote that a major source was from his mentor, Hitler and the "basic argument behind Hitler's madness was pure social Darwinism."[17] As Hitler explained to Goebbels

> One might well ask why there are any Jews in the world order? That would be exactly like asking why there are potato bugs? Nature is dominated by the law of struggle. There will always be parasites who will spur this struggle on and intensify the process of selection between the strong and the weak. The principle of struggle dominates also in human life. One must merely know

---

14 McGovern, *Martin Bormann*, 106.

15 McGovern, *Martin Bormann*, 102.

16 Von Lang, *The Secretary: Martin Bormann*, 201.

17 Jonathan Steinberg, *All or Nothing: The Axis and the Holocaust, 1941–1943* (New York: Routledge, 1990), 195.

the law of this struggle to be able to face it. The intellectual does not have the natural means of resisting the Jewish peril because his instincts have been badly blunted. Because of this fact nations with a high standard of living are exposed to this peril first and foremost. In nature, life always takes measures against parasites; in the life of nations that is not always the case. From this fact the Jewish peril actually stems. There is therefore no other recourse left for modern nations except to exterminate the Jew.[18]

BORMANN'S HATRED OF CHRISTIANITY

Although the Nazis were forced to tolerate religion, the major conflict between Christianity and Nazism was very clear

> as Martin Bormann exclaimed: "National Socialism and Christianity are irreconcilable." Hitler supported this view, stating: "One day we want to be in a position where only complete idiots stand in the pulpit and preach to old women." The Nazis viewed Christianity as a faith tainted by the Jews. In response, the Nazis offered the German people a new religion based around blood, soil, Germanic folklore and the Thousand Year Reich. The Nazis were no different here from earlier revolutionaries who tried to offer the people a brave new secular world. It was no surprise that racial supremacy played a large part in the new "religion."[19]

Bormann made his absolute disdain for Christianity and his open hostility and support of breaking the church as rapidly as possible absolutely clear.[20] He was one of many high-level Nazis who "intended eventually to destroy Christianity" for the reason that "National Socialism and Christianity are irreconcilable" because Nazism is based on science and science had superseded the Christian church,

---

18 Cited in Steinberg, *All or Nothing*, 195

19 Matthew Hughes and Chris Mann, *Inside Hitler's Germany: Life under the Third Reich* (New York: MJF Books, 2000), 80.

20 Joseph Keysor, *Hitler, the Holocaust, and the Bible* (New York: Athanatos, 2010), 180–181.

which he regarded as anti-science.[21] He added "National Socialism and Christian concepts are incompatible" because the Christian churches were all built on

> the ignorance of men and strive to keep large portions of the people in ignorance because only in this way can the Christian Churches maintain their power. On the other hand, National Socialism is based on scientific foundations. Christianity's immutable principles, which were laid down almost two thousand years ago, have increasingly stiffened into life-alien dogmas. National Socialism, however, if it wants to fulfill its task further, must always guide itself according to the newest data of scientific researchers.[22]

Bormann added, "Christian Churches have long been aware that exact scientific knowledge poses a threat to their existence" and instead they have relied on pseudo-science such as theology. Furthermore, Bormann concluded, the church takes "great pains to suppress or falsify scientific research. Our National Socialist worldview stands on a much higher level than the concepts of Christianity."[23]

One reason why Bormann hated Christianity was because he believed that "the concepts of Christianity…in their essential points have been taken over from Jewry" and therefore, Bormann concluded, Christianity must be obliterated. He added that when Nazis speak of a belief in God, they do not understand God to be that of the

> naïve Christians and their spiritual opportunists, [as] a human-type being, who sits around somewhere in space…. The force of natural law, [in the universe]…we call the Almighty or God…. The more accurately we recognize and observe the laws of nature

---

21 William L. Shirer, *The Rise and Fall of the Third Reich* (New York: Simon and Schuster, 1960), 240.

22 Martin Bormann, 1942; cited in George L. Mosse, *Nazi Culture: Intellectual, Cultural, and Social Life in the Third Reich* (Madison: University of Wisconsin Press, 1981), 244.

23 Martin Bormann, 1942; cited in Mosse, *Nazi Culture*, 244.

and of life, the more we adhere to them, so much the more do we conform to the will of the Almighty.[24]

He also believed that "No one would know anything about Christianity if pastors had not crammed it down "their throat as children" and when "in the future our youth no longer hear anything about this Christianity, whose doctrine is far below our own, Christianity will automatically disappear."[25] These statements were, ironically, originally published in *Kirchliches Jahrbuch für die Evangelische Kirche in Deutschland, 1933–1944* (Ecclesiastical Yearbook of the Evangelical Church in Germany).

Bormann's hatred of Christianity was so extreme that he "instructed his wife to 'make sure that none of our children get depraved and diseased by the poison of Christianity, in whatever dosage.'"[26] His wife agreed with her husband that their children must never be allowed to become infected with the "poison" of Christianity.[27] Ironically, their eldest son became an active Catholic and, on August 20, 1958, was ordained a Roman Catholic priest in the order of the Missionaries of the Sacred Heart at the Jesuit Church in Innsbruck, Austria.[28]

Many other examples exist of the fact that Bormann did everything in his power to destroy Christianity.[29] In Poland, Bormann required Germans and Poles to attend separate churches, and ruled that all church property was to be confiscated by the state excepting only the church building itself. Furthermore, all monasteries and cloisters were closed because they "worked against German morality," i.e., the Darwinian survival of the fittest morality.[30] Furthermore, "the seizure of church property...was consistent with the well-established animosity the Nazis showed toward this institution."[31]

---

24 Martin Bormann, 1942; cited in John S. Conway, *The Nazi Persecution of the Churches, 1933–1945* (New York: Basic Books, 1968), 384

25 Martin Bormann, 1942; cited in Conway, *The Nazi Persecution of the Churches*, 384

26 McGovern, *Martin Bormann*, 190.

27 McGovern, *Martin Bormann*, 102.

28 McGovern, *Martin Bormann*, 190.

29 Conway, *The Nazi Persecution of the Churches*.

30 Richard Steigmann-Gall, *The Holy Reich: Nazi Conceptions of Christianity, 1919–1945* (New York: Cambridge University Press, 2003), 228–229.

31 Steigmann-Gall, *The Holy Reich*, 229.

Bormann even required the German Protestant churches to raise one million Reichsmarks per month, and the German Catholic Churches 800,000 Reichsmarks a month, to help finance a war that many Christians opposed.[32] Furthermore, as Head of the Nazi Party Chancellery, Bormann was able "to indulge his long-held prejudice in a direct and sinister fashion." In this role he could easily

indulge his hatred of Christianity. Like many of the Nazi leaders …he had done everything he could to harass both the Roman Catholic and Protestant Churches. He despised Christianity as a corrupting and softening influence, interfering with the creation of the new Nordic man.[33]

Bormann, "one of the Nazi Party's most powerful functionaries and greatest anticlericals," also tried, often successfully, to block Nazi officials and others who attempted to mitigate Germany's disenfranchisement and suppression of Christianity.[34] Bormann not only fought for separation of church and state, but also church and political party.

For example, he did what he could to keep the clergy out of not only the party but also the National Socialists Teachers League. He forbade the wearing of party uniforms at church services and other religious activities.[35] The only exception was Christian funerals. In addition "The Nazi authorities brought great pressure on members of the police and armed forces to renounce their church membership."[36]

One of the very few high-level Nazis who was a practicing Christian was Josef Wagner. Bormann, though, was determined that not a single party leader be a practicing Christian. Consequently, Bormann

worked to have Wagner expelled in November 1941. Wagner appealed his case to Buch's[37] party court, defending himself by

---

32 Von Lang, *The Secretary: Martin Bormann*, 183.

33 McGovern, *Martin Bormann*, 65,

34 Steigmann-Gall, *The Holy Reich*, 215.

35 Steigmann-Gall, *The Holy Reich*, 215.

36 Hughes and Mann, *Inside Hitler's Germany*, 81.

37 Walter Buch was Bormann's father-in-law and head of the Nazi Party court.

referring to Point 24 of the Party Program[38] and insisting that he
had known nothing of his wife's [kind] conduct toward the Pope.
Buch and the six members of the party jury... accepted Wagner's
defense and reversed the expulsion order. Hitler, however,
refused to ratify the decision, thereby upholding Wagner's expulsion. Buch believed that it was his son-in-law ... who was really
responsible [for Hitler's decision].[39]

As expected, the forced expulsion of "pastors from positions of
power in the party, together with the withdrawal of party members
from the churches, paints an unambiguous picture of increased hostility between Nazism and Christian institutions after 1937."[40] As one
authority wrote, "the Nazis' attempts at *Gleichschaltung* for Protestantism failed," but this failure

> did not stop the Nazis persecuting religious opponents, including
> [Martin] Niemöller, who was imprisoned in 1937 and subsequent-
> ly sent to a concentration camp. When the Protestant Churches
> went on record in 1935 to say that the entire Nazi racial-folk
> *Weltanschauung*[41] was nonsense, 700 ministers were arrested,
> humiliated and their civil liberties restricted. Ultimately...by the
> late 1930s the policies of repression had effectively stifled open
> opposition within the Protestant movement.[42]

To replace religion, Germany needed "something scientific, 'real'
and non-metaphysical" to "replace the operations of the World-Spirit."
Historian Jonathan Steinberg wrote that to replace religion, the Nazis

> almost unconsciously, inserted biology. Darwin had discovered
> the "laws" of the evolution of species. It was obvious, wasn't it,

---

38 Point 24 proclaimed "positive Christianity" as one of the tenets of the Nazi
Party's Constitution.

39 Steigmann-Gall, *The Holy Reich*, 230.

40 Steigmann-Gall, *The Holy Reich*, 230

41 Meaning "worldview."

42 Hughes and Mann, *Inside Hitler's Germany*, 82.

that those laws applied to human species, peoples, races? ...all too obvious. A version of Darwin's ideas swept Germany in the last third of the nineteenth century.... Darwinian ideas explained everything: why blacks were poor and backward and why, therefore, Europeans had to rule them; why Germanic peoples had free institutions and Asiatics did not; why northern peoples were more enterprising than Latins and so on.... To minds accustomed to thinking of history in...[this] way the laws of racial struggle were irresistible and were, indeed, not resisted. From the murder of the feeble-minded by so-called "euthanasia" actions in 1940 to the ethnic policies of the German army in the Balkans, the fatal...legacy can be traced.[43]

BORMANN'S END

During the final stages of the war, when it became clear that Germany had lost the war, Bormann attempted to break through the Red Army lines in an effort to escape. What happened then has been debated for decades. Several witnesses claimed they saw him killed by a Russian tank. Others believed he escaped to South America as did several other leading Nazis.[44]

Bormann was tried at Nuremberg in *absentia* and sentenced to hang. In December 1972, two skeletons were unearthed during construction near the Lehrter Station where Bormann's diary was found in a discarded leather jacket in 1945, and close to where an eyewitness claimed that he had seen Bormann's body.

After extensive forensic examination by Professor Hugo Blaschke using Bormann's dental records (Blaschke was also Hitler's dentist), the shorter of the two skeletons was identified as that of Martin Bormann. German authorities then officially declared him dead. This forensic identification was validated by celebrated American forensic expert Dr. Reidar F. Sognnaes.

Nonetheless, journalist Jim Marrs makes the case that Bormann was well-connected among world elites and too smart to be haphazardly killed as described in what he calls "the legend of his death."

---

43 Steinberg, *All or Nothing*, 232.
44 McGovern, *Martin Bormann*.

This, he argues, was staged to avoid harassment for war crimes.[45] He adds that Bormann had been planning extensively for his post-war future and claims that Bormann escaped successfully to South America where he died many years later.

SUMMARY

After Martin Bormann became a disciple of Hitler and Darwin, he rapidly progressed into a racist and hater of Christianity. He was active in doing whatever he could to destroy the Christian church and eliminate as many people as possible who were members of what the Nazis regarded as inferior races, including Jews, Slavic peoples and all other so-called non-Aryan races. Under Hitler, Bormann was one of the most powerful men in Germany, and was able to put into practice his hatred, contributing to the terror caused by the Nazis during their twelve-year rule.

---

45 Jim Marrs, *The Rise of the Fourth Reich* (New York: William Morrow, 2009).

Heinrich Himmler:
Darwinist and mass murderer

INTRODUCTION

Heinrich Himmler, as head of the infamous SS, was one of the worst mass murderers in history. He was directly or indirectly responsible for the systematic murder of over 11 million innocent people. Himmler was both tenaciously anti-Christian and anti-Semitic. The number of lives lost under his administration included about 6 million Jews and over 5 million others, including Catholics priests, intellectuals and high-level military personnel.[1]

For this reason, the name Heinrich Himmler "stands today as the symbol of the mass murders committed by the Third Reich.... Himmler *was* Nazism."[2] Himmler was head of the infamous SS (*Schutzstaffel*, or Security Squad) and the chief architect of the Final Solution to the Jewish "problem," namely, their total annihilation.[3]

---

1 Richard Lukas, *The Forgotten Holocaust: The Poles under German Occupation 1939–1944* (New York: Hippocrene Books, 1997).

2 Bradley Smith, *Heinrich Himmler: A Nazi in the Making, 1900–1926* (Stanford: Hover Institution Press, Stanford University, 1971), 1, 172.

3 Linda Schmittroth and Mary Kay Rosteck, *People of the Holocaust*, Vol. 1: A-J (Detroit: Gale, 1998), 222.

Under his command, the SS who worked as concentration camp guards enslaved over 15 million innocent people. The two most important architects of the Holocaust were Heinrich Himmler and Reinhard Heydrich. Himmler was determined that what he referred to as the Jewish race "must disappear from the face of the earth."[4]

HIMMLER'S BACKGROUND

Himmler's mother was a pious Catholic, his family solidly middle class, and his father a respected German school headmaster. Historian Oswald Dutch wrote that nothing in Himmler's background "gives a hint of the source of his cruelty and persecution mania."[5] As a youth, he was a creationist, viewing the "scientific picture of life in the universe as the detailed record of God's design."[6] All of this was soon to change when he went to college and became involved in the Nazi movement.

All of Himmler's birth family members were very supportive of higher education, and were "directly involved in the scramble for academic success."[7] A diligent student, Himmler attended the University of Munich where, as an agriculture science student, he studied Darwinism. In college, his doubts would eventually result in abandoning both his creationism and his Catholic faith. He also probably learned about Darwinism and racism either directly, or most likely indirectly, through the writings of people such as Houston Stewart Chamberlain and the famous German professor Dr. Ernst Haeckel "who had transformed Darwinian evolution into the science of race."[8]

In December 1924, Himmler read Haeckel's book, *The Riddle of the Universe*, and, although he did not at that time agree with all of it, the book exposed him to the implications of the Darwinian worldview as

---

4   Schmittroth and Rosteck, *People of the Holocaust*, 1:222–223.

5   Oswald Dutch, *Hitler's 12 Apostles* (New York: Robert M. McBride & Company, 1940), 42.

6   Smith, *Heinrich Himmler*, 87.

7   Smith, *Heinrich Himmler*, 29.

8   Christopher Hale, *Himmler's Crusade: The Nazi Expedition to Find the Origins of the Aryan Race* (New York: Wiley, 2003), 102.

Heinrich Himmler (1900–1945)

Considered one of the worst mass murderers in history, Himmler was head of the SS and responsible for millions of deaths.

Bundesarchiv, Bild 183-L24943 / photographer: unknown, July 1941

interpreted by Haeckel.[9] Himmler learned some of his anti-Semitic ideas from Haeckel who "hated cities," which he associated "with Jews, whom he hated."[10]

At this time, the intellectual life in Germany, including at the University of Munich, was influenced by a

> trend of thought which was to become significant as the second cardinal principle of the National Socialist "purification" policy.... "Social Darwinism," a movement that gained a great deal of support after 1890, and had a profound effect upon Hitler's mind.[11]

It was also at the University of Munich where he adopted many of his anti-Semitic values. An important factor was his reading of numerous anti-Semitic books, such as those by Houston Stewart Chamberlin.[12] Furthermore, Himmler not only "lost his religious faith" in college, but came to believe that Christianity was "merely another manifestation of Jewish superstition" that polluted German culture.[13] He became such a fanatical anti-Christian that he declared the Nazis "shall not rest until we have rooted out Christianity" from Nazi-controlled Europe.[14]

Drawn to politics at university, he graduated in 1922 and become active in the Nazi party the following year. In 1927, Himmler married a Polish nurse —very ironic because a little over a decade later he became active in ordering the murder of millions of Poles, a race, along with Gypsies and Negroes, that were judged inferior by the Nazis.[15] When Germany attacked Russia, Himmler declared it was German's

---

9   Peter Longerich, *Heinrich Himmler. Biographie* (München: Siedler Verlag, 2008), 85; Smith, *Heinrich Himmler*, 177.

10   Hale, *Himmler's Crusade*, 102.

11   Helmut Krausnick, ed., Hans Buchheim, Martin Broszut and Hans-Adolf Jacobsen, contrib., *Anatomy of the SS State*, trans. Richard Barry, et. al. (New York: Walker & Company, 1968), 10.

12   Smith, *Heinrich Himmler*, 122, 147.

13   Hale, *Himmler's Crusade*, 83.

14   Paul Johnson, *A History of Christianity* (New York: Atheneum, 1976), 493.

15   Albert Speer, *Inside the Third Reich: Memoirs by Albert Speer*, trans. Richard and Clara Winston (New York: MacMillan, 1970), 188.

intention to "kill thirty million Russians," which the Nazi government called "sub-man...in mind and spirit lower than any animal."[16]

From the Darwinists, Himmler learned that the "origin of the species had laid down the laws of evolution as they affected all forms of life." English naturalist Charles Darwin further concluded that evolution was the result

> of a long, gradual development through a struggle for existence, in which the stronger and more efficient element always prevailed; the species had continually progressed and improved by a process of natural selection. The revolutionary significance of this theory, supported as it was by careful and detailed research, lay in the fact that it offered a simple mechanical explanation for life's phenomena (that is to say, it showed that these were naturally self-regulating) to replace the earlier acceptance of a supernatural power responsible for the creation of life on earth.[17]

Himmler was so driven by his attempt to apply "Darwin's theory of the survival of the fittest" to society that he concluded the "'struggle of the creative Teutonic-Aryan race' boiled down to the 'struggle against the parasitic Semitic race.'"[18] His hatred for Jews and other races he deemed inferior was so extreme that "various ministries of the Reich tried to tone down Himmler's Nordic ardour."[19]

An important factor that influenced the development and implementation of the Final Solution, which Himmler was charged with carrying out, was the fact that "Darwin's theory denied the existence of any essential difference in origin between men and animals" and some races were much closer to animals then other races.[20] Furthermore, those Germans who became Darwin's disciples

---

16 Norman Cohn, *Warrant for Genocide* (New York: Harper and Row, 1967), 188.

17 Krausnick, ed., *Anatomy of the SS State*, 11.

18 Marc Hillel and Clarissa Henry, *Of Pure Blood* (New York: McGraw-Hill, 1976), 23.

19 Hillel and Henry, *Of Pure Blood*, 27.

20 Krausnick, ed., *Anatomy of the SS State*, 11.

wanted to see the traditional Christian values governing the social behavior of mankind set aside. Darwin also explained that the biologically superior elements occasionally thrown up during the evolutionary process were, unfortunately, not *ipso facto* of greater value than the rest. As against this, those so-called "Social Darwinists," who were disciples of the modern creed of "natural forces" in their political outlook held that human society was also more or less a biological organism, and concluded, therefore, that the *biological factor was the one absolute* in all spheres of life.[21]

In a speech Himmler gave to the SS major generals in October 1943, he called Slavic peoples, which included not just Poles but also Russians and other Slavs, "subhuman beings," beasts that must serve "their superiors," i.e., the Germans.[22] Germans were the superior race, Himmler explained, because humans "are a product of the law of [natural] selection" and Germany's long history of war allowed selection to select out inferior Germans, making Germans superior to other ethnic groups.[23]

To achieve the Nazi racial goals, Hitler assigned Himmler the task of building the SS "into an organization of carefully selected men who would become the leaders of a new German race."[24] The SS eventually took the lead in carrying out the extermination of all Jews in German-controlled Europe.

Himmler attempted to divide the Polish people into two racial groups, the Aryans and those capable of being re-Germanized and, in contrast, the "other" Poles who were good only to work as slaves for the Germans.[25] The Nazis commissioned German anthropologists, such as Professor Eugen Fischer and other academics, to determine which Poles were "sufficiently Aryan" to Germanize.[26]

---

21 Krausnick, ed., *Anatomy of the SS State*, 11. Emphasis in original.

22 Michael Berenbaum, ed., *Witness to the Holocaust* (New York: HarperCollins, 1997), 177.

23 Berenbaum, ed., *Witness to the Holocaust*, 178.

24 Schmittroth and Rosteck, *People of the Holocaust*, 1:225.

25 Richard Weikart, *Hitler's Ethic: The Nazi Pursuit of Evolutionary Progress* (New York: Palgrave MacMillan, 2009), 67–68.

26 Weikart, *Hitler's Ethic*, 68.

Although Hitler originated the Holocaust machine, Himmler was the man who did his bidding "without showing or giving into moral qualms or doubts" about the mass murder he supervised.[27] Since most Soviets were Slavic, a people judged as an inferior race by the Nazis, Himmler and his associates also began plans to Germanize Soviet territory. This goal included eliminating most of the population of the cities by the "hunger plan," i.e., deliberately causing starvation.[28] The "push to build a pure, master race included the extermination of everyone Himmler and Hitler considered 'racially impure,'" which meant all non-Aryans.[29] Hitler's long-term goal was to return all Soviet cities to farmland by the extermination of most Slavic peoples. The German army and SS managed to murder over 12 million innocent people toward achieving this goal before they were finally driven out of Russia.

HIMMLER'S MANY ANTI-SEMITIC PROGRAMMES

The superior race idea dominated Himmler's goals.[30] He even set up a system to require SS men to obtain a certificate to marry in order to ensure that they "would not produce children of 'contaminated' blood," by which he meant had mixed race genes.[31]

Himmler's fixation on the scientific aspects of Darwinism and racism extended to the degree that he organized an extensive expedition to locate the genetic origins of the "Aryan race."[32] The leader of the expedition was zoologist Dr. Ernst Schäfer whose team of scientists examined Tibetan nobles for signs of "Aryan ancestry."[33] The cost of the expedition was over 250 million Reichsmarks, and they evidently never found any convincing scientific evidence to support their racist theory.

Himmler also set up the now infamous *Lebensborn* programme discussed in chapter 15. The "aim of these institutions was the breed-

27 Richard Breitman, *The Architect of Genocide: Himmler and the Final Solution* (New York: Alfred Knopf, 1991), 73.

28 Weikart, *Hitler's Ethic*, 174.

29 Schmittroth and Rosteck, *People of the Holocaust*, 1:225.

30 Breitman, *The Architect of Genocide*.

31 Schmittroth and Rosteck, *People of the Holocaust*, 1:225.

32 Hale, *Himmler's Crusade*.

33 Hale, *Himmler's Crusade*.

ing of a Nordic super-race with the aid of men and women carefully selected in accordance with the racial principles of the Third Reich."[34] Furthermore, throughout "Europe the Germans had kidnapped thousands of 'racially valuable' children, [and had] taken them from their families to Germanize them [as]...one of the ways of helping the super-race to be fruitful and multiply."[35] To increase the number of German births, in 1941 Himmler banned most contraceptives. The major exception was use of condoms to help deal with the German syphilis problem.[36] Evidently, the major influence that motivated Himmler to become a racist was not a direct study of Darwin, or even the German translations of Darwin, but the Nazi social Darwinists and Hitler himself:

> Euthanasia was for Hitler a program to rid the German people of anyone considered mentally or physically deficient—any perceived weakness in the collective gene pool. In that sense it was the logical extension of the mélange of late-nineteenth-century racist and Social Darwinist ideas that Hitler had picked up as a youth. In his 1929 speech at the Nuremberg Party Congress, he had stated that, if one million children were born in Germany in a given year, and if the weakest seven or eight hundred thousand were eliminated, the German people would be strengthened.[37]

As Himmler scholar Richard Breitman wrote, Nazi Germany from its very beginnings was a racial state, although it took several years to lead the country down the path to the Holocaust.[38] Nonetheless, we should not "overlook the racial hostility that contributed to [the] plans and early killings of Poles and Gypsies" and later Jews. War, Breitman wrote, was a cover to provide "appropriate opportunities for Hitler and other Nazi leaders to pursue their racial paranoia to extreme limits."[39]

---

34 Hillel and Henry, *Of Pure Blood*, 11.
35 Hillel and Henry, *Of Pure Blood*, 12.
36 Weikart, *Hitler's Ethic*, 157.
37 Breitman, *The Architect of Genocide*, 89–90.
38 Breitman, *The Architect of Genocide*, 75–76.
39 Breitman, *The Architect of Genocide*, 76.

PRODUCING A PURE GERMAN RACE

According to Elizabeth Wiskemann, "Himmler really believed that he could breed better Germans and arrange for all the sub-humans (*Untermenschen*) to die out or rot away or, in plain language, be murdered" to produce his mythical superior race.[40] The pure German race Himmler envisioned "was tall, blond, and blue-eyed," an ideal many Germans, including Himmler himself, did not measure up to. Himmler was so blinded by his ideology that he believed Germany would eventually win the war against the far more numerous Slavic masses because the Slavic people were evolutionarily inferior.[41] Germany had to win the war because, Himmler believed, the law of survival of the fittest will always prevail.

Himmler enjoyed major support for his racial programmes from German academics, including the German Society for Racial Hygiene, which had 1,300 members by 1933, many of which were academics.[42] The Society even published a peer reviewed academic journal, *Archiv für Rassen and Gesellschaftsbiologie*. The most important institute involved in this movement was the highly respected Kaiser Wilhelm Institute for Anthropology, Heredity and Eugenics. When the Nazis came to power, German universities began to train students in "racial studies and eugenics," which ensured the growth of a class of educated scientists that supported the Nazi racial programmes.[43]

In 1935, Himmler founded the *Ahnenerbe*, a well-funded research organization of scholars, both reputable and those less so, to find evidence that Aryans played a critical role in history. Himmler and other Aryan scholars believed that the Aryans evolved in the icy barrens of the Arctic where they ruled as the invincible master race.[44] The identification of the true Aryans and the eradiation of all other races

---

40 Elizabeth Wiskemann, "Introduction" in Krausnick, ed., *Anatomy of the SS State*, ix–x.

41 Breitman, *The Architect of Genocide*, 242.

42 Michael Burleigh and Wolfgang Wippermann, *The Racial State: Germany, 1933–1945* (New York: Cambridge University Press, 1991), 52.

43 Burleigh and Wippermann, *The Racial State*, 53.

44 Heather Pringle, *The Master Plan: Himmler's Scholars and the Holocaust* (New York: Hyperion, 2006).

became the cornerstone of the Nazi agenda.[45] The evidence for this theory, the scholars felt, would help to scientifically justify Germany's war and genocidal behaviour. They found little evidence for their theory in spite of long, expensive expeditions by researchers to various lands in the Arctic Circle.

HIMMLER BUILDS THE SS INTO A POWERFUL ORGANIZATION

During Himmler's sixteen years as head of the SS, he built it "into a vast empire, and in the process, he acquired the power of life and death over millions" of people by expanding

> the SS, a bodyguard unit whose membership originally totalled 280, into an enormous, cold-blooded military and economic empire totaling 50,000 members. Along the way, he acquired a number of new titles, including Chief of Police, Reich Commissioner for the Solidification of German Peoplehood, and Commander of the Political Police.[46]

Himmler also developed a "policy of turning Poland into a nation of illiterates" in an attempt

> to "sift out those with valuable blood and those with worthless blood." Polish children between the ages of six and ten would be examined, and those who were thought racially acceptable would be snatched from their families and raised in Germany; they would not see their biological parents again. The Nazi policy of stealing children in Poland is significantly less well known than is the extermination of the Jews, but it fits into the same pattern. It demonstrates how seriously a man like Himmler believed in identifying the value of a human being through racial composition. Removing these children was not for him—as it might seem today—some evil eccentricity, but an essential part of his warped worldview.[47]

---

45 Pringle, *The Master Plan*, Book jacket.

46 Schmittroth and Rosteck, *People of the Holocaust*, 1:225.

47 Laurence Rees, *Auschwitz: A New History* (New York: Public Affairs Press, 2005), 17.

Planning their conquest

The Deputy Führer, Rudolf Hess (centre), visited in Berlin by the Reichsführer-SS Heinrich Himmler, examining a model of a proposed rural settlement.

Bundesarchiv, Bild 146-1974-079-57 / photographer: unknown, March 20, 1941

One of the first direct steps that lead to the Holocaust was for the *Einsatzgruppen* in the occupied territories to murder select Jewish males. Many Jewish males were also sent to concentration camps. As more and more males died from overwork or were shot, Himmler was forced to begin the next step. Once you kill the family's breadwinner, the Nazis were faced with the problem of what to do with the women and children that were left behind. In the summer of 1941, Himmler made a watershed decision to murder the Jewish women and children as well, a decision authorized by Hitler that permeated down through the ranks to the mobile killing units, the *Einsatzgruppen*.

HIMMLER AS A MASS MURDERER

Himmler had no qualms about killing millions of people, especially those he deemed inferior races such as Jews, to achieve his Darwinian eugenic goal of producing a "superior" race. His goal was that all Jews will eventually be murdered and, with some exceptions, Himmler claimed that his "soldiers and *Einsatzgruppen* enthusiastically obeyed" his orders.[48] As noted, Himmler also wanted to eliminate all other "inferior races" especially the Slavic population, and once said the "purpose of the Russian campaign [was] to decimate the Slavic population by 30 million" persons. The rest would serve as slaves for Germany.[49]

Himmler also used his admiration for modern technology to achieve mass murder by using "some sort of streamlined and quiet procedure." Because of the enormous numbers, in the tens of millions of "inferior" people that must be eliminated, he reasoned, why not exploit

the most modern technology? Himmler's own handwriting thus provides the earliest evidence of a plan for a kind of death factory, with poison gas as the killing agent and crematoria to dispose of the bodies.[50]

Although Hitler raised the idea of gassing the Jews in his book *Mein Kampf*, and the T-4 Programme used carbon monoxide to gas mental

---

48 Hale, *Himmler's Crusade*, 345.

49 Rees, *Auschwitz: A New History*, 37.

50 Breitman, *The Architect of Genocide*, 88.

patients and others, it was Himmler who, in December 1939, came up with gas poison as the solution to the "Jewish Problem" which began on a large scale in earnest in December 1941.[51] To prevent the victims from resisting, they were told that they were going to be deloused in showers. The victims then undressed and were told to keep their clothes together so they could dress when the delousing was completed.

When inside of what they thought were delousing showers, the door was locked and Zyklon B crystals were dropped into the now sealed room. In minutes, everyone in the "showers" died. Their bodies were then removed by other prisoners, taken to the crematorium to be turned into ashes, and buried in an attempt to hide this horrendous crime from the world.

The murdering was previously carried out by shooting the victims at close range, a killing method that, contrary to Himmler's claims, caused much consternation among the mostly young German army recruits. Gassing reduced the gore that was caused by mass shootings and, consequently, reduced the demoralizing effect that the killings had on the Nazi soldiers.

HIMMLER'S END

After Germany was defeated, Himmler unsuccessfully attempted to flee from his homeland. When he was captured, rather than face his crimes, Himmler followed his master and committed suicide in 1945 by swallowing a cyanide capsule that he broke open with his teeth. He was buried in a secret grave—which is more respect than he gave his victims, millions who were buried in mass graves— so that his final resting place could not become a Nazi shrine.[52] He took his own life, historian Bradley Smith concluded, because "short of death he could draw no line between the [Nazi] party and himself."[53] In the end, both Himmler's "positive eugenics," encouraging the racially fit

---

51 David Cesarani, *The Final Solution: Origins and Implementation* (New York: Routledge, 1996), 75.

52 Roger Manvell and Heinrich Fraenkel, *Heinrich Himmler: The Sinister Life of the Head of the SS and the Gestapo* (New York: Skyhorse Publishing, 2007).

53 Smith, *Heinrich Himmler*, 172.

to rapidly multiply, and his "negative eugenics," killing the racially inferior, failed miserably.[54]

SUMMARY

Eugenics and race were so central to Himmler's worldview that he believed not only Jews, but other "inferior races" such as Slavs, must be exterminated or made slaves to the superior races, a policy the SS had begun to implement as early as 1939.[55] Toward this goal, he gave his life.

---

54 Lucy S. Dawidowicz, "The Failure of Himmler's Positive Eugenics," *Hastings Center Report*, Vol. 7, Issue 5 (October 1977): 43–44.

55 Manvell and Fraenkel, *Heinrich Himmler*, 23, 29, 99, 107, 126, 256, 260.

10

Dr. Joseph Goebbels: Darwinist father of the Holocaust

INTRODUCTION

Joseph Goebbels (October 29, 1897 – May 1, 1945) was a leading Nazi, one of Hitler's closest associates, and probably the second most infamous Nazi after Hitler. So important was Goebbels that, without him, some leading Nazi historians have concluded Hitler never would have gained totalitarian power.[1]

The son of working class Catholic parents, he was named Joseph "in honor of Dr. Josef Joseph, a revered local Jewish attorney and close family friend."[2] The deeply religious Goebbels family wanted Joseph to become a priest, but it was not to be. Instead, he became an anti-priest, conducting "acrimonious and vulgar campaigns against the Catholic clergy."[3]

A bright child, he devoured every book and encyclopedia he could obtain. He studied at eight universities, and earned degrees from the

---

1   Viktor Reimann, *Goebbels*, trans. Stephen Wendt (Garden City: Doubleday, 1976), 2–3.

2   David Irving, *Goebbels: Mastermind of the Third Reich* (London: Focal Point, 1996), xvii.

3   Helmut Heiber, *Goebbels* (New York: Hawthorn Books, 1972). 7.

University of Bonn, the University of Würzburg and the University of Freiburg.[4] Later, supported financially by the church, he earned his Ph.D. from the University of Heidelberg in Germany in 1921.

Little or no evidence existed of any anti-Semitism in Goebbels' background until much later in his life.[5] The love of his youth and the woman he wanted to marry, his "little rosebud," Fräulein Else, was Jewish, as were many of his friends.[6] Goebbels' major professor (and his favourite professor as well), Dr. Friedrich Gundolf, and his doctoral supervisor, Max Baron von Waldberg—both whom he praised to the skies—were also Jews, as was his wife's stepfather.[7]

Before receiving his doctorate, Goebbels read widely for his classes, and a major influence on his intellectual development included Darwin's ideas, as well as those of Friedrich Nietzsche, Alfred Rosenberg and Houston Stewart Chamberlain.[8] As early as 1915, he had begun to "have serious doubts about his religious beliefs" and in 1919, he openly rejected both the Catholic Church and Christianity. He once wrote "it hardly matters what we believe in, so long as we believe in something."[9] His rejection of the family faith bothered his father, as did his political move toward socialism.

GOEBBELS BECOMES A NAZI

Goebbels became a Nazi in 1925 when he met Hitler, who soon became his god and changed his life forever. He became enthusiastically committed and worked tirelessly to change Germany into the Nazi ideal. Nazism became his new religion as it also became "the religion of the German revolution."[10] When it became clear that "the

---

4 Paul Roland, *The Illustrated History of the Nazis* (Edison: Chartwell Books, 2009), 55.

5 Irving, *Goebbels: Mastermind of the Third Reich*, 12.

6 Irving, *Goebbels: Mastermind of the Third Reich*, 12.

7 Heiber, *Goebbels*, 248; Ralf Georg Reuth, *Goebbels* (New York: Harcourt Brace, 1993), 182.

8 Irving, *Goebbels: Mastermind of the Third Reich*, 20, 28.

9 Irving, *Goebbels: Mastermind of the Third Reich*, 11,13.

10 Hugh R. Trevor-Roper, *The Last Days of Hitler*, 3rd ed. (New York: MacMillan, 1962), 3.

Führer was intransigent on his anti-Semitism, Goebbels went along. And what he did, he did thoroughly."[11]

Under the influence of Hitler and the Nazis, Goebbels also became more and more anti-Semitic, eventually leaving Else Janke, whom he stated he would have married if she was not a Jewess. He once wrote that Jews were "inhumanly wicked…congenital money-grabbers who deliberately inflicted suffering on others to satisfy their greed."[12]

When Goebbels read *Mein Kampf* he had nothing but praise for the book, exclaiming that Hitler was "half plebeian, half god."[13] No doubt he also learned much of his Darwinism worldview from Hitler, about whom Bullock wrote the "basis of Hitler's political beliefs was a crude Darwinism." To defend this claim, Bullock quoted the following from Hitler's speeches

> "Man has become great through struggle…. Whatever goal man has reached is due to his originality plus his brutality…. All life is bound up in three theses: Struggle is the father of all things, virtue lies in blood, leadership is primary and decisive."… "The whole work of Nature is a mighty struggle between strength and weakness—an eternal victory of the strong over the weak. There would be nothing but decay in the whole of Nature if this were not so. States which offend against this elementary law fall into decay…through all the centuries force and power are the deter-mining factors…. Only force rules. Force is the first law." Force was more than the decisive factor in any situation: it was force which alone created right.[14]

Goebbels adopted this view, writing in his diary that "man is and remains an animal—here a beast of prey, there a house pet, but always an animal." This statement summed up his life quite well after he

---

11 Heiber, *Goebbels*, 248.

12 James M. Rhodes, *The Hitler Movement: A Modern Millenarian Revolution* (Stanford: Hoover Institution Press, 1980), 45.

13 Timothy W. Ryback, *Hitler's Private Library: The Books That Shaped His Life* (New York: Knopf, 2008), 77.

14 Alan Bullock, *Hitler: A Study in Tyranny* (New York: Konecky & Konecky, 1962), 398–399.

became a Nazi.[15] And, as one of the most educated and intelligent of the leading Nazis, Goebbels soon became head of the large Nazi party propaganda and public information machine.[16] Darwinism went beyond a theory applied to race, but also to nations:

> Historians like Heinrich von Treitschke, Max Lenz, and Erich Marks, as well as German history teachers, now saw the rivalry with England as a continuation of Germany's move toward global power. They buttressed their position with theories derived from Darwin; according to these theories, political expansion would enhance Germany's vitality and at the same time help fulfill the nation's mission by extending the influence of its culture, which they rated higher than that of other peoples.[17]

Goebbels was responsible for the massive Nazi propaganda rallies, parades, and impressive night time torchlight shows. He also controlled the media and supported a mass burning of those books that the Nazis objected to, especially books authored by Jews.[18] The book burning, set to begin at midnight, was organized by the German Student Association and supported by many professors.[19] As a result, at midnight "bonfires were blazing in many German University towns."[20] On May 3, 1933, about 20,000 books were burned in one day alone, which included "some of Germany's greatest intellectual and cultural resources" that Goebbels branded as "'intellectual filth' produced by 'Jewish asphalt literati.'"[21]

PROPAGANDA MINISTER

Called the virtuoso of lying propaganda, Goebbels is best known for his media and social manipulation in Nazi Germany.[22] As propaganda

---

15 Heiber, *Goebbels*, 5.

16 Linda Schmittroth and Mary Kay Rosteck, *People of the Holocaust*, Vol. 1: A-J (Detroit: Gale, 1998), 174.

17 Reuth, *Goebbels*, 11–12.

18 Schmittroth and Rosteck, *People of the Holocaust*, 1:174.

19 Reuth, *Goebbels*, 182.

20 Reuth, *Goebbels*, 182.

21 Reuth, *Goebbels*, 183.

22 Oswald Dutch, *Hitler's 12 Apostles* (New York: Robert M. McBride & Company,

minister, Goebbels created the myth—which he himself likely believed—that Hitler was "the man of destiny, the new saviour" of Germany.[23] Dr. Goebbels pushed the use of the term "Führer," meaning leader, to refer to Hitler alone, and made its use compulsory in Germany when referring to Hitler.

Goebbels also helped fashion the "Führer myth," the idea that Hitler was at the apex of human evolution, "superior to all other human beings."[24] It was Goebbels who made Hitler a god in the mind of the public and introduced pseudo-religious content into his rule. He also pushed use of the "Heil Hitler" greeting in everyday conversations

> arousing the protest of several party bigwigs. "Heil" sounded more like an exorcism or magic formula than a greeting. It was designed to replace the customary "*Grüss Gott*" or "*Guten tag*" ["Good Day"]. The personal Judaeo-Christian, western God was dead, as Nietzsche proclaimed. But a people without a god could hardly be expected to make sacrifices that went against their own material well-being. A new god, a god for the masses, was needed to spur them on to greater efforts. Goebbels had read Le Bon's *Psychology of the Masses*. He knew that what the masses needed was a god and human sacrifice. For a god he gave them Hitler; as sacrificial victims he offered them…the Jews.[25]

His chief propaganda theory was "the Big Lie": if something is repeated often enough, people will believe it no matter how false. This technique worked very well in disenfranchising the Jews. Goebbels took control of, not only the press, but also radio, film, theater, music, literature and publishing, purging Jews and all opposition to Nazism from them.

He was also behind the two most notorious anti-Semitic films in history, *The Eternal Jew* and *Jude Süss*.[26] Although a first class intellectual,

---

1940), 64.

23 Reimann, *Goebbels*, 2.

24 Schmittroth and Rosteck, *People of the Holocaust*, 1:174.

25 Reimann, *Goebbels*, 4.

26 Roger Manvell and Heinrich Fraenkel, *Dr. Goebbels: His Life and Death* (London: Greenhill, 2006), 192.

"Goebbels was guided almost exclusively by irrational factors" such as his faith in Hitler's worldview.[27] Nor was he guided by law but rather

> Goebbels had complained bitterly to the Führer about the Justice ministry's undersecretary Franz Schlegelberger, who often rejected Goebbels's requests for action against the Jews on the grounds that no legal basis existed. Since Auschwitz was located within the Reich, some legal basis would have to be created for taking Jews there, which had not been necessary for deportation to the ghettos in the Soviet Union.[28]

Instead of obeying German law, Goebbels became increasingly impatient because he believed that the

> extermination of the Jews was not progressing fast enough. He found a welcome opportunity to move things along when an anonymous attack was made on an anti-Soviet exhibition in the Berlin Lustgarten on 18 May. He immediately blamed the Jews.[29]

Ironically, Goebbels was physically not even close to the Nazi ideal—rather, he was closer to the exact opposite of it. Dutch described Dr. Goebbels, who was a small man with a large head, a crippled foot, and a fragile body, but a mesmerizing voice, as a

> small, ugly…deformed, dark and obviously not an Aryan type: yet daily and even hourly he preaches the principle of the great, blond, handsome Aryan-German "lordly race," a race which is to be allowed to seize the dominion of the world. In 1933…a local paper published a caricature showing an ugly, deformed, dark-haired little figure of a man, and below were the words: "And who may this man be? Why, to be sure, it is the representative of the well-built, healthy, blond, and blue-eyed Nordic race!"[30]

---

27 Reimann, *Goebbels*, 2.
28 Reuth, *Goebbels*, 304.
29 Reuth, *Goebbels*, 304.
30 Dutch, *Hitler's 12 Apostles*, 66.

Joseph Goebbels (1897-1945)

The effective and highly educated Minister of Propaganda, Joseph Goebbels, with his daughters Helga and Hilde, giving the Heil Hitler salute.

Bundesarchiv, Bild 183-C17887 / photographer: unknown, December 23, 1937

GOEBBELS' WAR AGAINST CATHOLICS

Around 1936, Goebbels launched a programme to persecute the Catholic Church because

> he wanted to eliminate a power from which millions of Germans derived spiritual strength and comfort. For this purpose he was going to proceed above all against the Catholic monks.... The drive against the Catholics was characterized by unprecedented violence, and its moral level could not have been lower. Every day the press published accounts filled with the basest accusations—stories of a type which no self-respecting newspaper ever would have printed before. On April 30, 1937, this resulted in the arrest of several thousand Catholic monks...articles against the Catholic Church followed, all of them slanted to show that the guilt of the defendants had already been established."[31]

Despite his best efforts, Goebbels' attempt failed because the German people would not accept his claims of criminality by the Catholic monks and

> it began to dawn on millions of Germans that, in the name of the state, they were being fed deliberate lies. Goebbels suffered a considerable loss of prestige, and people who for years had not seen the inside of a church now went there to demonstrate whom they believed, and whom they distrusted.[32]

Even his fellow government staffers saw that the attempt to discredit the Catholic Church by Goebbels had failed:

> "All of us working at the Propaganda Ministry could see which way things were going," Fritzsche later said.... Goebbels alone stubbornly refused to be convinced of his error. None of his friends and collaborators could make him change his mind.[33]

---

31 Curt Riess, *Joseph Goebbels: A Biography* (Garden City: Doubleday, 1949), 136.

32 Riess, *Joseph Goebbels: A Biography*, 136.

33 Riess, *Joseph Goebbels: A Biography*, 136.

Nonetheless, the bulk of his income came from his writings denouncing the Catholic church.[34] The Catholic Church's opposition to Nazism especially galled him. One example was the pivotal anti-racist papal encyclical *Mit brennender Sorge* given at the Vatican on Passion Sunday, March 14, 1937. Pope Pius XI appealed to "natural law, written by the Creator's hand on the tablet of the heart" directed at Nazi Germany

> to put a stop to the blasphemies, which, in words and pictures, are multiplying like the sands of the desert; to encounter the obstinacy and provocations of those who deny, despise and hate God, by the never-failing reparatory prayers of the Faithful, hourly rising like incense to the All-Highest and staying His vengeance.[35]

The Nazis knew that such words were directed to them.

Goebbles' anti-Christian attitudes were no doubt also influenced by Hitler. He wrote in his diary in 1939, "The Fuehrer is deeply religious, but deeply anti-Christian. He regards Christianity as a symptom of decay. Rightly so. It is a branch of the Jewish race."[36] Bullock adds the "truth is that, in matters of religion at least, Hitler was a rationalist and a materialist."[37]

GOEBBELS BECOMES A RADICAL ANTI-SEMITE

As indicated, no evidence existed that Goebbels' early home life was anti-Semitic, but as an adult he became a radical eugenicist and anti-Jewish racist.[38] He lost his Catholic faith during his university days and replaced it with his new heroes: Nietzsche, Hitler and Darwin. One man who worked closely with Goebbels, Rudolf Semmler, wrote that

---

34 Manvell and Fraenkel, *Dr. Goebbels: His Life and Death*, 212.

35 Pius XI, *Mit brennender Sorge;* http://www.vatican.va/holy_father/pius_xi/encyclicals/documents/hf_p-xi_enc_14031937_mit-brennender-sorge_en.html; accessed August 30, 2012; Para. 30, 12.

36 Jonathan Steinberg, *All or Nothing: The Axis and the Holocaust, 1941–1943* (New York: Routledge, 1990), 130.

37 Bullock, *Hitler: A Study in Tyranny*, 389.

38 Schmittroth and Rosteck, *People of the Holocaust*, 1:176.

"Goebbels' hatred of Jews was fanatical. Everything Jewish is to him like a red rag to a bull. The hatred is so strong that he becomes incapable of even recognizing facts when he has to deal with them."[39] Gilbert notes that Goebbels rejected the church's teachings and replaced it with those of the Darwinists, adding that

> Pope Pius XI challenged the Nazi claim of Aryan racial superiority, insisting that there was only a single human race. His assertion was challenged by the German Minister of Labour, Dr. Robert Ley, who declared in a speech in Vienna on November 22 [1938]: "No compassion will be tolerated for the Jews. We deny the Pope's statement that there is but one human race. The Jews are parasites."[40]

Of note is a comment by Semmler about Dr. Robert Ley, leader of the German Labour Front. Semmler described Dr. Ley as one of the "worst of the many drunkards in the higher ranks of the Nazi Party."[41] Dr. Ley, one of Hitler's closest associates, committed suicide in prison while on trial for war crimes at Nuremberg.[42]

In reaction to the "complete ban on the entry of Jews into theatres, concerts, cinemas, music halls, dance floors and other places of entertainment," Goebbels commented that any

> "places that allowed Jews to attend would be punished.... But the Jews who are attending them will be punished even more severely." In defending the exclusion of Jews from all places of entertainment, Goebbels told a Berlin audience on November 13 [1938]: "It is equivalent to degradation of German art to expect a German to sit next to a Jew in a theatre or cinema. If the parasites had not been treated much too well in the past, it would

---

39 Rudolf Semmler, *Goebbels: The Man Next to Hitler* (London: Westhouse, 1947), 98.

40 Martin Gilbert, *Kristallnacht: Prelude to Destruction* (New York: Harper Collins, 2006), 171–172.

41 Semmler, *Goebbels: The Man Next to Hitler*, 126.

42 Trevor-Roper, *The Last Days of Hitler*, 79.

not have been necessary to make such short work of them now." The very fact that such legislation was possible, he added, "proved to the world that the Jews had been having much too good a time in Germany."[43]

Goebbels was also responsible for the 1938 *Kristallnacht* riots against Jews that resulted in the murder of over 90 Jews, sending thousands to concentration camps, most of whom died there, and destroying about 300 synagogues.[44] Goebbels was one of the Nazi leaders most adamant on the "necessity of actually exterminating the Jews."[45] To do this, the Nazis set up concentration camps that, from the Nazis' viewpoint, were designed to be a

microcosm of the outside world. "This idea of struggle is as old as life itself," Hitler said in a speech as early as 1928. "In this struggle the stronger, the more able, win, while the less able, the weak, lose. Struggle is the father of all things.... It is not by principles of humanity that man lives or is able to preserve himself above the animal world, but solely by means of the most brutal struggle." This quasi-Darwinian attitude, at the vary core of Nazism, was evident throughout the administration of the concentration camps. The *Kapos*, for example, could "justly" mistreat those in their charge because they had proved themselves superior in life's "struggle."[46]

Goebbels also claimed that the mere sight of Jews

make me physically sick...I cannot even hate the Jew. I can merely despise him. He has raped our people, soiled our ideals, weakened the strength of the nation, corrupted morals. He is the poisonous eczema on the body of our sick nation. That has

---

43 Gilbert, *Kristallnacht*, 172.

44 Gilbert, *Kristallnacht*.

45 Schmittroth and Rosteck, *People of the Holocaust*, 1:177.

46 Laurence Rees, *Auschwitz: A New History* (New York: Public Affairs Press, 2005), 7.

nothing to do with religion [but rather race]. Either he destroys us, or we destroy him.[47]

Remember, these words are from the man considered by historians as the leading Nazi intellectual. The foolishness of his claims about world Jewry being the real enemy of all humanity was elegantly expressed by historian Curt Riess as follows:

> Goebbels asserted in all seriousness that the Axis and its satellites—in all about two hundred million people—were threatened in their existence by approximately fifteen million people who were widely scattered over the globe, with no state, no army, no fleet, and no air force of their own. Ridiculous as his thesis was, it must nevertheless be admitted that Goebbels presented it very adroitly and carried it through with great logic.[48]

Goebbels even thought Germany's Axis partners were inferior to the Germans and "his inner conviction of their racial inferiority to the Germans" affected his relations with them.[49] For example, he once said the "Italians fight tooth and nail against being regarded as racially inferior to, or even different from, ourselves"—but he believed they were racially inferior in spite of all the evidence to the contrary.[50]
Of the Russians, Goebbels said,

> they are not a people but a conglomeration of animals. The greatest danger…is the stolid dullness of this mass…this racial propensity of the Russian people…. The human mind cannot possibly imagine what it would be like if this opponent were to pour into western Europe like a flood.[51]

Statements such as this caused Manvell and Fraenkel to be amazed

---

47 Manvell and Fraenkel, *Dr. Goebbels: His Life and Death*, 24–25.

48 Riess, *Joseph Goebbels: A Biography*, 216.

49 Manvell and Fraenkel, *Dr. Goebbels: His Life and Death*, 216.

50 Manvell and Fraenkel, *Dr. Goebbels: His Life and Death*, 216.

51 Manvell and Fraenkel, *Dr. Goebbels: His Life and Death*, 214.

over the "mixture of shrewdness and sheer ignorance in a man of his intelligence."[52]

Goebbels opinion of Americans was equally devastating:

American soldiers are human animal material which can in no way stand comparison with our own people. One has the impression one is dealing with a herd of savages.... They are uneducated and know nothing.[53]

Even the English were regarded as inferior humans. Goebbels' list of inferior races was long and equally uninformed. No wonder he had few qualms about killing so many millions of non-Germans during the war.

DARWINISM AND WAR

Darwinism also influenced Goebbels' enthusiastic support for war:

Another consequence of the biologically grounded racism of the Nazis was the continual underestimation by their leaders of the military capabilities of the Russians. Goebbels, for example, repeatedly wrote in his diaries that the Bolsheviks would collapse like a "house of cards," that their army was "scarcely battleworthy," probably because "the low intelligence level of the average Russian makes the use of modern weapons impossible."[54]

Goebbels firmly believed "all is fair in love and war"—but especially war. As a result, he demanded that Germany throw out the Geneva Convention rules for the treatment of prisoners of war and murder all of the over 40,000 allied airmen prisoners held in Germany.[55] He believed the world "belonged to him who took it."[56] So fanatical was Goebbels that, when the allies had entered Berlin and it was abundantly

---

52 Manvell and Fraenkel, *Dr. Goebbels: His Life and Death*, 214.

53 Manvell and Fraenkel, *Dr. Goebbels: His Life and Death*, 215.

54 Mike Hawkins, *Social Darwinism in European and American Thought, 1860–1945* (New York: Cambridge University Press, 1997), 281.

55 Trevor-Roper, *The Last Days of Hitler*, 79.

56 Heiber, *Goebbels*, 323.

clear that the war was lost, Goebbels remarked, "If a single white flag is hoisted in a Berlin street, I shall not hesitate to have the whole street and all its inhabitants blown up."[57]

Goebbels once stated that he was a misanthropist and has "complete contempt for men and their behaviour."[58] German historians Linda Schmittroth and Mary Rosteck wrote that Goebbels, although a formidable personality and a first class intellect, was an excellent

> example of the fact that morality does not necessarily go along with high intelligence. This very well-educated man, who influenced the minds of millions of Germans, used his talents to spread hate and violence. Having no respect for people whose ideas differed from his own, he ordered the large-scale burning of books and the murder of political opponents of German leader Adolf Hitler before and during World War II.[59]

In the end, Goebbels intellect and education led to the Holocaust and the systematic murder of over 11 million innocent men, women and children by the use of modern technology. As late as April 20, 1945, when it was obvious to almost everyone that the war was lost, Goebbels was still asking Germans to trust blindly in the Führer and his government who together would lead them out of their present difficulties.[60] At this point the Führer and the government could no longer do anything to help their people because they realized it was hopeless. Goebbels then "emphatically" recommended bombing civilian populations if any group attempted to surrender. Some feel this order was motivated partly to punish his own people for losing the war.[61]

On April 30th, 1945, Hitler with his new wife, Eva Braun, committed suicide in their Berlin *Führerbunker* and Goebbels became Reich Chancellor. His tenure was brief. In the late afternoon of the following day, Goebbels and his wife, actress Magda Goebbels, sedated, then

---

57 Semmler, *Goebbels: The Man Next to Hitler*, 190.

58 Semmler, *Goebbels: The Man Next to Hitler*, 29, 104.

59 Schmittroth and Rosteck, *People of the Holocaust*, 1:172.

60 Trevor-Roper, *The Last Days of Hitler*, 106.

61 Semmler, *Goebbels: The Man Next to Hitler*, 23.

murdered their six young children with cyanide.[62] Soon after, Joseph Goebbels committed suicide with a bullet to his head.[63] His self-annihilation was the logical consequence of his ideological nihilism.

GERMAN INTELLECTUALS SUPPORT GOEBBELS

During World War II, Germany had the highest level of education of any nation in the world. The Nazis also valued education, and Goebbels surrounded himself with well-educated Germans, often those with Ph.D.s, for government ministers and other high-level positions. For example, his right-hand man, Dr. Erich Naumann, was state secretary and Dr. Otto Dietrich was Undersecretary for Propaganda Ministry.[64] Dr. Glasmayer was the radio minister who, even at the end of the war, was still encouraging Goebbels' wild fanaticism.[65]

Dr. Hans Lammers, "the bullhead," was head of Hitler's Reich Chancellery and Secretary of the German War Cabinet. Hans Lammers served only six years in prison for his war crimes, specifically his responsibility for the many anti-Jewish decrees that Germany instituted which resulted in the slaughter of millions of Jews.[66] Dr. Walter Funk was an undersecretary in the ministry of propaganda and Dr. Wilhelm Stuckart was Permanent Undersecretary to the Ministry of the Interior.[67]

Dr. Hans Hagen, a political officer attached to the Berlin Guards Regiment, described as a "highly excitable and self-important young man," worked with Dr. Goebbels at the Propaganda Ministry.[68] Other educated Nazis associated with Goebbels included Dr. Karl Goerdeler, the Reich price controller and Dr. Werner Best head of the Gestapo in occupied France and, later, the German minister in Copenhagen.[69]

---

62 Manvell and Fraenkel, *Dr. Goebbels: His Life and Death*, 296–298.

63 Trevor-Roper, *The Last Days of Hitler*, 213; Irving, *Goebbels: Mastermind of the Third Reich*.

64 Semmler, *Goebbels: The Man Next to Hitler*, 13, 33.

65 Semmler, *Goebbels: The Man Next to Hitler*, 187.

66 Semmler, *Goebbels: The Man Next to Hitler*, 66; William L. Shirer, *The Rise and Fall of the Third Reich* (New York: Simon and Schuster, 1960), 965.

67 Semmler, *Goebbels: The Man Next to Hitler*, 125.

68 Semmler, *Goebbels: The Man Next to Hitler*, 132; Shirer, *The Rise and Fall of the Third Reich*, 1061

69 Semmler, *Goebbels: The Man Next to Hitler*, 139, 152.

SUMMARY

This chapter reviewed the life and work of Dr. Joseph Goebbels, Nazi head of propaganda and public information, focusing on his racism and the influence of Darwinism on his beliefs. One of the most educated Nazis, he was also the leading propagandist for Hitler's racist programme that transformed the Germanic nations and the lands they conquered into a massive killing machine unequaled in world history.

Goebbels was a "malevolent genius whose oratory once inspired a nation to fight a total war and to hold out to the very end" rather than to surrender, even when it was clear that surrender was the only rational choice.[70] He was behind Hitler—the architect of the most devastating war in history that in only six years took the lives of a total of over 55 million people, most of whom were innocent civilians.[71] Goebbels, as a committed Darwinian eugenics advocate, was determined to produce what he judged was the superior race by any means he could. His racial programme failed and cost the lives of over 11 million innocent victims.

---

70 Irving, *Goebbels: Mastermind of the Third Reich.*
71 Roland, *The Illustrated History of the Nazis,* 198.

11

Hermann Göring comes under the influence of Hitler and Darwinism

INTRODUCTION

Hermann Wilhelm Göring (1893–1946) is "an example of a decent man who became corrupted by power" and Nazism.[1] His birth family had once stressed the equality of all persons, and were even willing to risk their careers for these beliefs. For example, Hermann Göring's father's career "reached a dead end because he advocated that black people be treated as human beings."[2]

As a young man, Hermann took after his father, Dr. Heinrich Göring in the area of human equality. While an eleven-year-old student in a private boarding school, he was condemned for writing an essay admiring his Jewish godfather, Austrian physician Hermann von Epenstein. That very night, young Göring returned to his hometown, never to return to this school again.[3]

GÖRING BECOMES A PILOT

After graduating from high school with honours, Göring went on to

---

1   Linda Schmittroth and Mary Kay Rosteck, *People of the Holocaust,* Vol. 1: A-J (Detroit: Gale, 1998).

2   Schmittroth and Rosteck, *People of the Holocaust,* 1:181.

3   Schmittroth and Rosteck, *People of the Holocaust,* 1:181.

become an ace fighter pilot in the First World War, and was awarded Germany's highest honour, *Pour le Mérite*, also known as "the Blue Max."[4] He also commanded *Jagdgeschwader* 1, the fighter wing once led by the most famous German pilot, Manfred von Richthofen, widely known as the Red Baron because he flew a bright red airplane and shot down over eighty enemy planes.

GÖRING'S TRANSFORMATION AND RISE TO POWER

When Nazism swept over Germany, Göring joined the party in 1921. At first he "resisted Hitler's strong anti-Jewish or anti-Semitic beliefs" and even saved a number of Jewish family friends when the Nazis came to power.[5] When he was wounded during the failed 1923 putsch (coup d'état) led by Hitler, a Jewish doctor treated his injuries.[6]

Nonetheless, Göring eventually "fell completely under Hitler's spell" and, for Göring, loyalty and faithfulness were the highest of all human virtues.[7] Eventually, "Göring totally worshipped Hitler [and]…soon abandoned his own tolerant views and went along with the Nazi leader's anti-Jewish speeches and writings."[8]

It was largely from Hitler and intellectuals such as Haeckel that Göring obtained his Darwinian ideas. Historian James Rhodes reported that at the start of the last century, when Göring was a young follower of Hitler, "Darwinism was the greatest intellectual fad in Europe." Many intellectuals

applied the catchwords "natural selection" and "survival of the fittest" to human affairs, and a loosely defined movement known as "social Darwinism" arose. In Germany, social Darwinism was promoted by an accomplished scientist and *völkisch* ideologue

---

4   Schmittroth and Rosteck, *People of the Holocaust*, 1:181.

5   Schmittroth and Rosteck, *People of the Holocaust*, 1:181.

6   Paul Roland, *The Illustrated History of the Nazis* (Edison: Chartwell Books, 2009), 65.

7   Richard J. Evans, *The Coming of the Third Reich* (New York: The Penguin Press 2004), 191.

8   Schmittroth and Rosteck, *People of the Holocaust*, 1:182.

named Ernst Haeckel. The enormously popular Haeckel argued that peoples were involved in the struggle for survival.[9]

Haeckel also established an organization, called the Monist League that strove to preserve the German *Volk*. The term *Volk* or "folk" is a term Hitler used to refer to the German history, spirit, mythology, language, religious nature and customs—in which the whole is greater than the sum of its parts. More than just a nationalistic concept, it was used as a reason to reject Jews and other "inferior races" as Germans, and declare the need for the expansion of the German people, an idea called *Lebensraum*. Hitler likely obtained some of his ideas about race from professors such as Haeckel. Rhodes wrote that

> Hitler, who probably read Haeckel as a teenager, took up Darwinian ideas with a vengeance: "The whole of nature is a powerful struggle between the strong and the weak, an eternal victory of the strong over the weak." He extended this doctrine to peoples and argued: "A stronger race will drive out the weak, for the vile urge in its ultimate form will, time and again, burst all the absurd fetters of the so-called humanity of individuals, in order to replace it by the humanity of Nature which destroys the weak to give his place to the strong."[10]

Hitler concluded that the "laws of eternal fight and upward struggle" caused him to conclude that the most important goal of the German people is "the worth and freedom" of their existence, and that their nation

> must defend this with the last drop of its blood; that it has no holier duty to fulfill, no higher law to obey." In practice, this meant that a *Volk* always had to be at war: "...those who do not want to fight in this world of eternal struggle do not deserve to live." The purpose of war was not only to destroy competitors but

---

9 James M. Rhodes, *The Hitler Movement: A Modern Millenarian Revolution* (Stanford: Hoover Institution Press, 1980),123.

10 Rhodes, *The Hitler Movement*, 123.

also to acquire living space and slaves, goods to which the stronger had perfect rights. Having achieved these goals, the mighty could enjoy "the happiness of survival on this earth."[11]

The living space goal meant war for land and slaves, mostly Polish and Russian land and Slavic slaves.

Göring soon became, in Dutch's words, "the first Apostle" of Hitler and not only accepted but worked to implement the ideology documented by Rhodes noted above.[12] It was Göring who persuaded von Hindenburg that the only man who could lead Germany out of its deep economic depression was Hitler.[13] In 1934, Göring became head of the *Luftwaffe* (the German air force) and, by 1936, when Hitler began planning for war, Göring became second in command in Germany.

Two years later, Göring presided over the passage of laws designed to limit the freedoms of certain Germans, especially Jews. It was Göring who created the Gestapo and established the first concentration camps in Germany.[14] Clearly

Hitler's Darwinian myth was the least elevating of all his [Göring's] ideologies. It reduced the meaning of life to mere biological subsistence, offering the individual a salvation that amounted to nothing more than a temporary share in the collective immortality of one of the fittest peoples and told an individual that he was nothing more than an insignificant, transitory member of a species scraping and clawing for continued life.[15]

As soon as President Hindenburg appointed Hitler as head of the German Government "thousands of Germans were arrested for being Jews or Catholics."[16] Göring eventually went with the party line and

---

11 Rhodes, *The Hitler Movement*, 123.

12 Oswald Dutch, *Hitler's 12 Apostles* (New York: Robert M. McBride & Company, 1940), 44.

13 Schmittroth and Rosteck, *People of the Holocaust*, 1:183.

14 Roland, *The Illustrated History of the Nazis*, 55.

15 Rhodes, *The Hitler Movement*, 123.

16 Schmittroth and Rosteck, *People of the Holocaust*, 1:183.

was attracted at first to the idea of expelling all German Jews, either to Madagascar or to the western powers. But he argued that it would only be possible to deal adequately with the problem in wartime because war released the Nazis from the constraints of international law and the pressure of public opinion. After the outbreak of war the seizure of Jewish assets increased in scale, as did the exploitation of Jewish labour.... Goering's home contained numerous works of art acquired on the same grounds.... It was during the "cleansing" of the European economy that the Nazi leadership moved toward a final solution to the Jewish question.[17]

To achieve these goals, Göring founded the Secret State Police, called the Gestapo, who had the authority "to murder the opponents of National Socialism" which included Jews.[18] Göring soon became even more deeply involved in the Jewish "question," believing that the so-called Jewish problem was by far the most important task of Germany. As a result:

> Throughout the war, Göring's officials remorselessly carried out the policies of expropriation and Aryanisation which he repeatedly authorized. Through his interest in the economics of Aryanisation, and the use of Jewish concentration camp labour, Goering was inextricably caught up in the effort to find a solution to the "Jewish question." In the winter of 1938–9 he had acquired powers to organize the economic exploitations of the Jewish population. The wider question of what to do with the Jews thus excluded from public life he delegated to Heydrich and the SS, under his loose supervision.[19]

His irrational racism resulted in expressing, both in private and public, his "fierce hostility to the Jews." Furthermore, Göring imagined

17 Richard Overy, *Goering: Hitler's Iron Knight* (New York: Barnes and Noble Books, 1984), 127–128.

18 Dutch, *Hitler's 12 Apostles*, 55.

19 Overy, *Goering: Hitler's Iron Knight*, 127–128.

Zionist conspiracies everywhere and, like Hitler, expected a final settlement of the scores between Jew and German. The only reservations he had were expressed in terms of economic necessity. He insisted that Jewish labourers working on arms orders in Germany should not be moved eastward while they could still work, but he removed even this constraint in August 1942. Otherwise he left Heydrich free to carry out his instructions "for the achievement of the final solution to which we aspire."[20]

Göring did defend his Jewish friends in several cases, such as Luftwaffe Field Marshall Erhard Milch whose father was Jewish. Göring obtained for him a "German Blood Certificate" declaring him an Aryan. When confronting the Gestapo's objections, Göring made his famous statement, *"Wer Jude ist, bestimme ich!"* or, "I will decide who is a Jew."[21]

Some claim Göring might merely have been repeating or paraphrasing the statement made by others. No doubt others made the same claim when defending their Jewish friends. This fact illustrates the irrationality of Darwinist racism.

In Göring's view as a Nazi, "the end always justified the means," and that meant the extermination of the Jews was justified because, he believed, it would result in a superior race and, as a result, a greater Germany.[22] For Göring, in warfare "neither justice nor morality had a part to play; the strong won, the weak perished," and that was justice as taught by classical Darwinism.[23] It soon became very obvious where this ethic led.

GÖRING'S HATRED FOR THE CATHOLIC CHURCH

Although reared a Catholic, Göring came to hate the Catholic Church because he correctly believed that they were opposed to Nazi policy. The reason was that the Church taught such doctrines as the need to

---

20 Overy, *Goering: Hitler's Iron Knight*, 128.

21 Eric Metaxas, *Bonhoeffer—Pastor, Martyr, Prophet, Spy: A Righteous Gentile vs. The Third Reich* (Nashville: Thomas Nelson, 2010), 511.

22 Evans, *The Coming of the Third Reich*, 191.

23 Evans, *The Coming of the Third Reich*, 191.

Hermann Göring (1893-1946)

Adolf Hitler and Göring, in uniform as Reich Marshal of the Greater German Reich.

Bundesarchiv, Bild 183-2007-0316-500 / photographer: Heinrich Hoffmann, circa 1940/1942

help the weak and poor. Journalist Stewart Herman wrote that the "teaching of mercy and love of neighbor is foreign to the German race and the Sermon on the Mount is, according to Nordic sentiment, an ethic for cowards and idiots."[24] Göring bought into this worldview and wrote that

> Catholic believers carry but one impression from attendance at divine services and that is that the Catholic Church rejects the institutions of the National Socialists [Nazi] state. How could it be otherwise when they are continuously engaging in polemics on political questions or events in their sermons![25]

Göring also decreed that the "Heil Hitler" salute was the only public religious observance allowed in Nazi Germany.[26] Very "aware that the churches could be dangerous," Göring "was determined that the price the priests must pay for the luxury of being left unmolested was silence in political matters."[27] Those who refused to remain silent about the horrors of the Nazi regime were punished severely, often with their lives.

The Nazi government declared they would "smite without mercy all those whom Goebbels called 'priest politicians' and whom they accused of collusion with Marxists and Jews."[28] On July 15, 1935, Göring ordered the police to "prosecute with all the rigor of the law any political activity of the clergy or of the Catholic organizations…; Göring concluded with the threat to suppress all youth organizations which meddle in politics."[29] In other words, the church must stay out of the way of what the Nazis wanted to do with Jews and others, or else their members would also be punished.

---

24 Stewart W. Herman, *It's Your Souls We Want* (New York: Harper, 1943), 57.

25 Henri Lichtenberger, *The Third Reich*, trans. and ed. Koppel S. Pinson (New York: Greystone Press, 1937), 210.

26 Bruce Walker, *The Swastika against the Cross: The Nazi War on Christianity* (Denver: Outskirts Press, 2008), 17.

27 Roger Manvell and Heinrich Fraenkel, *Goering* (New York: Simon and Schuster, 1962), 137.

28 Lichtenberger, *The Third Reich*, 211.

29 Lichtenberger, *The Third Reich*, 212.

GÖRING'S HITLER-INSPIRED HATRED FOR THE SLAVIC PEOPLE

Adolf Hitler considered the Slavic people a class of born slaves because of what he called "their bottomless stupidity" and "those stupid masses of the East"—words that he "endlessly repeated in his mealtime diatribes." This was not only a measure "of his racism, but of intellectual laziness, of complacency in the face of a vast, fast-changing and secretive country of which he and his advisers knew very little."[30] Göring went along with this idea. The best example of Göring's hatred for Slavs is the Siege of Leningrad (now Saint Petersburg), the deadliest blockade in history. The Nazis "did not want just to annex useful territory and create a new balance of power, but to wipe out a culture and an ideology, if necessary a race."[31] Consequently existing cities in Russia

were to be stripped of their valuables and destroyed (Moscow was to be replaced with an artificial lake), and the delightful new villages populated with Aryan settlers.... Within twenty years, Hitler dreamed, they would number twenty million. Russians—[the] lowest of the Slavs—were to be deported to Siberia, reduced to serfdom, or simply exterminated, like the native tribes of America. Putting down any lingering Russian resistance would serve merely as sporting exercise. "Every few years," Speer remembered, "Hitler planned to lead a small campaign beyond the Urals, so as to demonstrate the authority of the Reich and keep the military preparedness of the German army at a high level." As a later SS planning document put it, the Reich's ever-mobile eastern marches...would "keep Germany young."[32]

So surreal is this vision, so risible in its...shallowness.... What was the sense in occupying a country so as to destroy it? ... [requiring] troops to hold half a continent in permanent slavery?

---

30 Anna Reid, *Leningrad: The Epic Siege of World War II, 1941–1944* (New York: Walker and Company, 2011), 23.

31 Reid, *Leningrad*, 20.

32 Reid, *Leningrad*, 20–22.

For the Nazi leadership, though, it was no daydream. In July 1940, weeks after the fall of France, Hitler ordered the commander-in-chief of the army, Field Marshal Walther von Brauchitsch, and his military chief of staff, General Franz Halder, to start planning the conquest of the Soviet Union.[33]

Furthermore, individual Nazi officers were allowed to

treat the Russians they came across as they saw fit. Also assumed from the outset was ruthless food requisitioning. The occupying troops were to live off what they could commandeer locally, even if it meant that civilians starved. "The Russian has stood poverty for centuries!" joked Herbert Backe, state secretary in the Ministry for Food and Agriculture. "His stomach is flexible, hence no false pity!" Goebbels quipped that the Russians would have to "eat their Cossack saddles"; Goering predicted "the biggest mass death in Europe since the Thirty Years War."[34]

Hitler's "grand vision of extermination" had putative justifications that on the surface appeared rational, such as to obtain for

Germany agricultural land and oil wells, and eliminate an inimical regime. But it was [ultimately]...about race: a *Vernichtungskrieg*, a war of extermination. Bolsheviks, Jews, Slavs—they were vermin, brutes, cankers, poison; their very existence anathema to the National Socialist dream. Liquidating or enslaving them was not just a means to territorial domination, but part of its purpose.[35]

GÖRING'S END

As the war progressed, Hitler became even more unreasonable and irrational than Göring. In the end, Göring became disillusioned with the Nazi government and eventually lost Hitler's favour. It was too late,

---

33 Reid, *Leningrad*, 22.
34 Reid, *Leningrad*, 22.
35 Reid, *Leningrad*, 24.

though, because by this time the Nazis were all but defeated. The Allies then put the leading Nazis on trial for war crimes. Göring was condemned to death at the Nuremberg Trials, but just after he was found guilty and before he was to be hanged, he managed to take his own life by poison someone smuggled into his prison cell.[36]

SUMMARY

Hermann Göring was the second most powerful German Nazi, and one of the leaders in persecuting the churches. His example illustrates the corrupting influence of both Hitler and Darwinism on a once decent man. Although Göring had a leading role in the Holocaust, he eventually became disillusioned with Nazi philosophy—but too late—and ended his life, like so many leading Nazis, by suicide. He is a prime example of the adverse effects that an immoral life philosophy can have on a person, and illustrates the central importance of one's worldview in society.

---

36 Roland, *The Illustrated History of the Nazis*, 197.

Reinhard Heydrich (1904-1942)

Head of the intelligence agency of the SS, Heydrich organized a massive spy network to accumulate information and arrest Nazi opponents.

Reinhard Heydrich:
Fervent anti-Christian and
Holocaust mastermind

~~~~~~

INTRODUCTION

Reinhard Tristan Ergen Heydrich (March 7, 1904 – June 5, 1942) was the head of the SD (*Sicherheitsdienst*, or Hitler's so called security police) and deputy to SS leader Heinrich Himmler. He also was the chief organizer of Nazi Germany's plan to murder all European Jews.[1] In short, Heydrich was the "true architect and brain behind the concept of the future SS state."[2] He was also "the Generalissimo of the racial war" against the Jews and the "extensions of international Jewry," which he considered to have occurred in the Soviet Union. For this reason, Heydrich concluded that by "conquering the Soviet Union, he would be striking a decisive blow at the worldwide conspiracy of Judeo-Bolshevism."[3]

HIS EARLY LIFE

A shy, unhappy child, his parents were cultured musicians and Heydrich

---

1   Edouard Calic, *Reinhard Heydrich: The Chilling Story of the Man Who Masterminded the Nazi Death Camps*, trans. Lowell Bair (New York: William Morrow, 1985), 214.

2   Joachim C. Fest, *The Face of the Third Reich: Portraits of the Nazi Leadership* (New York: Pantheon, 1970), 98.

3   Calic, *Reinhard Heydrich*, 235.

appreciated music his entire life. Although reared as a devout Catholic, he grew up in a fiercely anti-Semitic home, a contradiction that he never openly dealt with. Eventually, his religion became Nazism, and he evolved into an active virulent anti-Catholic.

A very bright youth, Heydrich did exceptionally well in school and also excelled as an athlete. His family, though, as a result of their losses after the First World War, could no longer afford to send Heydrich to college. Like many Germans, Heydrich's family lost most of their fortune after the war. Many otherwise rational Germans blamed the Jews for their economic losses due to the unfounded theory that the Jews were somehow "trying to take over the world" by causing Germany to lose the war.

Consequently, to obtain an education, the embittered young Heydrich became a German naval cadet. Although he advanced quickly, becoming a second lieutenant in 1926, he proved unpopular with some, allegedly because of his arrogant attitude. He eventually was expelled from the German navy for "conduct unbecoming an officer and a gentleman" because, among other offences, he was accused of getting the daughter of a shipyard director pregnant and refusing to marry her.

HEYDRICH BECOMES A NAZI

Heydrich joined the Nazi Party in 1931 and his fortunes soon changed. That same year, Heydrich married nineteen-year-old Lina von Osten, who was also a doctrinaire anti-Semite.[4] Heydrich was described as a man of "Luciferian coldness" with an insatiable greed for power, who "shared a conscious awareness of the omnipotence of man" in government.[5] Fest noted in his chapter on Heydrich that this "epitome of a Nazi" was at the "core" of National Socialism, a movement whose foundational belief, as well as that of the Third Reich government, was

the idea of race. Whatever aspect of ideology or practical policy was uppermost at any given moment—whether nationalist, socialist, monarchist or other tendencies—it only served to a greater or lesser degree to distract attention from the all-powerful

---

4 Calic, *Reinhard Heydrich*, 215.
5 Fest, *The Face of the Third Reich*, 98.

racial doctrine. It has rightly been pointed out that "the doctrine of the racial enemy is as essential to National Socialism as the doctrine of the class enemy is to Bolshevism." It welded together old emotions and prejudices which had been given a pseudo-scientific veneer during the nineteenth century.… In itself, the mythological exaltation of their own race above the so-called lower or opposed races served the tactical purpose of increasing the masses' self-confidence and mobilizing their will to violence.[6]

Under Heydrich and Himmler, Germany became a police state. Heydrich's success in achieving this goal helped to skyrocket his career. He became an SD Major (*Sicherheitsdienst des Reichsführers-SS*, or *SD*, was the intelligence agency of the SS in Nazi Germany) by the end of 1931 and, in 1932, was promoted to SD Colonel with complete control of the SD intelligence service. The following year, before he was even thirty, he was appointed SD Brigadier General.[7]

Heydrich rapidly built the SD intelligence service into a massive network designed to spy on Hitler's opponents, especially those in the Nazi Party whose loyalty was questionable. Ever aware of the importance of new technology, Heydrich used secret cameras and hidden microphones to document any potential opposition to Hitler. He then rapidly collected an enormous amount of information on party members and others.

This information was used to achieve a purge that began in 1933 when Heydrich assisted Himmler in carrying out the large-scale arrest of Nazi opponents, including religious leaders and all of those who had openly spoken out against Hitler. Soon German prisons were filled to capacity with those Heydrich had entrapped, forcing the construction of concentration camps to hold the growing overflow.

HEYDRICH'S MILITANT ANTI-CATHOLIC CRUSADE

Although a baptized Catholic, Heydrich left his faith as he became more involved in Nazism. For Heydrich, the enemies of the Nazi state were "all equally dangerous, whether Jew, Freemason or political

---

6 Fest, *The Face of the Third Reich*, 99.
7 Calic, *Reinhard Heydrich*, 215.

Churchman."[8] Historian Mario Dederichs described Heydrich's anti-Catholicism as a "cold hatred" which "assumed at times paranoid features."[9] Historian John S. Conway wrote that

> Heydrich's hatred of the churches...bordered on the pathological.... Blinded by an apostate's hatred, his evaluation of the church situation was always so biased and his suggestion so radical, that even Hitler, perhaps for tactical reasons, was obliged to restrain his subordinate.[10]

According to his wife, Lina, of all the many enemies of Nazism, Heydrich "considered the Church the most dangerous."[11] His hatred toward Catholics was important in his goal to murder, first, all Polish Catholic priests and, then, Polish Catholic intellectuals and others.

Historian Richard Steigmann-Gall calls Heydrich the most important anti-Christian in Nazi Germany besides Himmler and, of course, Hitler.[12] Steigmann-Gall concluded that Catholicism was the Nazis' major political opponent and for this reason "was at the forefront of most anticlerical actions taken by the Nazi state."[13]

In his book, *The Fortunes of Our Struggle*, Heydrich argued that all opposition to Nazism ultimately originated from either Jews or "politically active Christian clergy," by which Heydrich meant those clergy or laymen who opposed Nazism or its policies, especially the Nazi policies opposing Jews. He once commented that "Pope Pius XII was a greater enemy of the Third Reich than either British Prime Minister Winston Churchill or US President Franklin D. Roosevelt."[14]

---

8 Mario R. Dederichs, *Heydrich: The Face of Evil* (London: Greenhill Books, 2006), 74

9 Dederichs, *Heydrich: The Face of Evil*, 75.

10 John S. Conway, *The Nazi Persecution of the Churches, 1933–1945* (New York: Basic Books, 1968), 287.

11 Dederichs, *Heydrich: The Face of Evil*, 75.

12 Richard Steigmann-Gall, *The Holy Reich: Nazi Conceptions of Christianity, 1919–1945* (New York: Cambridge University Press, 2003), 133.

13 Steigmann-Gall, *The Holy Reich*, 133.

14 Cited in Brenda Ralph Lewis, *A Dark History: The Popes: Vice, Murder, and Corruption in the Vatican* (New York: Metro Books, 2011), 226.

To achieve his goals against both the church and the "inferior races" Heydrich established a nationwide network of informers to ensure that his policies noted above were carried out. Any comment that opposed Heydrich, even to neighbours or friends, could be reported and the non-conformist would most certainly suffer serious repercussions.[15] Because Heydrich "was more openly hostile to the churches [than other leading Nazis] and advocated breaking them as swiftly as possible by direct persecution," his spy network rendered their opposition largely ineffective.[16] As a result, the opposition by the churches, Christians and others was often effectively put down.

HEYDRICH'S ANCESTRY QUESTIONED
One problem Heydrich faced was the claim that his father, Bruno Heydrich, was a Jew.[17] This allegation was found to be false, but rumours persisted. Historian Edouard Calic notes that, despite the recurrent rumours about his Jewish ancestry, evidently with little hard evidence,

Hitler decided not to force Heydrich out of the Nazi Party. Hitler described the six-foot-tall Nazi as "a highly gifted but also very dangerous man, whose gifts the movement had to retain... [because he will be grateful that we did not expel him and he will] obey blindly." Always haunted by the ever-present rumors that he might be Jewish, Heydrich's hatred toward the Jews grew even stronger. He also was tormented by a severe lack of self-esteem. One story tells of his returning home one night, drunk, seeing himself in the mirror, and using his pistol to shoot at his own reflection, shouting "filthy Jew."[18]

The threat by Hitler to keep Heydrich in line worked exceptionally well. Heydrich became a fanatical Nazi and loyal Hitler disciple.

---

15 Joseph Keysor, *Hitler, the Holocaust, and the Bible* (New York: Athanatos, 2010), 171.

16 Keysor, *Hitler, the Holocaust, and the Bible*, 180.

17 Heinz Höhne, *The Order of the Death's Head: The Story of Hitler's SS*, trans. Richard Barry (London: Pan Books, 1969), 147.

18 Calic, *Reinhard Heydrich*, 215.

HEYDRICH MOVES GERMANY TOWARD THE HOLOCAUST

An important step toward the Holocaust was the establishment of creative measures to apply Darwinian eugenics that included

> racial hygiene, eugenic choice of marriage partners, the breeding of human beings by the methods of selection on the one hand and extirpation on the other. The guiding aide of the "race-attached soul" made all cultural and creative achievements dependent on external appearance and at the same time linked the ability and hence the right to found states and empires.[19]

Fest noted that behind these programmes was the vision of creating a "people of pure blood," which was described by race theorist Hans F.K. Günther as men who were

> "blond, tall, long-skulled, with narrow faces, pronounced chins, narrow noses with a high bridge, soft fair hair, widely spaced pale-coloured eyes, pinky-white skin colour." The efficacy of this racial image, however, was so repeatedly undermined—particularly by the physical appearance of most of the leading National Socialists—that it must not be seen as too binding. Yet there were frequent attempts to reconcile the leaders of the Third Reich to this racial picture, some of them so outrageous as to be comic.[20]

The motive for solving the Jewish "problem" was based on the fact that the Nazi

> race theory contained a utopian element that gnawed into the ideology of Hitler and his closer followers with the force and exclusiveness of an obsession. Hitler was influenced above all by the theories of the nineteenth-century social Darwinist school, whose conception of man as biological material was bound up with impulses toward a planned society. He was convinced that the [Aryan] race was disintegrating, deteriorating through faulty

---

19 Fest, *The Face of the Third Reich*, 99.
20 Fest, *The Face of the Third Reich*, 99–100.

breeding as a result of a liberally tinged promiscuity that was vitiating the nation's blood.[21]

The "useless eaters" and those the eugenicists regarded as inferior humans, including the Jews and Slavics, must all be eliminated because, as Heydrich explained, if any survived they would "form a new germ cell from which the Jewish race would again arise. History teaches us that."[22] Some, such as Höhne, claimed that Heydrich did not personally hate Jews—"he was no racial fanatic"—but was just doing his job.[23]

Others have argued, with much justification, that Heydrich did his job far too well for someone who did not have a strong personal commitment to the Nazi Darwinist goals. For example, Heydrich chaired the 1942 Wannsee Conference, held near Berlin in what some claim was a confiscated home of a Jewish family, where they planned and implemented the rapid extermination by the gassing of all Jews in German-occupied territories. In 1941, Göring ordered Heydrich to develop a programme to resolve the

Jewish problem using any means available. Heydrich announced this at the Wannsee Conference on 20 January, 1942, using it as a carte blanche from the movement's leaders to proceed to annihilation. Goering was not present at the meeting, but was represented by his state secretary, Neumann. It was his wish that he be kept closely informed about the SS policy toward the Jews and it can be assumed that the SS carried out their tasks with Goering's knowledge and blessings.[24]

Already by 1941, besides the elimination of many "inferior" humans including Asians, Slavs, Gypsies and German Jews, "Heydrich informed the Führer that 363,211 other Jews had been killed."[25] After

---

21 Fest, *The Face of the Third Reich*, 99.
22 Mitchell Geoffrey Bard, ed., *The Complete History of the Holocaust* (San Diego: Greenhaven Press, 2001), 76.
23 Höhne, *The Order of the Death's Head*, 150.
24 Fest, *The Face of the Third Reich*, 128.
25 Calic, *Reinhard Heydrich*, 242.

Germany invaded Poland, Heydrich organized the killing of various racial groups including Jews, Catholic clergy and others the Nazis judged as undesirable.[26] He had a list of 61,000 names slated for death and by 1939, about 50,000 Poles were murdered, including 7,000 Jews.

Next, the Soviet Union was targeted for racial eugenics. The purpose of invading the Soviet Union was to eliminate or subjugate the "inferior" Slavic humans and clear the way for German colonization of their land. When the Soviet invasion ended, over 20 million Soviets had been murdered, many in the effort to eliminate "inferior" races.[27] To determine who was racially superior, "Heydrich appointed racial experts to examine all applicants for German citizenship." These racial experts often were professors or university-trained eugenicists.

Although the "physical appearance of most of the leading national Socialists" did not fit the ideal blond, blue-eyed Aryan racial character "Reinhard Heydrich seemed to be the exception."[28] Heydrich looked like an Aryan because he "was tall, blond, athletic, and combined high intelligence with a metallic streak in his nature which was regarded as proof of a special racial grace."[29]

Heydrich may have looked like the Nazi racial ideal, but inside he was a "nervously irritable individual, subject to secret anxieties and continually plagued by tension, bitterness and self-hatred."[30] Höhne described Heydrich as one of the "radical, merciless rebels against tradition, morality and all humanitarian rules of conduct."[31] The Nazi ideal was very superficial, at least for some of the leading Nazis such as Heydrich.

HEYDRICH'S END

Heydrich's personality and policies engendered the enmity of an enormous number of people, resulting in an assassination attempt by several Czechs on May 29, 1942 in a suburb of Prague called Kobylisy.

---

26 Richard Weikart, *Hitler's Ethic: The Nazi Pursuit of Evolutionary Progress* (New York: Palgrave MacMillan, 2009), 67.

27 Calic, *Reinhard Heydrich*, 242.

28 Fest, *The Face of the Third Reich*, 100.

29 Fest, *The Face of the Third Reich*, 100.

30 Fest, *The Face of the Third Reich*, 100.

31 Höhne, *The Order of the Death's Head*, 149.

At the time, Heydrich was driving in an open car to his new country estate and was injured in the attempt. He eventually succumbed to his injuries and died on June 5, 1942.[32] The Nazis gave Heydrich an elaborate funeral and showered many accolades upon him.

Even after his death, Heydrich was the cause of enormous suffering and the murder of many innocent people. For example, in retaliation for his death, Hitler ordered the execution of 10,000 randomly selected Czechs that lived in the villages that sheltered the underground operatives who assassinated Heydrich. His staff, recognizing that this response would alienate many of his Czech supporters, convinced Hitler to respond less irrationally. Nonetheless, the Nazi retaliation still was brutal, and close to

13,000 people were arrested, deported, imprisoned, or killed. On 10 June [1942] all males over the age of 16 in the village of Lidice, 22 km north-west of Prague, and another village, Lezáky, were murdered. The towns were burned and the ruins leveled.... Among those tortured and killed was Bishop Gorazd, who is now revered as a martyr of the Orthodox Church.[33]

Hitler fumed that men as important to the Reich as Heydrich should not be "driving in an open, unarmored vehicle or walking about the streets of Prague unguarded," behavior that Hitler said is "just damned stupidity, which serves the country not one whit." Hitler added that a Nazi "as irreplaceable as Heydrich should" never have exposed himself to unnecessary danger as he did which was "stupid and idiotic" because men

like Heydrich should know that they are eternally being stalked like game, and that there are any number of people just waiting for the chance to kill them.... So long as conditions in our territories remain unstable, and until the German people has [sic] been completely purged of the foreign rabble, our public men must exercise the greatest care for their safety.[34]

---

32 Ralf Georg Reuth, *Goebbels* (New York: Harcourt Brace, 1993), 304.

33 Calic, *Reinhard Heydrich*, 215.

34 Reuth, *Goebbels*, 415.

Three years later, the Nazis were defeated, their leaders who were still alive were tried as war criminals and many were hung in Nuremberg. Although Heydrich was never brought to trial for his crimes, he has been justly condemned by society ever since, and his inclusion in this book is one example.

SUMMARY

Reinhard Heydrich was the chief organizer of Nazi Germany's plan to murder all European Jews and other inferior races. He was one of the few high-level Nazis who physically looked like the "ideal" German, yet was once accused by his enemies of being a Jew. He worked within the system, conforming to the Nazi culture to the extent of heading the Wannsee Conference that "resolved the Jewish problem" by planning their extermination.[35] The critical influence of eugenics and the influence of the prevailing Darwinist culture on his beliefs is well documented.

---

35 Roger Manvell and Heinrich Fraenkel, *Dr. Goebbels: His Life and Death* (London: Greenhill, 2006).

13

Dr. Alfred Rosenberg: The "scribe of the new gospel" of Darwinism

INTRODUCTION

Alfred Rosenberg (January 12, 1893 – October 16, 1946) was a major ideological leader in the Nazi party, especially at its inception. Rosenberg was "the father of Nazi ideology and the author of the book that had a profound effect on Hitler, namely, *Der Mythos des 20 Jahrhunderts* (*The Myth of the Twentieth Century*) published in 1930.[1] This influential racist anti-Semitic and anti-Catholic book also had an influence on early Nazi party policy. Rosenberg also contributed to the book *Germany's Renewal*, a volume Hitler recommended that all party members read.[2]

Through his writings, Rosenberg became the "scribe of the new gospel," the philosophy of Nazism based on social Darwinism.[3] This philosophy was racist, anti-Semitic, pan-German, militaristic and

---

1 Oswald Dutch, *Hitler's 12 Apostles* (New York: Robert M. McBride & Company, 1940), 80–81; Joachim C. Fest, *The Face of the Third Reich: Portraits of the Nazi Leadership* (New York: Pantheon, 1970), 164.

2 Richard Weikart, *Hitler's Ethic: The Nazi Pursuit of Evolutionary Progress* (New York: Palgrave MacMillan, 2009), 14.

3 Fest, *The Face of the Third Reich*, 163.

pseudo-religious. He was called the Nazi theorist of the Holocaust.[4]

As editor, and later publisher, of the main German newspaper that Hitler read daily, *Völkischer Beobachter* ("People's Observer"), Rosenberg played a major role in shaping the thinking of millions of Germans.[5] His influence was so great that he became the "cultural leader" of the Third Reich.[6] He was also, some claim, the author of the designation "The Third Reich" for Hitler's government that was envisioned to last a thousand years. In the end, it lasted *only* a dozen years. Hitler recognized that he must have a philosophic basis for his programme, and for this he turned to one of his earliest allies, Rosenberg.[7] Rosenberg's ideology was

> ultimately related to race (racism, Nordicism, racial soul, ethnicity, blood-and-honor, etc.—terms which he used largely interchangeably). Certainly his contributions to the idea of anti-Semitism, to the National Socialist concept of the state, to anti-universalism and to Germanic or Germanicized religion are closely allied to his pervasive ideology of race.[8]

Furthermore, he often covered the topic of

> racial admixture (adulteration), cross-breeding and miscegenation (most frequently referred to by him as racial shame, disgrace, and infamy). Essentially, Rosenberg believed Nordic racial purity spearheaded the battle of white Europe against racial destruction ("blood poisoning"); it was vital, he admonished, that racial purity be considered a principle not only of domestic, but also of

---

4 Fritz Nova, *Alfred Rosenberg: Nazi Theorist of the Holocaust* (New York: Hippocrene Books, 1986).

5 James Biser Whisker, *The Philosophy of Alfred Rosenberg: Origins of the National Socialist Myth* (Torrance: The Noontide Press, 1990).

6 Paul Douglass, *God among the Germans* (Philadelphia: University of Pennsylvania Press, 1935), 30.

7 Arthur Duncan-Jones, *The Struggle for Religious Freedom in Germany* (London: Victor Gollancz, 1938), 24.

8 Nova, *Alfred Rosenberg*, 31.

foreign policy. For Rosenberg this was not the responsibility of Germany alone.[9]

For example, in his 1927 book, *Zukunftsweg einer deutschen Aussenpolitik (The Future Course of German Foreign Policy)*, Rosenberg formulated a crude method for guaranteeing worldwide racial purity.

In the early 1940s the Holocaust became one of Hitler's main objectives for Germany. On March 1, 1942, he signed a decree on Germany's "systematic spiritual struggle against Jews, Freemasons, and their allies" ostensibly because these groups were all opponents of the goals of National Socialism.[10] This "necessary war mission" decree ruled that not only Jews, Freemasons, and their allies but also the ideological opponents of National Socialism must be annihilated. Furthermore the Nazi directive stated that these groups were

the authors of the war presently directed against the Reich. The systematic spiritual struggle against these powers is a necessary war mission. I have therefore instructed *Reichsleiter* Alfred Rosenberg to carry out this mission in conjunction with the chief of the high command of the *Wehrmacht*. His operational staff for the occupied territories is authorized to search for relevant materials in libraries, archives, lodges, and other ideological or cultural institutions of all types, and to have this material confiscated for the ideological work of the Nazi Party and subsequent research work at the National Socialist Academy.[11]

Presumably, this project, which Rosenberg had a mission to carry out, would aid Hitler and his academic supporters who were going to "research" the confiscated material to find evidence to support their goal of exterminating those regarded as inferior races.

Rosenberg's life goal, which he partly fulfilled, was "to become the custodian of the party ideology and the author of his *magnum opus* which would provide National Socialism with a definitive theory of

---

9 Nova, *Alfred Rosenberg*, 31.

10 Max Domarus, *The Essential Hitler: Speeches and Commentary* (Wauconda: Bolchazy-Carducci, 2007), 403.

11 Cited in Domarus, *The Essential Hitler*, 403.

history as a function of race.[12] Rosenberg believed, in contrast to the biblical account and historical Christian teaching, that God created separate human races, and that the Aryan race was superior to all others. Historian Raymond Feely concluded that as early as 1940, "Outside of *Mein Kampf*, Herr Rosenberg's [*The*]*Myth of the Twentieth Century* is in one sense the most important treatise in the Third Reich."[13] It has been translated into English and is kept in print by many of the white supremacist groups existing today.

Next to *Mein Kampf*, this two-volume work became the most important book of National Socialism and sold close to two million copies.[14] How much *The Myth of the Twentieth Century* was actually read and understood, though, is unknown. Historian Paul Roland claimed that the massive book, with its hundreds of footnotes, has the distinction of being one of the most unread bestselling books in history—nonetheless, it still had a seminal influence on early Nazi ideology.[15]

The Myth of the Twentieth Century also "made a direct and deep impression on Hitler" at least during the early period of the Nazi movement.[16] Dutch claimed that Rosenberg "imported into Hitler's original program...the doctrine of racial value, that is the superiority of German Aryan blood."[17] Professor Richard Evans documented that Rosenberg, more than anyone else "turned Hitler's attention toward the threat of...a Jewish conspiracy. ...through Rosenberg, Russian anti-Semitism, with its extreme conspiracy theories and its exterminating thrust, found its way into Nazi ideology in the early 1920s."[18]

Hitler was happy to learn that *The Myth of the Twentieth Century* was given a large boost in sales when the German Cardinal von Faulhaber of Munich condemned the book and placed it on the Catholic index

---

12 Peter Peel, "Preface," in Alfred Rosenberg, *The Myth of the Twentieth Century* (Torrance: The Noontide Press, 1982), v.

13 Raymond T. Feely, *Nazism versus Religion* (New York: The Paulist Press, 1940), 26.

14 Feely, *Nazism versus Religion*, 167.

15 Paul Roland, *The Illustrated History of the Nazis* (Edison: Chartwell Books, 2009), 57.

16 Dutch, *Hitler's 12 Apostles*, 85.

17 Dutch, *Hitler's 12 Apostles*, 26.

18 Richard J. Evans, *The Coming of the Third Reich* (New York: The Penguin Press 2004), 178.

Alfred Rosenberg (1893-1946)

Rosenberg's books and writings influenced many in Nazi Germany to adopt
racist, anti-Semetic and anti-Christian views.

Bundesarchiv, Bild 183-1985-0723-500 / photographer: Friedrich Franz Bauer

as a heretical work.[19] After its formal condemnation, its sales picked up considerably. Its flaws were such the even Hitler ridiculed parts of it to his insiders.

Rosenberg's importance is further illustrated by his inclusion among the ten people regarded at the Nuremberg Trials as most responsible for the Holocaust still living at the end of the war. Called "the theorist of the party," he "gathered together the confused ideas of Hitler and clarified them." The result was that Hitler built on "Rosenberg's ideas and allow[ed] himself to be influenced by Rosenberg in all his decisions."[20] According to a former insider, Rosenberg's role changed when, for various reasons, he lost some of his Nazi status after 1940.

Rosenberg also actively promoted other racist authors, giving them both more credibility and sales. One example was Professor Hans Weinert, who discussed racial policy designed to foster evolutionary progress in his book on the origin of human races. He concluded that the path to higher levels of evolution included eugenics and a prohibition against racial mixing.[21]

Professor Weinert's views on the evolution of human races were largely well received by the Nazi movement as shown by the official National Socialist Racial Policy Office publication listing Weinert's books, including *Die Rassen der Menschheit* (*The Races of Mankind*), as valuable books on racial theory. *The Nationalsozialistische Monatshefte*, edited by Alfred Rosenberg, included an article by Heinz Brücher on Weinert's work promoting one of Weinert's books on race and human evolution.[22]

THE THESIS OF ROSENBERG'S BOOK

The theme of Rosenberg's book was not only blood purity, anti-Semitism and the rejection of Christianity but the importance of the

---

19 Adolf Hitler, *Hitler's Secret Conversations, 1941–1944*, trans. Norman Cameron and R.H. Stevens; intro. H.R. Trevor-Roper, "The Mind of Adolf Hitler" (New York: Farrar, Straus and Young, 1953), 342.

20 Dutch, *Hitler's 12 Apostles*, 82.

21 Hans Weinert, *Entstehung der Menschenrassen*, 2nd ed. (Stuttgart: Fredinand Enke Verlag, 1942), 314–315.

22 Heinz Brücher, "Lebenskunde," *Nationalsozialistische Monatshefte* (1937), 8:190–192.

domination of society by "those who are racially superior."[23] The book outwardly appeared to be very scholarly bolstered by its detailed erudition documented by hundreds of footnotes, some longer than an entire page. And, not surprisingly Rosenberg's major target

> was the Jews. His monumental, consistent, and practically unqualified anti-Semitism requires a separate chapter [in his book]. In addition, Rosenberg was outspoken in his frequent derogatory references to Negroes (referred to him usually as "Niggers"). He normally discussed them in connection with the problems of miscegenation, and often deliberately equated Negroes with Jews.[24]

Furthermore, Rosenberg judged

> European history as the struggle of the German people against the debilitating influences of Judaism and the Roman Catholic Church, and he pillaged literary and historical sources for material to support his thesis. He was enabled more readily to do this by adopting a purely subjective concept of race. ...what he strongly approved of was, *ipso facto*, Germanic; what he profoundly rejected was, in accordance with the same definition, Jewish.[25]

The Myth of the Twentieth Century was inspired by Rosenberg's "intellectual mentor," Stewart Chamberlain, and also by Arthur de Gobineau who wrote *An Essay on the Inequality of the Human Races*, as well as Friedrich Nietzsche who preached the superman superiority theory. According to James Whisker, Professor of Political Science at West Virginia University, the theme of Rosenberg's book was to reinterpret all of history in terms of race conflicts.[26]

Both Chamberlain and Rosenberg "believed that humankind was divided absolutely into superior and inferior beings."[27] Furthermore,

---

23 Dutch, *Hitler's 12 Apostles*, 83.

24 Nova, *Alfred Rosenberg*, 31.

25 Robert Cecil, *The Myth of the Master Race: Alfred Rosenberg and Nazi Ideology* (New York: Dodd and Meade, 1972), 12.

26 Whisker, *The Philosophy of Alfred Rosenberg*, 190–191.

27 Whisker, *The Philosophy of Alfred Rosenberg*, 191.

the superior race must not commit "racial pollution" by "sexually intermixing with inferior beings."[28] Rosenberg concluded the biological genes that produced a superior culture and political system were unique to Nordic men. He wrote that the "German people are not marked by original sin, but by original nobility."[29] His racism, he stressed, was based on Darwinism and the best science of the day supported by the leading German scientists.[30]

As was true of many Nazis, Rosenberg was influenced by Arthur de Gobineau. Gobineau was a major proponent of White supremacy theory. In his

> most influential work, the four-volume, mid-1850s *Essai sur l'inégalité des races humaines (Essay on the Inequality of Human Races)*, de Gobineau declared the superiority of the white race over others. He argued that the white race would prosper only if it did not become contaminated by mixing with other races. This belief eventually became one of the major principles of Nazi philosophy.[31]

RACISM AT THE CORE OF ROSENBERG'S NAZI IDEOLOGY

In his introduction to Rosenberg's book, to document the book's importance to Nazism, Professor Peel wrote that Nazi

> orthodoxy was never as monolithic nor as all-embracing as that of Marx and Lenin. There was, of course, agreement on the major issues—that World Jewry was the irreconcilable enemy of all Aryan civilization and culture and especially of Germany.[32]

Although Rosenberg's beliefs about Darwin were mixed, he openly supported Darwin's "survival of the fittest" and "superior race" ideologies. The fact is, the Nazis

---

28 Whisker, *The Philosophy of Alfred Rosenberg*, 191.

29 Cited in Fest, *The Face of the Third Reich*, 168.

30 Whisker, *The Philosophy of Alfred Rosenberg*, 202.

31 John Grabowski, *Josef Mengele* (Farmington Hills: Lucent Books, 2004), 20.

32 Peel, "Preface," in Rosenberg, *The Myth of the Twentieth Century*, xv.

combined their racial theories with the evolutionary theories of Charles Darwin to justify their treatment of the Jews. The Germans, as the strongest and fittest, were destined to rule, while the weak and racially adulterated Jews were doomed to extinction.[33]

Rosenberg stressed the Darwinian idea that "life arises out of struggle, out of death."[34] He openly "denied absolutely" creation *ex nihilo* for several reasons, including the fact that he thought "a creationist view" of origins was "an Asian-Jewish idea, passing from Paul (Saul) through the Roman Catholic Church to Luther."[35] Rosenberg also taught that Jews were sons of the "Jewish Jehovah" who was a "swindler, a promoter of lies and a murderer."[36]

In short, the major ideas that inspired Rosenberg to compose his new "German Bible" were anti-Semitism, rejection of Christianity and the right of "those who are racially superior" to dominate the racially inferior.[37] For all of these reasons, he aggressively attacked the Judeo-Christian idea of creation. A major factor for the success of Rosenberg's ideas and Nazi politics in Germany was that they appealed to professors, students and civil servants. It was this ideology that drove Hitler to commit his crimes against humanity.[38]

Rosenberg and others believed that the Jews and other inferior races must be eradicated for another reason: they spread pathogens such as bacteria.[39] As evidence of this claim they turned to the German public health research that

studied the medical data concerning typhus epidemics through the prism of race as a biological reality rather than as a social construct. Noting the prevalence of typhus outbreaks among the impoverished and overcrowded populations of urban Jews in

---

33 Mitchell Geoffrey Bard, ed., *The Complete History of the Holocaust* (San Diego: Greenhaven Press, 2001), 34.

34 Douglass, *God among the Germans*, 45.

35 Whisker, *The Philosophy of Alfred Rosenberg*, 98, 136.

36 Whisker, *The Philosophy of Alfred Rosenberg*, 28.

37 Dutch, *Hitler's 12 Apostles*, 83.

38 Whisker, *The Philosophy of Alfred Rosenberg*, 181.

39 Cecil, *The Myth of the Master Race*.

Eastern Europe, they mistook correlation for causality, ignored the obvious environmental factors, and attributed the spread of typhus to alleged Jewish cultural and genetic defects.[40]

For example, in one 1940 article about "spotted fever and ethnic identity," the German head of the public health department in Nazi-occupied Poland, Dr. Jost Walbaum, proclaimed that

> "The Jews are overwhelmingly the carriers and disseminators of the infection. Spotted fever endures most persistently in the regions heavily populated by Jews, with their low cultural level, their uncleanliness, and the infestation of lice unavoidably connected with this." One of his associates, Dr. Erich Weizenegger, similarly argued: "The sickness occurs...especially among the Jewish population. This is caused by the fact that the Jew totally lacks any concept of hygiene."[41]

This "lack" they assumed, was presumably caused by genetic racial defects. It is also ironic in view of the Jewish law on hygiene given in Leviticus.

ROSENBERG AS AN ANTI-CATHOLIC

Rosenberg was "almost as violent an anti-Catholic as he was anti-Jewish and only relatively less anti-Protestant. He is, in fact, anti-Christian."[42] *The Myth of the Twentieth Century* openly assaulted "Christianity and all that it stands for."[43] His hatred of the Catholic Church "was exceeded only by his hatred of Jews."[44] This was true because the core of Rosenberg's racial philosophy of the "absolute value of pure blood and race" brought him in "direct collision with Christian theology."[45] Roland wrote that few Germans

---

40 Christopher R. Browning, *Remembering Survival: Inside a Nazi Slave-Labor Camp* (New York: W.W. Norton, 2010), 122.

41 Browning, *Remembering Survival*, 122.

42 Peel, "Preface," in Rosenberg, *The Myth of the Twentieth Century*, xv.

43 Fest, *The Face of the Third Reich*, 168.

44 Nova, *Alfred Rosenberg*, 22.

45 Douglass, *God among the Germans*, 36, 38.

dared to speak out publicly against the [Nazi] regime, but certain members of the clergy, both Protestant and Catholic, criticized the Nazis from the pulpit when it became clear that they intended to supplant Christianity with a new pagan religion. The Christian cross was to be replaced with the swastika, and pictures of saints were to be removed from all chapels, churches and cathedrals.[46]

Another reason Rosenberg hated Catholicism was because of what he regarded as their

"abusive," "Jesuitic-Roman" system which consistently preached and practiced the "spineless" Roman principles of love and non-heroic, non-Germanic pity and compassion. In the name of the Church, love and pity had undermined the honor and hero-oriented subjective conception of the Germanic people. According to Rosenberg, the Church had, with the help of all possible alliances, extirpated all that was free, proud, and honor-loving, cleverly falsifying the Nordic tribal system, customs and independence.[47]

A third reason for Rosenberg's anti-Christian view was the Catholic Church's opposition to the Nazi goal of breeding a superior race just as humans breed horses. For example

in 1939, when Hitler instructed the SS to embark on a discreet, but widespread, campaign for elimination of the incurably sick and insane, public opinion in Germany was by no means ready for it. The counterattack, led by the Bishop of Muenster, slowed up the euthanasia program and, even if it did not stop it, drove it further underground, thus showing how effective resistance could be achieved by the Churches on an issue attracting the support of their flocks.[48]

---

46 Roland, *The Illustrated History of the Nazis*, 115.
47 Nova, *Alfred Rosenberg*, 21.
48 Browning, *Remembering Survival*, 144.

Lastly, the Nazis' goal was to replace the Bible with *Mein Kampf*. All of these goals alienated many Christians, for example, Martin Niemöller (1892 –1984), a Lutheran Pastor. He was a submarine commander in the First World War, and initially welcomed the new Nazi government. He soon became "disillusioned by their plans for a state-controlled Reich Church and by the rabidly anti-Christian sentiments expressed by Alfred Rosenberg and other members of Hitler's inner circle."[49]

Rosenberg concluded that Christianity would soon die in Germany:

> When Hermann Goering asked Rosenberg on August 22, 1939, "Do you believe that Christianity is approaching its end and that a new form [of religion] designed by us will arise?" Rosenberg answered: "Indeed! The religious value system has already ceased to be recognized."[50]

One major result of applying Rosenberg's ideas was

> the incoherence, imprecision and irrationality of the [Nazi] ideology itself…defeated all efforts to drive out what remained of the humane and Christian values of earlier centuries. When professor Walter Frank exclaimed at Tuebingen in 1936 that "all German history…must be seen as only the prehistory of National-Socialism," this could only have the impact of rhetoric.… Nazi biologists, avid for promotion, might measure the long skulls of their prehistortoric ancestors, but there would be others who knew that the size of the human head could be affected by rickets, as well as by race. The Nazis…[treated] as dogma their simplified and distorted version of theories put forward in the nineteenth century by such pioneers as Darwin.[51]

ROSENBERG'S END

After being convicted by the Allies at the Nuremberg Trials for crimes against humanity, Rosenberg was hanged on October 16, 1946. A major

---

49 Roland, *The Illustrated History of the Nazis*, 115.

50 Nova, *Alfred Rosenberg*, 23.

51 Browning, *Remembering Survival*, 150.

factor in his guilty verdict was that as Minister of Eastern Occupied Territories during the war, he carried out Nazi policy in the areas where most of the atrocities occurred. His book, *The Myth of the Twentieth Century*, and his anti-Semitic activities were also contributing factors. A witness to his execution called him the "arch-priest of Nazi culture in foreign lands."[52] Rosenberg hid forty-seven crates of Nazi records in a Bavarian barn that contained "an almost unbelievable admission of systemic killings, lootings, etc."[53] These detailed records of war crimes were important in the decision to hang him and the other Nazis on trial for war crimes.

SUMMARY

Alfred Rosenberg was a leading Nazi whose writings, primarily his best selling book, *The Myth of the Twentieth Century*, were responsible for influencing many people in Nazi Germany—from those high in the Nazi heirarchy to the wider audience who read his works—to murder so-called inferior races. He also was a vehement anti-Catholic and influenced not only the Jewish Holocaust, but also the Christian Holocaust in Poland and other nations. For these reasons, he was executed by the Allies after World War II.

---

52 Kingsbury Smith, "The Nuremberg Trials: The Execution of Nazi War Criminals," *International News Service* (October 16, 1946): 1.

53 Bard, ed., *The Complete History of the Holocaust*, 371.

Julius Streicher (1885–1946)

Publisher of the radical anti-Jewish newspaper *Der Stürmer*, Streicher incited widespread hatred of Jews and worked toward their total annihilation.

14

Julius Streicher: Anti-Catholic Darwinist and Hitler's mentor

INTRODUCTION

Julius Streicher (February 12, 1885 – October 16, 1946) was the founder and editor of the now infamous and vehemently anti-Semitic newspaper *Der Stürmer*—loosely translated *The Attacker*—the only newspaper that Hitler read "from beginning to end...from the first to the last line."[1] The paper's sole aim was the "incitement of the German nation against the Jewish race."[2]

Der Stürmer focused especially on what Streicher called the "race shame" crime, which was romance between an Aryan and a non-Aryan. This view came from the "scientific" belief that, in its purer forms "this racial doctrine, by no means limited to Germany, developed there with all the trappings of pseudoscholarship."[3] The doctrine taught that the Jews as a race were so degenerate that they could not to be improved,

---

1   Oswald Dutch, *Hitler's 12 Apostles* (New York: Robert M. McBride & Company, 1940), 154.

2   Dutch, *Hitler's 12 Apostles*, 154.

3   Eugene Davidson, *The Trial of the Germans: An Account of the Twenty-two Defendants before the International Military Tribunal at Nuremberg* (Columbia: University of Missouri Press, 1997), 41.

presumably even by Darwinian methods "since they were racially inferior, as were the black and yellow peoples."[4]

Called "the man who persuaded a nation to hate Jews," Herr Streicher relentlessly pursued Jews for much of his life in speeches and college lectures, but mostly in print.[5] *Der Stürmer* regularly featured allegations of ritual murder by Jews and claimed "world conspiracy of Jewry" myths that were of very questionable validity. Nazi historian Oswald Dutch called *Der Stürmer* the "lowest and least reputable newspaper that has ever been circulated in any country as an official news organ."[6] Davidson wrote that Streicher's

> anti-Semitism was of the brass-knuckles kind. He had delighted in the destruction of the synagogues, the beatings, the smashing of people and storefronts, in every turn of the screw, up to the Final Solution in the pits and gas chambers. He had always wanted the Jews exterminated. Streicher was the core within the core of the Party. He stood for the one thing all the [Nazi] defendants had in common. Although the others did their best to keep their distance from him, all had believed, in some part, at least, in the endlessly repeated message he wrote as editor of *Der Stuermer*, which had as a subtitle, "Nuremberg weekly for the fight for truth."[7]

Called one of the "pornographic, neurotic Jew-baiters," Streicher was later joined by Joseph Goebbels, propelling his position forward until it eventually dominated Nazi policy, especially after 1935.[8] Exactly why Streicher hated Jews is unclear and many theories have been offered. As Dutch wrote, "It is not entirely clear what impelled Julius Streicher...to make anti-Semitism not only his life work, but also his almost exclusive source of remuneration."[9]

---

4   Davidson, *The Trial of the Germans*, 41.

5   Randall L. Bytwerk, *Julius Streicher: The Man Who Persuaded a Nation to Hate Jews* (New York: Dorset Press, 1983), 1.

6   Dutch, *Hitler's 12 Apostles*, 154.

7   Davidson, *The Trial of the Germans*, 40.

8   Heinz Höhne, *The Order of the Death's Head: The Story of Hitler's SS*, trans. Richard Barry (London: Pan Books, 1969), 303.

9   Dutch, *Hitler's 12 Apostles*, 155.

One rumor, likely false but which caused Streicher a lot of problems, is that a girl he took a liking to as a young man turned him down for a Jew. More likely, he came under the influence of men like Hitler, Professor Otto Dickel of Augsburg University and other anti-Semites. He had a "close connection" with Hitler since 1923.[10] Professor Dickel taught that Jews were the greatest threat, not only to Germany, but also to the entire European continent.

STREICHER ACCEPTS SOCIAL DARWINIAN RACISM

Although Streicher's views on Darwinism are mixed, it is well documented that he accepted the social Darwinian inferior race theory, and concluded that Jews were one of the worst of all biologically inferior races. He believed that a single act of sexual intercourse with a Jew would contaminate an Aryan woman for life. For this reason, he condemned mixing what he judged as superior races with inferior races. He also accepted the ideas of the social Darwinists, such as Arthur de Gobineau and Ernest Renan who

> declared race, instead of economics or geography or politics, to be the decisive factor in history, and the Nordics to be the most creative and illustrious of the planet's inhabitants—[this] had been eagerly seized upon by German writers like Wilhelm Marr, who seems to have invented the term "anti-Semite," and the economist Eugen Duehring, who believed that the Jewish religion was a sign of the inferior race and monotheism a sign of the Jews' desire to rule other people. Racists of many varieties flourished. The Social Darwinists held that above all the species must be maintained, the unfit should be sterilized, the stronger races had the right to stamp out the weaker...[and] the Germans [were the] superior people.[11]

Streicher's hatred of "race mixing," though, went far beyond the simple rejection of a behaviour or a people. It was translated into, not just words, but inhuman actions. For example, he repeatedly

---

10 Dutch, *Hitler's 12 Apostles*, 159.
11 Davidson, *The Trial of the Germans*, 40.

forced Aryan women who had been too friendly with Jews or even half-Jews,

> to parade the streets with large sandwich-boards. On these appear the words, "I [then follows her full name] have given myself to [here is given the man's full name], a Jewish hog." In July 1933, in Nuremberg, Streicher had a nineteen-year-old Catholic girl arrested because she had fallen in love with a Jew, and Streicher scented "culpable relations." The girl's head was shaved bare, and she was compelled by the S.A. to trail the Nuremberg theaters and cabarets, accompanied by her Jewish lover. Wherever they were both dragged on to the stage, the S.A., on Streicher's orders, explained, by obscene commentary and action, the crime that these two young people, honestly in love with each other, had been guilty of.[12]

Streicher's own private sex life was scandalous in spite of the fact that he was described by some Nazis as an unattractive bombastic man lacking in character. He reportedly attempted to seduce even the wives of his friends. He also told a graduating class of high school girls, it "is your duty to bear sons for the fatherland. Have them in wedlock if possible, out of wedlock if necessary. The state will look after them."[13]

Streicher's father was a schoolteacher, an occupation he also followed. Julius began his anti-Semitic activities as early as 1919 and founded *Der Stürmer* in May 1923. Called pornographic, his paper became an instant hit, and was sold to both Christian and Jewish homes. His independence and rash ways caused even some fellow Nazis to call him a "dung heap" and to write about Streicher, "*Du bist ja ein Narr*"— "You're a fool, yes, you are."[14]

A LEADING AND INFLUENTIAL NAZI

No minor Nazi, it was Streicher who was able to keep the party going after Hitler's failed 1923 putsch. It was also Streicher who lavishly

---

12   Dutch, *Hitler's 12 Apostles*, 155.

13   Cited in Louis Lochner, *What about Germany?* (New York: Dodd, Mead & Co., 1942), 71.

14   Dutch, *Hitler's 12 Apostles*, 160.

supplied Hitler with money in the early days to support his political work. In 1935 Streicher, the man *Time Magazine* wrote had a Hitler-like mustache and was the "No. 1 Jew Baiter," was given an assembly attended by 50,000 people to "honor Hero Streicher."[15] The storm troopers who led the massive rally earnestly chanted the following little hymn of hate: "We must unite against the Enemy of Humanity.... We must crush those who combine everything bad."[16] As the crowd left the rally for home they chanted "Perish the Jew! ...where is the Jew? Let's get him!"[17]

STREICHER'S PUBLISHING HOUSE

Streicher established a publishing house in Nuremberg which became the leading publisher of anti-Semitic literature. He published "some of the most vile anti-Jewish passages to be recorded in modern history."[18] One of the most well-known examples was a book titled, *The Poison Mushroom*, a collection of seventeen short stories illustrated with full colour drawings showing that the Jews were the most dangerous of all poisons. Written by schoolteacher Ernst Hiemer, the illustrations effectively conveyed a strong message about the evil Jews who were like poisonous vermin that must be destroyed or they will destroy German society and people. The book was enthusiastically introduced into the classrooms of Germany and influenced German youth to accept the Nazi belief that Jews were not just biologically inferior, but also poisonous to society.

Streicher's claims in *Der Stürmer* were not solely for entertainment, but in the end resulted in the murder of many hundreds of Jews.[19] He "has succeeded beyond the limits of his immediate office in obtaining influence over the party."[20] Streicher also was involved in the meetings leading up to the infamous Nuremberg Laws that formally initiated the Holocaust.[21]

---

15 "50,000 for Streicher," *Time Magazine* 9, Vol. 26 (August 26, 1935): 22.

16 "50,000 for Streicher," 22.

17 "50,000 for Streicher," 23.

18 Gregory Wegner, *Anti-Semitism and Schooling under the Third Reich* (New York: RoutledgeFalmer, 2002), 158.

19 Dutch, *Hitler's 12 Apostles*, 161.

20 Dutch, *Hitler's 12 Apostles*, 161.

21 Richard Weikart, *Hitler's Ethic: The Nazi Pursuit of Evolutionary Progress* (New

His relentless war against Jews continued even after hardly any free Jews remained in Germany and "one of the mainsprings of National Socialism—the struggle against Jewry" can "be traced back primarily to Streicher's, Hitler's, Himmler's and the Nazi party's eugenic anti-Semitism that triumphed over all intellectual considerations, and was one of the chief propaganda messages of the German government."[22]

The reasons Streicher offered for condemning the Jews—their genetic immorality, their greed and their causing Germany to lose the First World War—were recognized by many Nazis as false—in their words, "poppycock" even "poisonous agitation."[23] The real reasons for Streicher's and the Nazis' anti-Semitism, Höhne wrote, were because

the SS subscribed to the theory culled from Darwin and adapted [it] to their own purposes [namely], that a people's valuable characteristics could be increased and improved by a process of selection. The SS racial mystics recognized only one criterion of value—the Nordic Germanic race. The political twist given to Darwin's biological theory presented his concept of the struggle for existence in a new light. What Darwin had regarded as a law of nature, the social Darwinists wished to impose from without through measures of coercion decreed by the authoritarian State; this culminated in the belief that the superior and stronger race had the right to eliminate racially inferior beings.[24]

The normal "task of any State is to protect the weak, the handicapped and the minorities" but, as a result of their Darwinian beliefs, the goal of a "normal civilized State's social policy was inverted." In Nazi Germany the task "was to reinforce the 'good blood' and root out those elements of the race considered 'bad blood'":

The SS looked upon nations not as formed entities but, in Buchheim's words, as "a plantation overgrown with weeds, which

---

York: Palgrave MacMillan, 2009), 145.

22 Dutch, *Hitler's 12 Apostles*, 162.

23 Höhne, *The Order of the Death's Head*, 302–303.

24 Höhne, *The Order of the Death's Head*, 300–301.

must be cleared by isolating the incorrigible, cutting out the "ferment of decomposition," cultivating the worthwhile elements and allowing the sub-standard to wither."[25]

Associating the idea of race and Darwinism was not original with the Nazis, but the notion of race was at the forefront of early social Darwinian ideology

As early as 1903 Wilhelm Schallmayer, the biologist, had proposed "fertility selection"; in his view, good racial characteristics could be cultivated by methods of racial selectivism, such as control or banning of marriages and sterilization of inferior members of society. This was clearly the forerunner of Himmler's racial fantasies with his "clan oaths," marriage permits and racial hygiene examinations. In his social-Darwinistic phraseology Himmler once said: "Unless the blood of leadership in German veins, by which alone we stand or fall, can be increased by the admixture of good blood from elsewhere, we shall never achieve world mastery."[26]

For all these reasons, Darwinism was critical to the development of the Nazi state. James M. Rhodes identified six major Nazi ideologies. One, which Rhodes identified as the Neo-Manichaean race cosmology, seems to fit Streicher the closest.[27] This view evaluated the proportion of Aryan and "ape blood" in the individual according to Table 1.

As late as 1941, Hitler called Streicher "brilliant" and "irreplaceable," even arguing that he "fought like a buffalo in our cause."[28] Davidson wrote that Streicher's convictions about the baseness and wickedness of the Jews matched those of Hitler, and even went beyond

---

25 Höhne, *The Order of the Death's Head*, 300–301.

26 Höhne, *The Order of the Death's Head*, 300–301.

27 James M. Rhodes, *The Hitler Movement: A Modern Millenarian Revolution* (Stanford: Hoover Institution Press, 1980), 106.

28 Adolf Hitler, *Hitler's Secret Conversations, 1941–1944*, trans. Norman Cameron and R.H. Stevens; intro. H.R. Trevor-Roper, "The Mind of Adolf Hitler" (New York: Farrar, Straus and Young, 1953), 127.

Table 1

The Neo-Manichaean race cosmology which evaluated the proportion of Aryan and "ape blood" in the individual according to the following chart:

SPECIES	BLOOD MIXTURE
Nordic (blond, blue-eyed)	Close to pure Aryan
Germanic (brown-haired, blue-eyed or, less desirable, brown-eyed)	Predominantly Aryan
Mediterranean (white but swarthy)	Slight Aryan preponderance
Slavic (white but degenerate skull structure)	Close to half-Aryan, half-ape
Oriental	Slight ape preponderance
Black African	Predominantly ape
Jewish (fiendish skull)	Close to pure ape

the anti-Jewish regulations imposed by the Nuremberg Laws.[29] Hitler, though, felt that *Der Stürmer* did not go far enough, noting that— "the Jew is baser, fiercer, [and even] more diabolical than Streicher depicted him."[30]

STREICHER THE ANTI-CATHOLIC

Streicher was also stridently anti-Catholic. One reason was because he concluded Nazi teachers often "told their pupils the truth about the Jews, whereas priests and pastors taught the same children from the Old Testament, presenting stories in which Jews were heroes."[31] The public reaction by Christians to such teachings of Streicher was so vehement that "outraged Christians protested throughout Germany, and *Der Stürmer* received many letters" objecting to Streicher's characterization of priests.[32]

---

29 Davidson, *The Trial of the Germans*, 39.
30 Hitler, *Hitler's Secret Conversations*, 126.
31 Bytwerk, *Julius Streicher*, 112.
32 Bytwerk, *Julius Streicher*, 112.

One result of Streicher's *Der Stürmer* articles was that his disciples and many Nazis stepped up their campaign against Christians. Some Christian leaders argued that Christians must understand the Old Testament to understand the Jew, an idea that Streicher condemned. Ministers were also condemned for marrying Germans and Jews—and, as occurred occasionally, the marriage of a Negro and a German Aryan was anathema.

STREICHER'S END

Streicher was one of the few high-level Nazis who remained faithful to the Führer to the very end.[33] He was tried, found guilty and hanged for crimes against humanity by the Allied Military Tribunal at Nuremberg in 1946. A witness to his execution wrote that Streicher, "after glancing around the room where he would die, uttered in a piercing scream: 'Heil Hitler!'"[34]

His last words, directed to his executioners and as translated by the prison interpreter, were, "The Bolsheviks will hang you one day."[35] The specific reason for his execution was because of his quarter century of "speaking, writing, and preaching hatred of the Jews." A contemporary report about "Jew-Baiter Number One"[36] said:

> In his speeches and articles, week after week, month after month, he infected the German mind with the virus of anti-Semitism, and incited the German people to active persecution. ...Streicher's incitement to murder and extermination at the time when Jews in the east were being killed under the most horrible conditions clearly constitutes persecution on political and racial grounds in connection with war crimes...and constitutes a crime against humanity.[37]

---

33 Davidson, *The Trial of the Germans*, 40.

34 Kingsbury Smith, "The Nuremberg Trials: The Execution of Nazi War Criminals," *International News Service* (October 16, 1946): 4.

35 Smith, "The Execution of Nazi War Criminals," 4.

36 Dutch, *Hitler's 12 Apostles*, 154.

37 Quoted in Smith, "The Execution of Nazi War Criminals," 4.

His campaign worked—at least until reality hit the German people and Germany lost the war.

SUMMARY

Julius Streicher was a leading propagandist for racism, especially against Jews in Nazi Germany. He believed the Darwinian idea that certain races were inferior and, for the sake of the superior race, must not be allowed to reproduce with the superior race because the result would be racial degeneration. He had a major influence on the Nazi movement and Hitler as well, especially during the early part of the war. Streicher was found guilty at the Nuremberg Trials and executed by the Allies for his role in the anti-Semitism movement that led to the Holocaust and Nazi war crimes.

15

Lebensborn: Breeding better Nazis using Darwinism

INTRODUCTION

In December 1935, Heinrich Himmler established the infamous *Lebensborn*[1] homes to help accomplish the Nazi goal of achieving a superior human race by deliberate racial selection.[2] The *Lebensborn*'s two main goals were numerical quantity and racial quality, two somewhat antagonistic ideals.[3] Its "ultimate goal was to develop a racially superior stock, in accordance with pseudo-scientific notions" of eugenics.[4]

Breeding superior humans, Himmler declared, would eventually provide superior men for leadership of a superior people, the Aryans. Aryan is not a precise category, but in colloquial modern English, Aryan signifies the Nordic for Norway, the racial ideal promoted by the Nazis, which actually included most people in Scandinavia, Germany, Austria

---

1 Meaning "well of life."

2 Larry V. Thompson,"*Lebensborn* and the Eugenics Policy of the *Reichsführer-SS*," *Central European History*, 4, No. 1 (March 1971): 54–77; Marc Hillel and Clarissa Henry, *Of Pure Blood* (New York: McGraw-Hill, 1976), 22, 45.

3 Hillel and Henry, *Of Pure Blood*, 35.

4 Lucy S. Dawidowicz, "The Failure of Himmler's Positive Eugenics," *Hastings Center Report*, Vol. 7, Issue 5 (October 1977): 43.

and people originally from these regions. Of course, the definition excluded all Jews, including all native German-speaking Jews.

This programme was the result of the Nazi conclusion, based on Darwinism, that "some human races are infinitely superior to other human races," and intermarriage works against this goal because "even if the bad stock is raised [up by interbreeding] the good is lowered."[5] Furthermore, the Nazis believed that inferior races breed more rapidly then the superior ones, resulting in a gradual increase in the percentage of inferior humans in the population. This belief was not a marginal view among Nazis, but rather was "central to national socialist racial theory and practice."[6]

The *Lebensborn* was no small project. In the nine years it was in existence, about 12,000 children, close to half illegitimate, were born in its fifteen homes.[7] Professor Thompson wrote:

> Racial purity was an obsession with Himmler, consistently emphasized in his speeches and writings, even while he was engaged on many fronts in extending the power and influence of himself and the SS. He believed that not only physical attributes but character traits, such as loyalty, determination, courage, and a sense of honor, could be biologically transmitted. Since, in his estimation, the "Aryan race" possessed these and other virtues in abundance, Himmler demanded proof of such ancestry from his men and their wives or prospective brides. Marriages consummated on this basis would biologically ensure a future SS elite, and they would also establish the SS as the racial nucleus from which Germany could replenish an Aryan inheritance now dangerously diluted through generations of race-mixing.[8]

In the *Lebensborn*, "the scientists and Hitler found common ground. German eugenicists, long frustrated in their dreams of selective breed-

---

5 William Montgomery McGovern, *From Luther to Hitler: The History of Fascist-Nazi Political Philosophy* (Cambridge: Riverside Press, 1941), 449.

6 Elizabeth D. Heineman, "Sexuality and Nazism: The Doubly Unspeakable?" *Journal of the History of Sexuality*, 11, No. 1 & 2 (January/April 2002): 22.

7 Dawidowicz, "The Failure of Himmler's Positive Eugenics," 43.

8 Thompson, "*Lebensborn* and the Eugenics Policy of the *Reichsführer-SS*," 55.

ing, looked with hope to the Nazi Party."[9] Professor Fritz Lenz, a leading German biologist, called Nazism "applied biology." He concluded that around a third of the German population were genetically inferior and, for this reason, should be sterilized—especially the racial inferior people such as the Jews and Slavs—and that "genetic purification was the nation's first priority."[10] It was not just the biologists that supported Nazism, but "Nazism was actively and enthusiastically espoused and promoted by...the medical profession."[11]

For centuries, Germany had been a set of city-states, such as Bavaria and Saxony, and was unified as a single nation only in 1871. One major goal of the German nationalist movement was to produce a great nation of Teutonic people, referring to those persons whose native language was German.[12] The belief that Teutonic people were racially superior to all other races was bolstered by their belief that Darwin's theory of the survival of the fittest applied to humans. Toward this end, the German nationalists "did not hesitate to maintain that the 'struggle of the creative Teutonic-Aryan race' boiled down to the 'struggle against the parasitic Semitic race.'"[13]

As a result, German "doctors, psychologists, biologists...scholars, scientists" concluded that the pure Germans were "the good, the true and the beautiful, while the bad, the false and the ugly" was the "work of inferior, meaning non-German" people.[14]

In this view, the "master race" must exterminate the "weak for the benefit of the strong" because evolution has given the strong "the right to exterminate whole races and peoples." These views were

Nazi ideas that were accepted by the Germans when Adolf Hitler attained power in 1933.... Thus the leaders of the Third Reich... used the pretext of purifying the German race to initiate a pro-

9 George Victor, *Hitler: The Pathology of Evil* (Washington: Brassey's, 1998), 173.

10 Victor, *Hitler: The Pathology of Evil*, 173.

11 John Cornwell, *Hitler's Scientists: Science, War, and the Devil's Pact* (New York: Viking, 2003), 174.

12 Jonathan Rose, *The Holocaust and the Book: Destruction and Preservation* (Amherst: University of Massachusetts Press, 2001).

13 Hillel and Henry, *Of Pure Blood*, 23.

14 Hillel and Henry, *Of Pure Blood*, 23.

cess of planned reproduction on the one hand and extermination [on the other hand].[15]

To achieve this goal, German girls were told it was the "duty of every German woman to bear children for the Führer."[16] *Lebensborn* homes were established to help achieve this goal. The criteria used to select ideal parents for breeding the Nazi so-called super-race included over twenty

characteristics, including the applicant's height, standing and seated; the shape of the skull, face and forehead; colour and location of the eyes and distance between them; length, breadth and curvature of the nose; length of arms, legs and body; colour, growth and quality of body hair; skin colour; back of the head, cheek-bones, lips, chin, eyelids; thorax (male applicants), pelvis (female applicants). In addition to all this, the SS man's bride had to be able to provide evidence that neither she nor her parents suffered from any physical or mental disease. Also she had to submit to an examination by SS doctors to make sure she was not sterile. Finally, provided she overcame all these hurdles, she had to produce a family tree showing there had been no Slavonic, let alone Jewish, blood in her family since 1750.[17]

The candidate parent for breeding also had to submit full-length photographs, usually nude or in a bathing suit, for evaluation. Last, the scientific "'race experts' subjected the question of [the candidates'] …future harmony to microscopic examination. The final decision rested with the Reichsführer" Hitler.[18] The problem was that few Germans fit this ideal—most were too dark, too short, too thin, too fat or in other ways too non-Nordic.[19]

The "aim of these institutions was the breeding of a Nordic super-race with the aid of men and women carefully selected in accordance

---

15 Hillel and Henry, *Of Pure Blood*, 23.
16 Hillel and Henry, *Of Pure Blood*, 43.
17 Hillel and Henry, *Of Pure Blood*, 31.
18 Hillel and Henry, *Of Pure Blood*, 31.
19 Hillel and Henry, *Of Pure Blood*, 27.

with the racial principles of the Third Reich."[20] The women did not need to be married and the fathers could have a wife and still sire at least one child with a *Lebensborn* woman. Himmler evidently followed his own advice and, in the 1940s, fathered two children by one of his several mistresses.[21]

Highly educated people were given a disproportionate responsibility for breeding better Germans, while many people deemed inferior were sterilized. For example, the chief medical officer of the *Lebensborn* organization, Dr. Gregor Ebner, "personally ordered the sterilization of many children and supervised the selection and Germanization of thousands of kidnapped children in the occupied territories."[22] When interviewed as an old man, Dr. Ebner stated that he had no regrets about what he had done and still felt that applying science to breed a better race of humans was morally proper.

All of the racial breeding was "supervised by doctors who were experts in 'racial science.'"[23] The "race examiners" believed that it was "possible to eliminate all traces of impure blood within a few generations, a century at most."[24] To do this, Himmler envisaged importing Norwegian girls to Bavaria for the purpose of "rapidly transforming the Dinaric into a pure Nordic race by means of selective breeding."[25]

Dinaric people were tall, mostly of mesomorph bodily build (of medium build and neither thin nor fat), had relatively long legs, medium arm span and a short trunk. This was an imprecise classification that is today regarded as close to worthless, and was most closely associated with the writings of German biologist Hans F.K. Günther and Harvard professor Carleton S. Coon.

KIDNAPPING CHILDREN

To achieve this goal more rapidly, throughout Europe the Germans had "kidnapped thousands of 'racially valuable' children, [and had]

20 Hillel and Henry, *Of Pure Blood*, 11.

21 Richard Weikart, *Hitler's Ethic: The Nazi Pursuit of Evolutionary Progress* (New York: Palgrave MacMillan, 2009), 133.

22 Hillel and Henry, *Of Pure Blood*, 18.

23 Hillel and Henry, *Of Pure Blood*, 25.

24 Hillel and Henry, *Of Pure Blood*, 25.

25 Hillel and Henry, *Of Pure Blood*, 25.

taken them from their families to Germanize them. That was one of the ways of helping the super-race to" multiply more rapidly.[26] Himmler, on his first tour of occupied Poland was

> amazed by the Nordic appearance of many "Slavic" children and decided to kidnap them from their parents and send them to *Lebensborn* foster homes and orphanages in Germany. Two special SS agencies—the *Volksdeutsche* Liaison Office and the Race and Settlement Office—searched Europe for "human specimens considered suitable for Germanization." They also "cleared" vast areas of land of "inferior" Poles and Jews by killing or enslaving the inhabitants, and put to death thousands of Germans who were considered feebleminded, infirm, mentally ill, or crippled. (The gas chambers were originally invented to weed out "unfit" Germans and were later applied to the genocide of entire "undesirable races," particularly Gypsies and Jews.)[27]

An estimated 250,000 children were forcibly taken away from their parents, most never to return.[28] The Nazis often tried to convince the children that they were abandoned by their birth parents. Although some of the children were successfully adopted by SS families, many adoptions did not work out and these children often ended up in Nazi concentration camps where a large number died.[29] Dawidowicz concludes that in the end, tragically,

> Tens of thousands of these children—no one will ever know how many—were murdered, perhaps because it turned out that they had "bad blood," that is, characteristics that did not fit the stereotype of the "Aryan"—blond hair, blue eyes, and an obedient nature.[30]

---

26 Hillel and Henry, *Of Pure Blood*, 12.

27 Richard Milner, *Darwin's Universe: Evolution from A to Z* (Berkeley: University of California Press, 2009), 277.

28 Dawidowicz, "The Failure of Himmler's Positive Eugenics," 43.

29 John Grabowski, *Josef Mengele* (Farmington Hills: Lucent Books, 2004), 28.

30 Dawidowicz, "The Failure of Himmler's Positive Eugenics," 43.

The Lebensborn programme

A nurse with baby strollers in front of a Lebensborn institution. Here, under Himmler's SS flag, the German "super-race" was being bred.

Bundesarchiv, Bild 146-1973-010-11 / photographer: unknown, 1943

Only about 25,000 of the children were ever returned to their parents after the war. As German zoologist and geneticist Ludwig Plate wrote at the time, the death of so many children was worth it because "progress in evolution goes forward over millions of dead bodies" of "inferior" humans.[31]

To justify this cruel policy, Himmler wrote in a speech delivered on October 14, 1943, that in all foreign nations, even in Poland, there are inevitably

> some racially good types. In these cases…it is our duty to take their children, to remove them from their present environment, if need be even by stealing them…. Either we bring this good blood home here, use it and integrate it into our people or—gentlemen, you may call this cruel, but nature is cruel—we destroy it.[32]

Soon after the Nazis took over the German government, the racial propaganda machine became active in indoctrinating the general population into the ideal created by the university "race experts" in order to return Germany to the Teutonic ideal, "warning the population against the dangers involved in mixing true Aryan blood with that of inferior races."[33] To help achieve this goal, the Nuremburg Laws were passed on September 15, 1935, "to preserve German blood from all [race] contamination and protect the German race to the end of time."[34]

A major means used to achieve this goal was to outlaw marriage and sexual relations between Jews and Aryans.[35] The logic for this law was that the Nazi leadership believed that the "progressive deterioration of the German race" was occurring due to the "inability of twentieth-century man to produce pure-blooded and racially valuable children" for the reason that

31 Cited in Christopher Hutton, *Race and the Third Reich* (Cambridge: Polity, 2005), 212.

32 Cited in Dawidowicz, "The Failure of Himmler's Positive Eugenics," 43.

33 Hillel and Henry, *Of Pure Blood*, 28.

34 Hillel and Henry, *Of Pure Blood*, 28.

35 Hillel and Henry, *Of Pure Blood*, 28.

inferior races, the Jews in particular, had been permitted to mix with the superior races. Every effort was therefore to be made to reverse this "degeneration of the species," which was discernible right up to the highest levels of the State. By Himmler's orders, the RuSHA laid down a series of principles: insistence on racial hygiene, improving the racial stock by means of selection, supervision of the marriages of individuals of pure blood, and the bringing up of children in State institutions.[36]

Many German race theorists proposed various means to "purify the German race, but the race experts...relied most heavily on the works of the Bavarian Dr. Wilhelm Schallmayer."[37] In 1900, he received an award for his book on producing a superior German race titled, *Inheritance and Selection in the Life of Nations*. One subject that Dr. Schallmayer dealt with was: "Racial hygiene and its control in the national interest."[38] This document listed eight major ways to achieve this goal:

1. girls should be made to realize that no nobler career exists for them than that of wife and mother;
2. a woman's social position should depend on the number of children she has borne;
3. a cult of the family should be created and developed;
4. women should marry young;
5. the inheritance laws should be reformed to conform with the population policy;
6. work by women outside the home must be reduced to a minimum;
7. sexual disease must be fought; and
8. special homes should be created for returning soldiers, by which preference was to be given to those against whom there were no objections on the grounds of racial hygiene and from whom an improvement of the birth rate was to be expected.[39]

36 Hillel and Henry, *Of Pure Blood*, 28.
37 Hillel and Henry, *Of Pure Blood*, 28–29.
38 Hillel and Henry, *Of Pure Blood*, 28–29.
39 Hillel and Henry, *Of Pure Blood*, 28–29.

Dr. Schallmayer "was responsible for not only the *Lebensborns* but also the concentration camps as a result of his stressing that science has proved 'an essential part of any breeding policy was to insure that the most unsuitable heritable variations were not reproduced.'" These ideas were all taught in the German biology textbooks to reinforce Nazi racial ideals. For example, one biology book stated that it is "the SS man's duty to choose a biologically flawless wife and, moreover, [the Nazi party] has constantly reminded him of his obligation as a member of an elite formation to have a large number of children."[40]

It was no easy task to persuade German men to select Nordic ideal women for brides. In fact, Himmler was puzzled "by the problem of why men fell for the non-Nordic, more sexy type of girl, and right up to the collapse of Nazi Germany the problem of recruiting the right type of future mother was one of his major preoccupations."[41]

Himmler felt that the *Lebensborn* system could solve this problem. Consequently, on July 3, 1944, Himmler issued the following order: "no more applications to marry women who do not comply in every respect with the racial criteria in force." Himmler actively tried to sell his idea to his military officers by preaching the law of Darwinism:

> Nature teaches us…that the principle of selection rules over it, that the stronger remains victor and the weaker succumbs. It teaches us that what often appears to an individual as brutality, because he himself is affected or because through his education he has turned away from the laws of nature, is nonetheless fundamentally necessary, in order to bring about a higher evolution of living organisms.[42]

In the end, the experiment failed and no evidence exists that superior people resulted from the experiment. Furthermore, after the war, the Race and Settlement Main Office, including its spin-off *Lebensborn*, was brought to trial before the Nuremberg Military Tribunal in 1947–1948.[43]

---

40 Hillel and Henry, *Of Pure Blood*, 30.
41 Hillel and Henry, *Of Pure Blood*, 48.
42 Cited in Weikart, *Hitler's Ethic*, 175.
43 Case No. 8, Green Series.

Compared to the crime of genocide against the Jews, the *Lebensborn* did not appear to reach the level of evil that resulted in the Holocaust. Dawidowicz concluded that when

assessing the accomplishments of *Lebensborn* and the SS's related racial eugenics programs, it is clear that "positive" racial eugenics in Hitler's Germany failed to attain its goals. In dramatic contrast, Germany's "negative" racial eugenics—the murder of the crippled, the sick, the insane, the Gypsies, and the Jews—succeeded beyond belief. The Germans found it easy to organize and carry out mass murder, to take life. They never discovered how to organize mass procreation, to make life.[44]

SUMMARY

The Nazis established the *Lebensborn* programme to produce racially superior children more rapidly than could be achieved in an open society. Women judged to be racially superior were selected to produce babies often fathered by Nazi officers judged to be racially superior. Furthermore, close to 250,000 children were kidnapped from occupied nations and sent to Germany to be "Germanized" in *Lebensborn* institutions.

The *Lebensborn*, although supported by many, if not most, of the leading biologists in Germany and other nations, produced a tragedy that caused enormous suffering and failed for reasons that we understand very well today. These reasons include the realization that hereditary diseases and medical conditions are far more complex than the scientists infatuated with Darwinism dreamed possible.[45]

Both the environment and epigenetics are now recognized as critically important, as well as the fact that genes form an enormously complex system whose interrelations still elude scientific researchers. In the end, the *Lebensborn* was "one of the most horrifying programmes instituted by the Nazis."[46] The few informal attempts to follow up on

---

44 Dawidowicz, "The Failure of Himmler's Positive Eugenics," 44.

45 Mitchell Geoffrey Bard, ed., *The Complete History of the Holocaust* (San Diego: Greenhaven Press, 2001), 28.

46 Grabowski, *Josef Mengele*, 28.

the children born from the programme indicate that, as a whole, they were in almost every way close to average. Unfortunately, as yet no comprehensive scientific medical study has been completed on the children of the *Lebensborn*. The information we do have indicates that, in the end, the experiment failed horribly.[47]

---

47 Bernt Engelmann, *In Hitler's Germany* (New York: Pantheon, 1986).

16

Darwinism in the biology textbooks of the Third Reich

INTRODUCTION[1]

The content of textbooks played a critical part in the goal of spreading Nazi ideology and Darwinian theory throughout Germany. This is indicated by a statement attributed to Hitler: "Let me control the textbooks and I will control the state."[2] The Nazis ensured that Darwinism was taught in detail using textbooks and classrooms for the reason that ideas derived from "Darwinian theory became important truths in Hitler's ideology."[3] Furthermore, the Nazi government ensured that not only were all teachers and professors to be Darwinists, committed to "Hitler's racial doctrines," but also that all textbooks were revised to conform to this goal.[4]

---

1   I relied heavily on the research of Professor Richard Weikart for this chapter, specifically his unpublished essay, "The Role of Darwinism in Nazi Racial Thought." Any mistakes that remain are mine.

2   Cited in Christopher J. Klicka and Gregg Harris, *The Right Choice: The Incredible Failure of Public Education and the Rising Hope of Home Schooling* (Gresham: Noble Publishing Associates, 1992), 89.

3   Gilmer W. Blackburn, *Education in the Third Reich: A Study of Race and History in Nazi Textbooks* (Albany: State University of New York Press, 1985), 22.

4   William L. Shirer, *The Rise and Fall of the Third Reich* (New York: Simon and Schuster, 1960), 249.

1. Chimpanzee

2. Gorilla.

3. Orang.

4. Negro.

Figure 1
Pictures a Negro next to an Orang, a Chimpanzee and Gorilla. The racist
implications are obvious.

Source: Ernst Haeckel, *The Evolution of Man* (New York: D. Appleton and Company, 1879), frontispiece.

Fig. 345.⁵⁵⁹

Orang-Outan.

Fig. 346.⁵⁶¹

Hottentot Wagoner — Caffre War.

Fig. 347.⁵⁶⁰

Chimpanzee.

Fig. 348.⁵⁶²

Hottentot from Somerset.

Fig. 349.

Mobile Negro, 1853.

Fig. 350.

Mobile Negro, 1853.

Figure 2
Comparisons of Negroes and apes. Note the similarity between the Orang-Outan and the Hottentot Negro and the Chimpanzee and the Hottentot Negro.
Source: J.C. Nott and G.R. Gliddon, *Types of Mankind: or Ethnological Researchers* (London: Lippincott, 1857), 459.

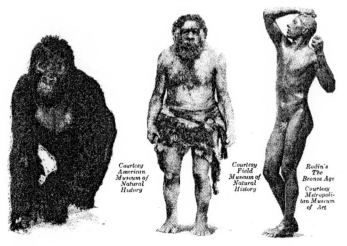

Figure 3
Pictures of gorillas, then widely believed to be our closest living common evolutionary ancestor, to Neanderthals, now recognized to be another race of modern man, to modern man as shown by French sculpture Rodin.

Source: Orland Kay Armstrong, "Beating the Evolution Laws," *Popular Science Monthly*, Vol. 115, No. 3 (September 1929): 19.

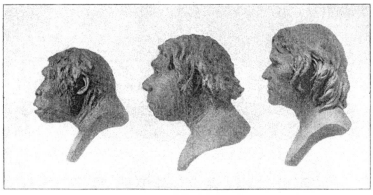

FIG. 258. Three stages in human development

Restorations to suggest the probable appearance of primitive types of human beings. From left to right, *Pithecanthropus erectus* (Java), *Homo neanderthalensis* (Germany), and the " Man of Cro-Magnon," *Homo sapiens* (France). These photographs are of figures molded by Professor J. H. McGregor on the basis of fragments of primitive man discovered from time to time in various parts of the world

Figure 4
The evolution of man showing Java man, Neanderthal man and modern man.

Source: Benjamin Gruenberg, *Elementary Biology* (Boston: Ginn and Company, 1924), 495.

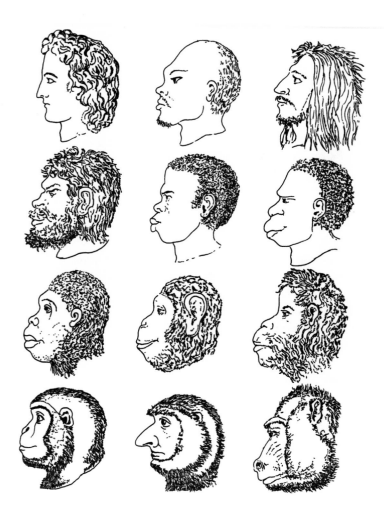

Figure 5
This illustration from Ernst Haeckel's book purports to show the evolution of man from an ape. The Negro (2nd row, middle) and the Mongol (top row, middle) are shown to be "less evolved" than the "ideal" man, shown with a Greco-Roman profile.

Source: Ernst Haeckel, *Natürliche Schöpfungsgeschichte* (Berlin: Georg Reimer, 1868), frontispiece (ed. note: numbering has been removed).

Nobel laureate Konrad Lorenz noted that "evolution not only supported the National Socialist worldview" but also the "fact that human beings" evolved from lower life forms. "The logical force" of evolution,

> Lorenz insisted, would do more than anything to win over people to Nazi ideals. [Kiel University professor] Paul Brohmer came down closest to the thinking of Lorenz on the issue of evolution in biology instruction. He saw in Darwin's work one of the greatest expressions of the human spirit. Brohmer thought it wholly inappropriate for biology teachers to treat Darwinism as false doctrine.[5]

Because the idea that all life was part of a "Darwinian struggle for existence" was central to Nazi ideology, the battle for Darwinian indoctrination was "waged without end." Consequently, German educators ensured that this ideology was openly taught in the schools and textbooks.[6] Because many teachers had a difficult time teaching the blunt Nazi survival of the fittest doctrine, German educators were forced to refine "Hitler's crude militaristic and social Darwinist ideas and made them somewhat more palatable to the educated."[7] They did this by requiring the teaching of a somewhat kinder, gentler Darwinism in the schools, but Darwinism just the same.[8] Furthermore, in intellectual circles

> every opportunity was taken to drive home the Nordic Germanic [eugenic] message. All disciplines emphasized the…inferiority and biological unattractiveness of the "non-Aryan" races. This was not particularly aimed at the non-Aryan students, but was part of the indoctrination of their German peers. It was as if the "alien blood" students did not exist as sentient beings.[9]

---

5 Gregory Wegner, *Anti-Semitism and Schooling under the Third Reich* (New York: RoutledgeFalmer, 2002), 72.

6 Blackburn, *Education in the Third Reich*, 21–22.

7 Blackburn, *Education in the Third Reich*, 127.

8 Wegner, *Anti-Semitism and Schooling under the Third Reich.*

9 Lynn H. Nicholas, *Cruel World: The Children of Europe in the Nazi Web* (New York: Alfred A. Knopf, 2005), 84.

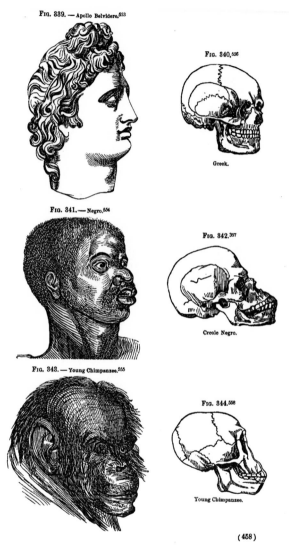

Fig. 339. — Apollo Belvidere.[553]

Fig. 340.[556]

Greek.

Fig. 341. — Negro.[554]

Fig. 342.[557]

Creole Negro.

Fig. 343. — Young Chimpanzee.[555]

Fig. 344.[558]

Young Chimpanzee.

(458)

Figure 6
Illustrations of the highest evolved men, the Greeks, and the primitive
ape-men, the "negro" compared to the ape. Note the Creole Negro skull is far
more ape-like than the modern man skull.

Source: J.C. Nott and G.R. Gliddon, *Types of Mankind: or Ethnological Researchers*
(London: Lippincott, 1857), 458.

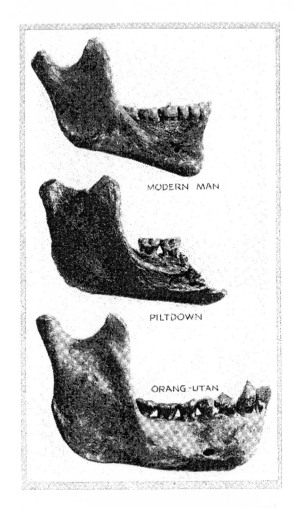

From top to bottom, jaw of a modern man, Piltdown man, and orang-utan. A study of these
shows how the ape jaw is shortened and slightly
lightened in the Piltdown specimen and has
been reduced and given a chin in modern man.

Figure 7
**The jaws from Orang-utan, also once believed to be the closest common
ancestor to modern man bridged by Piltdown man, now proven to be a hoax.**

Source: W.K. Gregory and Michel Mok, "How Man-Apes Became Men," *Popular Science Monthly,*
Vol. 119, No. 4 (October 1931): 22.

Bendiscioli wrote that the Nazi Government was centred

around the idea of the "race" or "nation" (*Volk*).... It aims at the biological preservation, the eugenic perfection, and the purity of the race. As a result of this attitude the teaching of biology has become a subject of primary importance in German schools. The governments of the various states have made the theory of heredity, racial doctrine, racial hygiene, and demographic politics, obligatory subjects on scholastic curricula.[10]

BERNHARD RUST–DARWINIST MINISTER OF SCIENCE, EDUCATION AND NATIONAL CULTURE

Bernhard Rust (1883 –1945) was introduced to Darwinism and eugenics in college and graduated with a doctorate in German philosophy. Dr. Rust joined the Nazi party in 1922. A zealous Nazi, he eventually controlled every level of the German educational system.

Soon after Hitler became Chancellor in 1933, Dr. Rust was selected *Reichsminister für Wissenschaft, Erziehung und Volksbildung* (Reich Minister of Science, Education and National Culture), and set about to reshape the German educational system to conform to the racist and anti-Christian goals of Nazism.

It was Dr. Rust who, in 1933, issued the rule requiring students and teachers to greet each other with the Nazi salute as a symbol of loyalty to Nazi Germany. His major educational goal was to immerse German youth in Nazi philosophy, especially social Darwinism. Rust also was instrumental in purging German universities of Jews and other "enemies of the State." Teachers who were known to be critical of the Nazi Party were dismissed or, in Nazi ideology sent to be "retrained."

DARWINISM PERMEATES NAZI BIOLOGY TEXTBOOKS

As a further precaution against "wrong thinking," schools could use only books that had been approved by the Nazi party. In Dr. Rust's view, "the whole function of education is to create Nazis."[11] Rust also believed

---

10 Mario Bendiscioli, *Nazism versus Christianity* (London: Skeffington & Son, 1939), 193.

11 Abraham Wolf, *Higher Education in Nazi Germany* (London: Methuen, 1944), 24.

that non-Aryan science, such as Albert Einstein's "Jewish physics," was flawed. In an address to scientists, Rust said that the "problems of science do not present themselves in the same way to all men. The Negro or the Jew will view the same world in a different light from the German investigator."[12]

Dr. Rust also became the director of a national scientific research centre that oversaw the use of prisoners for the now infamous, often brutal, Nazi medical experiments. After the fall of Nazi Germany in 1945, the United Nations War Crimes Commission (UNWCC) indicted him for his involvement in human medical experiments—but Rust had beaten the hangman and already committed suicide.

After the Nazis took over Germany, biology instruction and textbooks rapidly became saturated with Darwinian evolution. Prior to this, the subject was rarely mentioned in the textbooks. In 1938, the Ministry of Education published an official school curriculum handbook that included a chapter on new biology requirements.[13] This curriculum included the biology goals developed by the National Socialist Teachers' League, no doubt influenced by Ernst Haeckel's writings and authored by Darwin's disciples, H. Linder and R. Lotze, emphasizing evolution. It was Haeckel who first translated Darwin's 1859 *On the Origin of Species* into German.

The biology curriculum included teaching plant and animal evolution in grades three and four, and human evolution in grade five. The required topics for biology instruction in the upper grades included human evolution and the origin of the human races.

The guidelines repeatedly stressed that evolution was central to both the Nazi worldview and the biology curriculum. The curriculum specifically mandated a detailed coverage of evolution, including the evolution of human races by "selection and elimination" of the less-fit races. It stipulated that students must accept as "self-evident this most

---

12 Maxine Block, ed., *Current Biography: Who's News and Why*, Vol. 2. (New York: H.W. Wilson, 1942), 727.

13 H. Linder and R. Lotze, "Lehrplanentwurf für den biologischen Unterricht an den höheren Knabenschulen. Bearbeitet im Auftrag des NSLB. Reichsfachgebiet Biologie," *Der Biologe*, Vol. 6 (1937): supplement, 239–246. [In English: "Draft syllabus for biology teaching at senior schools for boys. Adapted by order of the NSLB (National Socialist Teachers Association). Reich subject area 'biology.'"]

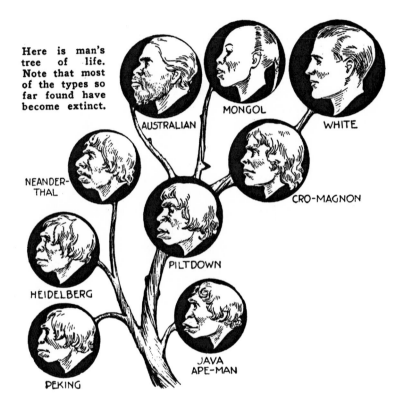

Here is man's tree of life. Note that most of the types so far found have become extinct.

AUSTRALIAN

MONGOL

WHITE

NEANDER-THAL

CRO-MAGNON

HEIDELBERG

PILTDOWN

PEKING

JAVA APE-MAN

Figure 8
A human evolution "tree" showing the then common racist hierarchy. Whites are shown as being descended from Cro-Magnon and Mongols and Australians from Piltdown man, the later now proven to be a hoax. The "negroes" are unexplainably absent from the tree.

Source: W.K. Gregory and Michel Mok, "How Man-Apes Became Men," *Popular Science Monthly*, Vol. 119, No. 4 (October 1931): 23.

essential and critically important natural law of elimination [of the unfit] together with evolution."[14] Eugenics, although introduced in geography and history, was

> developed much further in biology. The teaching of racial studies and eugenics soon was required in designated classes. This order was a bonanza for the extremists whose eugenics texts had gone unread for years. Hundreds of books and pamphlets were published for all levels of instruction. Written in turgid and propagandistic prose...the books, after providing minimal introductions to genetics and prehistory, were dedicated almost entirely to a totally [we recognize now] unscientific definition of races and their supposed characteristics.[15]

Teachers in the fifth grade were also required to cover the emergence of "primitive" human races "in connection with the evolution of animals." Eighth grade students were taught evolution in far more detail, including the worldviews of Lamarckism and Darwin, and their political implications, as well as the origin and evolution of the human races.

The race segment included material on putative prehistoric humans and the evolutionary history of contemporary "races," including the Nordic and Jewish "races." The Teachers' League material stressed that, while the "individual organism is temporary, the life of the species to which it belongs is lasting," and is ruled by the laws of evolution.[16]

BIOLOGY TEXTBOOKS TIE DARWINISM, NAZISM AND RACISM TOGETHER

The close connection between Nazism and Darwinism was explained in detail in many of the biology textbooks.[17] One text, written for fifth

---

14 Linder and Lotze, "Lehrplanentwurf für den biologischen Unterricht an den höheren Knabenschulen: 148–149.

15 Nicholas, *Cruel World*, 84–85.

16 Linder and Lotze, "Lehrplanentwurf für den biologischen Unterricht an den höheren Knabenschulen: 141, 157, 160.

17 Peter Kramp and Gerhard Benl, eds., *Vererbungslehre, Rassenkunde und Rassenhygiene: Lehrbuch für die Oberstufe Höherer Lehranstalten*, 2 vols. (Leipzig : G. Thieme, 1936). [In English: *Genetics, Study of Race and Race Hygiene: Textbook for Senior High Schools*.]

grade girls, after explaining that "all creatures, plants as well as animals, are in a continual battle for survival" added that the animal that does

> not secure sufficient territory and guard it against other preda-
> tors, or lacks the necessary strength and speed or caution and
> cleverness, will fall prey to its enemies.... The battle for exis-
> tence is hard and unforgiving, but is the only way to maintain life.
> This struggle eliminates everything that is unfit for life, and
> selects everything that is able to survive. ...the laws of nature are
> built on a struggle for survival.[18]

The implications of these ideas to Nazi war and racist policies are obvious. The textbook then provided a set of examples to support the above claim, concluding that "every creature has to fight for its survival... summarized in the principle: Each individual wants to maintain its existence in the struggle for survival (self preservation instinct, fighting will, individuality)."[19] The text then added that humankind is also "subject to these natural laws, and has won its dominant position through struggle" against inferior animals.[20] Support for this conclusion included the claim that people historically "had both to secure their own prey, and protect themselves against the larger carnivores." Furthermore, each person must fight for his place in his community and those who are less fit in the "struggle for survival...will perish. Our Führer tells us: 'He who wants to live must fight, and he who does not want to fight in this world of perpetual struggle does not deserve to live!'"[21]

In part two, the authors continue, noting that all living things which are successful

> in the struggle for survival are not satisfied merely with existence,
> but seek to preserve their species as well. Here too is a drive that

---

18 Hermann Wiehle and Marie Harm, *Lebenskunde für Mittelschulen. Fünfter Teil. Klasse 5 für Mädchen* (Halle: Hermann Schroedel Verlag, 1942), 168. [In English: *Biology for Middle School.*]

19 Wiehle and Harm, *Lebenskunde für Mittelschulen*, 168.

20 Wiehle and Harm, *Lebenskunde für Mittelschulen*, 168.

21 Wiehle and Harm, *Lebenskunde für Mittelschulen*, 169. See also, Adolf Hitler, *Mein Kampf* (Cambridge: Houghton Mifflin/The Riverside Press, 1962), 20.

corresponds to natural law. Without this drive, species would long since have vanished.... Maintaining the species also is a struggle. The deer ruts in the fall and offers battle to other deer in competition for females. The stronger and cleverer deer passes on his inheritance. The rooster defends his status and his hens courageously. The battle for females selects the fittest.[22]

The text, after stressing that the "drive for maintaining the species is stronger than the instinct for self-preservation," then details the importance of sacrificing one's life for the Nazi state and evolution. Examples provided to support the Nazi goal of sacrificing one's life for the Nazi state include the fact that a female rabbit defends her

young against hawks, often at the cost of her own life. A fox risks its life to secure food for its young. The life of the individual can be sacrificed to assure the continuation of the species. (The law of the species is stronger than that of the individual!)[23]

This text then claims that a natural law exists that applies to all life, namely, nowhere on earth is there a life form that exists which produces only one or two offspring because that

would inevitably lead to extinction.... [Therefore a] large number of offspring are an important means in the struggle for survival of the species. The house mouse can resist the field mouse simply through its larger number of young. In such instances, one can speak of a battle of births.[24]

This argument was used by the Nazis to develop their policy of encouraging German women to have large families. They used both propaganda and awards, such as money and honours, to achieve this goal. The Nazis also justified their wars for *territory* by Darwinism:

22 Wiehle and Harm, *Lebenskunde für Mittelschulen*, 169–170.
23 Wiehle and Harm, *Lebenskunde für Mittelschulen*, 170–172.
24 Wiehle and Harm, *Lebenskunde für Mittelschulen*, 172.

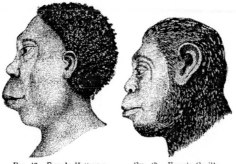

Fɪɢ. 46.—Female Hottentot.   Fɪɢ. 47.—Female Gorilla.

Figure 9
Drawings of female gorilla and a Hottentot (Khoikhoi from Southern Africa).
Note the drawings show little relationship with reality but are drawn to prove
the author's preconceived idea. The author concludes, "The physical aspects of
many native Africans gives them, beyond question, a decidedly beastly look."
Source: Alexander Winchell, *Preadamites; or a Demonstration of the Existence of Men Before Adam*
(London: S.C. Griggs and Co., 1880), 253.

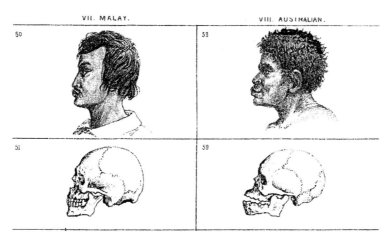

Figure 10
Malay and native Australian male profiles and their skull profiles. Note how
ape-like the skulls are pictured.
Source: J.C. Nott and G.R. Gliddon, *Types of Mankind: or Ethnological Researchers*
(London: Lippincott, 1857), lxxvi.

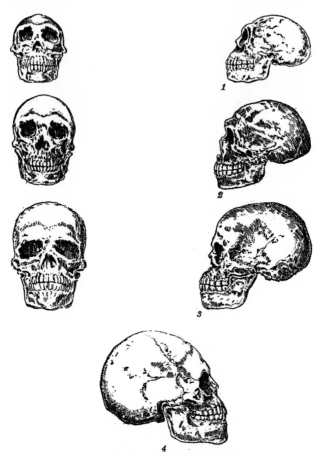

FIG. 256. Ancestors of man represented by remains of skulls

1, Pithecanthropus erectus, the " erect ape-man " of Java; *2,* the Neanderthal man; *3,* the negroid man of Laussel; *4,* Nebraska glacial man. These four types represent successive advances in the evolution of the human races, although we must not think of them as a straight series of our ancestors. Compare the size of the brain at different stages of development: Pithecanthropus, 850 cc.; Piltdown, 1300 cc.; Neanderthal, 1600 cc.; modern man, 1500–1800 cc.

Figure 11

An early picture of the now disproven progression from apes to man (1. Java Man; 2. Neanderthal man; 3. Negroid man of Laussel; 4. Nebraska glacial man). The caption gives the brain sizes at different stages: Pithecanthropus, 850 cc; Piltdown, 1300 cc; Neanderthal, 1600 cc; modern man, 1500-1800 cc.

Source: Benjamin Gruenberg, *Elementary Biology* (Boston: Ginn and Company, 1924), 493.

Each species strives to conquer new territory. The species goes before the individual. History provides us with enough examples to prove that mankind, too, is under this law. In the midst of their prosperity, the Romans lost the desire to have children. They sinned against the law of maintaining the species. Their state was undermined and overcome by foreign peoples ... Our nation, too, once hung in the balance. National Socialism restored to the German people the will to have children, and preserved our people from certain decline, which would have been inevitable under the law of species and the law of the greater number of offspring.

To support this argument, the authors again quoted Hitler who wrote:

"Marriage, too, cannot be an end in itself, but rather it must have the larger goal of increasing and maintaining the species and the race. That only is its meaning and its task."... The goal of female education must be to prepare them for motherhood.[25]

In part three, the text again stressed that humans "do not live as individuals like animals" do, but as a society that has "come together as ethnic states," adding

the individual has only one purpose: to serve the whole group. Major accomplishments are possible only by the division of labour. Each bee risks its life without hesitation for the whole. Individuals who are not useful or are harmful to the whole are eliminated. The species is maintained by producing a large number of offspring. It is not difficult for us to see the application of these principles to mankind: ...The ethnic state must demand of each individual citizen that he does everything for the good of the whole, each in his place and with his abilities.... "He who loves his people proves it only by the sacrifices he is prepared to make for it."
If a person acts against the general interest, he is an enemy of the people and will be punished by law. A look at our history proves

---

25 Cited by Wiehle and Harm, *Lebenskunde für Mittelschulen*, 172. See also, Hitler, *Mein Kampf*, 275, 460.

that we as a people must defend our territory to preserve our existence. "The world does not exist for cowardly nations." Military service is the highest form of education for the Fatherland. "The task of the army in the ethnic state is...to serve as the highest school for education in service of the Fatherland."[26]

The text concluded by stating that every citizen must be ready to serve "for the good of the whole, for the will of the Führer, even at the cost of sacrificing his own life.... The good of the nation goes before the good of the individual." Furthermore, these Darwinian

natural laws are incontrovertible; living creatures demonstrate them by their very survival. They are unforgiving. Those who resist them will be wiped out. Biology not only tells us about animals and plants, but also shows us the laws we must follow in our lives, and steels our wills to live and fight according to these laws. The meaning of all life is struggle. Woe to him who sins against this law: "The person who attempts to fight the iron logic of nature thereby fights the principles he must thank for his life as a human being. To fight against nature is to bring about one's own destruction."[27]

THE GOVERNMENT PRESSES FOR DARWINIAN INDOCTRINATION

One of the leading authorities on biology pedagogy during the Third Reich was Paul Brohmer, a professor at Kiel Teachers' College. His book, *Der Unterricht in der Lebenskunde* (*The Teaching of Life Sciences*), was part of a series devoted to "National Socialist Pedagogy in School Instruction."[28] Professor Brohmer stressed that Nazi ideology was based on the laws of biology.

---

26 Wiehle and Harm, *Lebenskunde für Mittelschulen*, 173. See also, Hitler, *Mein Kampf*, 474, 105, 459.

27 Wiehle and Harm, *Lebenskunde für Mittelschulen*, 174. See also, Hitler, *Mein Kampf*, 314.

28 Paul Brohmer, *Der Unterricht in der Lebenskunde*, 4th ed. (Osterwieck-Harz: A.W. Zickfeldt, 1943). [In English: *The Teaching of Biology.*]

Figure 12
Drawings of a "pre-adamite" man. This was a popular early attempt to harmonize creationism with evolutionism. These illustrations are from an 1880 book by a University of Michigan geology professor, Dr. Alexander Winchell. He was a major author at the time and published many semi-popular books on geology and related subject matter.

Source: Alexander Winchell, *Preadamites; or a Demonstration of the Existence of Men Before Adam* (London: S.C. Griggs and Co., 1880), frontispiece.

Figure 13
Evolution showing the Negro in between a chimpanzee and a white man.
Source: William K. Gregory, *Our Face from Fish to Man: A Portrait Gallery of Our Ancient Ancestors and Kinfolk Together With a Concise History of Our Best Features* (New York: G.P. Putnam Sons, 1929), frontispiece.

After glorifying Darwin for inaugurating a "new, more fruitful era of biology," he criticized Darwin for the individualism inherent in some of his writings because it reflected English liberalism. Brohmer believed that evolution should stress holism and collectivism rather than individualism. Brohmer stressed, however, that this criticism was not directed against evolution, which he fully supported, but only against certain parts of Darwin's writings.

Another instructor of biology teachers, Ferdinand Rossner, in a book approved by the Nazi Ministry of Education, also pressed for extensive coverage of evolution and eugenics in all biology classes.[29]

After the Nazis had sufficient time to revise the educational curriculum to correspond to their ideological agenda, all higher level German biology texts in the late 1930s and early 1940s included extensive discussion of evolution, including evolution of the human races and the biological ranking from low to high that resulted from evolution. The 1942 edition of the officially Nazi endorsed textbook titled, *Biologie für Oberschule und Gymnasium*, devoted an entire chapter on evolution and its importance for the Nazi worldview.[30] Dr. Graf went beyond Darwinian evolution as expounded in Darwin's 1871 book, *The Descent of Man*, stressing that evolution has proven humans were not specially created but rather are just another animal and, furthermore, that evolution substantiates the Nazi teaching of human inequality. In the chapter titled, "Racial Science," in the fifteen pages devoted to human evolution and the common ancestors of humans and apes, he included illustrations of our racial lineage as documented by a set of human skulls.[31]

The text included much discussion of the Jewish "race" in contrast to the superior Aryan "race."[32] In another biology text published in 1934, Europeans were "divided into five main racial types: Nordic,

---

29 Ferdinand Rossner, *Der Weg zum ewigen Leben der Natur: Gegenwartsfragen der biologischen Lebenskunde*, 2nd ed. (Langensalza: Verlag von Julius Beltz, 1937), 100. [In English: *The Way to Eternal Life in Nature: Contemporary Questions of Biology.*]

30 Jakob Graf, *Biologie für Oberschule und Gymnasium, Band 4, Ausgabe für Knabenschulen* (München: J.F. Lehmanns Verlag, 1942), 320–348. [In English: *Biology for High School and College, Edition for Boys' Schools.*]

31 Graf, *Biologie für Oberschule und Gymnasium*, 354–355.

32 Graf, *Biologie für Oberschule und Gymnasium*, 372–382.

Dinaric, Alpine, Mediterranean, and Eastern/Baltic."[33] To support this theory, the textbook used photographs and charts to compare physical characteristics of the various races and

> the best-looking and best-groomed were the Nordics. Eyes were compared, as were lips, chins, noses (Nordic—thin; Mediterranean—curved; Dinaric—quite fleshy; Eastern—thick, not curved; and so on), faces, heads, and body shapes. To this were added spiritual and intellectual qualities that…naturally, demonstrated the superiority of the Nordic race.[34]

A leading biology text for *Mittelschule* (middle school), with the official imprimatur of the Reich Ministry of Education, included extended attention to human evolution.[35] Of the ten main chapters, two were on evolution and one was devoted exclusively to human evolution. The human evolution chapter alone comprised over 14 percent of the main part of the text.

One text that covered evolution and the origin of humans in detail recommended that students visit a zoo to view primates to reinforce what the text claimed was the close similarity between humans and apes.[36] As this text made clear, all Third Reich German schoolchildren were to be taught that some lower primate was their evolutionary relative.

The Nazi Ministry of Education also published lists of books recommended for school libraries, many that taught Darwinism. One of the approved texts was *Abstammungslehre und Darwinismus* (*Darwinism and the Theory of Evolution*) by University of Berlin zoologist Richard Hesse, devoted to proving evolution. The 1936 edition contained a chapter titled, "Evolutionary Theory Is Valid Even for Humans."[37]

---

33 Nicholas, *Cruel World*, 85.

34 Nicholas, *Cruel World*, 85.

35 Wiehle and Harm, *Lebenskunde für Mittelschulen*, 173.

36 Wiehle and Harm, *Lebenskunde für Mittelschulen*, 132.

37 Richard Hesse, *Abstammungslehre und Darwinismus*, 7th ed. (Leipzig: B.G. Teubner, 1936), 48–55. [In English: *Darwinism and the Theory of Evolution*.]

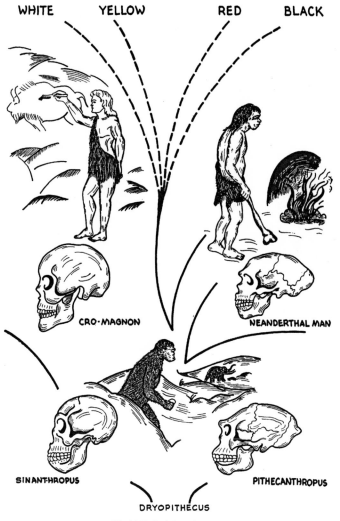

WHITE   YELLOW   RED   BLACK

CRO·MAGNON

NEANDERTHAL MAN

SINANTHROPUS

PITHECANTHROPUS

DRYOPITHECUS

FIG. 14-74. Evolution of man.

Figure 14

An illustration from a 1957 college zoology text written by University of
Michigan Professor Alfred Elliott. Note that while no mention is made of the
inferiority idea once common in textbooks, the illustration pictures four
distinct races that are shown to have evolved from an ape-like early prehuman.

Source: Alfred M. Elliott, *Zoology* (New York : Appleton Century, 1957), 376.

That same year, the Ministry of Education approved *Rassenpflege und Schule* in which professor Martin Staemmler taught neo-Darwinian evolution of human races by means of mutation and natural selection. He also expounded on the racial struggle for survival and the important role of *Lebensraum* (the need for more living space to allow the Aryan race to expand) in that struggle.[38]

A separate section of many texts was reserved to discuss Jews as an inferior race, but "not a 'pure' race," rather a "complicated mixture of Oriental and Middle Eastern peoples" that could be distinguished from the latter by their fleshier noses.[39]

THE MEYER-ZIMMERMANN TEXT

A leading higher grades biology textbook published in Nazi Germany was *Lebenskunde: Lehrbuch der Biologie für Höhere Schulen* (*Biology Textbook for Higher Level Technical Schools*) by Dr. Erich Meyer and Dr. Karl Zimmermann. This text came to the same racist conclusion as the popular text used in America, *A Civic Biology*, by George William Hunter, used in the famous Scopes Trial in 1925. Instead of "Negroes," which the Hunter text deemed inferior, the Meyer text focused on "Jews" and "Gypsies" as examples of "inferior races." This text concluded that "primitive races have found their last place of refuge" in remote areas of the world such as Africa, and that these "primitive races are physically, as well as mentally, far behind the highly developed races.... The most highly developed races are the master races; greater aptitude enabled them to found superior cultures and civilizations."[40]

The socialist collectivist ideology was also fostered in this text by teaching students that "the crown of the entire curriculum" was achieved by a

> thorough treatment of reproduction, heredity and evolution, formation [i.e., evolution] of races, racial science, racial care,

---

38 Martin Staemmler, *Rassenpflege und Schule*, 3rd ed. (Langensalza: Hermann Beyer und Söhne, 1937), 13, 32–36. [In English: *Racial Care and School*.]

39 Nicholas, *Cruel World*, 85.

40 Cited in Simone Arnold Liebster, *Facing the Lion: Memoirs of a Young Girl in Nazi Europe* (New Orleans: Grammaton Press, 2000), 388–390.

and population policy. Thus biology instruction leads to the biological-racial foundations of the People's Community and of the state leadership.[41]

This officially-approved biology text likewise discussed human evolution in some detail. For example, the authors stated that during the Ice Age, humans "improved physically and intellectually" because the harsh conditions then propelled the evolution of humans upward by elimination of the less fit. The "half-animal prehuman" evolved into a "primitive human who lived in caves and knew how to use fire and make stone tools and hunting weapons."

These typical examples illustrate the fact that both human evolution and the evolution of unequal races were standard topics in Nazi biology texts. The authors then claimed that all humans "are subject to the iron law of natural selection" as a result of

the development of higher cultures, the effect of natural selection was reduced, at times even neutralized.... Natural selection had, in the past, exterminated men ill with severe inherited weaknesses; however, in modern culture these are retained and not prevented from proliferating...modern culture has worked against nature. It has chiefly perpetuated the survival and propagation of the weakly and sick to the detriment of the one of outstanding ethnic value. What we observe here is sometimes called *Negative Selection, Anti-Selection*.[42]

The concern was

how swiftly the "ethnic value" of an entire nation can change when left alone to the same degree of selection and anti-selection. Let's assume one half of the population in a nation is less valuable yet produces four children per couple (given the same number

---

41 Erich Meyer and Karl Zimmermann, *Lebenskunde: Lehrbuch der Biologie für höhere Schulen*, Vol. 2 (Erfurt: Verlag Kurt Stenger, 1940), 333. [In English: *Biology Textbook for Higher Level Technical Schools.*]

42 Cited in Liebster, *Facing the Lion*, 388–390. Italics in original.

of deaths for each group, 15 of 1,000 per annum), the more valuable half having only two children would therefore be extinct within 300 years.[43]

The authors' next claim that the Jews are "a racial mixture of parasitic nature" and that the "disharmony of the Jewish racial mixture" is proven by the higher frequency of certain medical conditions among Jewish-Gentile offspring, such as flat feet. They also claim that diabetes is four times higher in Jews compared to other nationalities (a conclusion not supported by medical research). The authors then argued that the "most repugnant features of the Jewish people" are rooted in their inferior moral disposition, including

craftiness, physical and mental uncleanness, cruelty, greed, a distaste for physical labour, particularly the vocation of farmer or soldier.... It is therefore right to view Jews as a parasitic nation or a racial mix of parasitic characteristics that causes its host nation only disadvantage and spells disaster. The calamity brought upon Europe initiated by the emancipation of Jewry, which gave them equal civil and political rights, was nearly disastrous.... The Gypsy nation is also a foreign body and consequently has to be rejected.[44]

The text then concluded that, above all else, "it is our sacred and civil duty to protect our blood from being contaminated with alien blood, especially Jewish blood. No greater shame can be inflicted on the honour of the German nation than the breaking of this law."[45]

The authors also stressed that "racial reinvigoration of German blood" in German society requires drastic action, and that Nazi Germany, being the

first country on earth to recognize the mortal danger facing civilized nations on this globe due to a violation of fundamental laws

---

43 Cited in Liebster, *Facing the Lion*, 388–390.
44 Cited in Liebster, *Facing the Lion*, 389.
45 Cited in Liebster, *Facing the Lion*, 389.

of life, has therefore as a consequence adjusted its policies toward armed combat of these dangers.... After the assumption of power by National Socialism, our first concern was to protect the German nation from further increase of hereditarily ill individuals and to reduce to a minimum any further increases. The passing in 1933 of the *Law for the Prevention of Hereditarily Diseased Offspring* stems from this desire.[46]

The text concluded with the amazing statement that this new German race law "is an immense blessing" because it uses "advanced science to keep our race clean in a humane way, a method that otherwise is brought about in nature more brutally."[47]

Although some textbooks were more tactful, many, if not most, Nazi era texts came to similar conclusions. This was one reason for the high level of German support for Nazism. Another reason for teaching Darwinism in school was that Hitler's goal of "total militarization" required acceptance of war "as an integral part of a life of Darwinian struggle."[48]

Racism was not just limited to Jews, but extended to all putative inferior peoples, even those from India, which one text taught had unfortunately

gone downhill due to mixing with lesser races, but the fact that an Indian, Dr. Chandrasekhara Raman, had won the Nobel Prize for physics in 1930 made clear that the Nordic element in India had not yet been completely eradicated. In Africa, the Negro had "triumphed biologically" over the white settlers and would soon do the same in the hopelessly heterogeneous United States. What's more, the French, in...carrying on the Napoleonic Wars and World War I, had severely diminished their Nordic population, which accounted for their "intellectual decline."[49]

---

46 Cited in Liebster, *Facing the Lion*, 390. Italics in original
47 Cited in Liebster, *Facing the Lion*, 388–390.
48 Blackburn, *Education in the Third Reich*, 117.
49 Nicholas, *Cruel World*, 85.

Few national groups were left out of the racially inferior category:

Along with the Jews, Negroes and the yellow races were specifically mentioned, [in the textbook] and the reader was cautioned that mixing with "Middle Eastern" and "Oriental elements" to "the east of our Reich"...thus introducing the Slavs, who would be the next ethnic group to be designated subhumans, or *Untermenschen*.[50]

The texts discussed above are only a few of the many published during the Nazi era that endeavoured to indoctrinate students into Darwinism. Others include Hans Heinze's *Rasse und Erbe: Ein Wegweiser auf dem Gebiete der Rassenkunde, Vererbungslehre und Erbgesundheitspflege für den Gebrauch an Volks- und Mittelschulen (Race and Inheritance: a Guide to the Study of Race, Genetics and Heredity Hygene for Use in Elementary and Middle Schools)* from 1934 and Otto Steche's *Leitfaden der Rassenkunde und Vererbungslehre der Erbgesundheitspflege und Familienkunde für die Mittelstufe (Guide to Race and Genetics for Heredity, Hygiene and Genealogy for Junior High Schools)* from 1935.[51]

Nazi educators also published a journal titled, *Deutsche Wissenschaft Erziehung und Volksbildung: Amtsblatt des Reichsministeriums für Wissenschaft, Erziehung und Volksbildung und der Unterrichtsverwaltungen der anderen Länder (German Science and Education: Official Journal of the Reich Ministry for Science, Education, and Culture and the Education Authorities of the Other Countries)*.

SUMMARY

The evolution and eugenics content of German biology textbooks printed during World War II shows that a form of Darwinian racism was openly taught and necessarily influenced the Holocaust. Furthermore, the Nazi government control of German schools was driven by the need to indoctrinate German children into evolution. A central

---

50 Nicholas, *Cruel World*, 85.

51 The term *Erbgesundheitspflege* means "heredity health care," referring to practical measures to promote hereditary health (*erb* means heredity, *gesundheit* means health and *pflege* means care). It is often translated as "eugenics," which is derived from the Greek *eugenes*, meaning well-born.

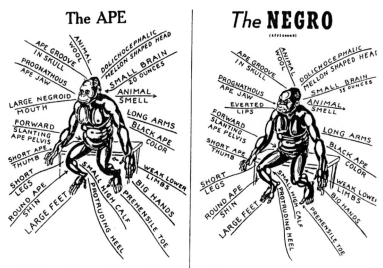

Figure 15
A Ku Klux Klan leaflet picked up at a Klan rally in Bryan, Ohio, in the late 1990s.
The tract used quotes and "scientific" claims from older, pre-1900 scientific
literature to justify its claims of Negro inferiority.

Source: author's collection.

Nazi policy was to ensure that Nazi racism and other programmes had as much support—and as little opposition—as possible.

The Nazis aggressively pushed the teaching of Darwinism in their schools during the entire time that they ruled Germany, just as is now being done in America and other nations.[52] In Germany, Darwinism indoctrination was part of the process to ready the population for the elimination of the Jews and other putative inferior races to achieve the goal of producing a superior race.

Racism, especially anti-Semitism, was a major Nazi party policy and Darwinism was part of the strategy that the Nazis used to spread it.[53] Clearly, "Darwinism provided support for Nazi propaganda campaigns warning of the threat of Jewish blood to [the] German population."[54] They failed, and we today view their attempt as one of the worst acts of inhumanity in history—yet the West is pursuing a similar Darwinian indoctrination policy today.

---

52 Klicka and Harris, *The Right Choice*.

53 Wegner, *Anti-Semitism and Schooling under the Third Reich*.

54 Wegner, *Anti-Semitism and Schooling under the Third Reich*, 71.

17

What can be learned from attempts to apply Darwinism to society

D arwinism, more than almost any other movement since 1850, had a lasting and profound influence on society. As one historian explained, the late nineteenth century

marked the high tide of Social Darwinism. A misbegotten child of Darwin's theory of natural selection, Social Darwinism rendered human life as a perpetual struggle, in which the fit survived and the unfit languished and died. Everything from *laissez-faire* economics to the supposed "vanishing" of Native Americans was cast in terms of these supposedly inescapable "natural" laws. Not surprisingly, African Americans became the object of Social Darwinist speculation, especially after the 1880 U.S. census reported an apparent decline in their numbers.[1]

Furthermore, it is clear "from *Mein Kampf* and Hitler's speeches that he viewed racial conflict as the determining factor in all of human history. 'The racial question gives the key not only to world history,

---

1   James T. Campbell, *Middle Passages: African American Journeys to Africa, 1787–2005* (New York: The Penguin Press, 2006), 117.

but to all human culture.'"[2] The specific race Hitler was concerned about first was the Jews, but Negroes and other "inferior races were not far behind in his mind. For proof of his racial theory one only had to look at the German census data. This data was later revealed to be erroneous because other factors had a "dramatic impact on contemporary debates about black [and other] people's character and progress." Nonetheless the census data

> was seeming proof that proslavery writers had been right, that Negroes were a naturally dependent race, able to survive in the protective custody of whites, but doomed to extinction (as Native Americans were allegedly doomed) once forced to survive on their own in a competitive, Darwinian world.[3]

Historian James Campbell adds that these ideas

> were not the property of racial extremists but fundamental axioms of late-nineteenth-century American thought, and they had immediate, real-world consequences. White life insurance companies, for example, almost universally refused to sell policies to African Americans on the grounds that they were bad risks, a practice that continued well into the twentieth century.[4]

Darwinism also had a major influence on Nazi governmental policy and, in the end, resulted in the total destruction of many major European cities and cost over 55 million lives. Many of these deaths were due directly to the racist ideas that were translated into government policies by Hitler and his disciples. How central racism was to World War II is revealed by the fact that "As the war ground on, Hitler believed that killing Jews was more important than winning the war."[5]

---

2   Jackson Spielvogel and David Redles, "Hitler's Racial Ideology: Conflict and Occult Sources," in *Simon Wiesenthal Center Annual*, Vol. 3, Chapter 9 (White Plains: Kraus, 2009), 228; also available online at http://motlc.wiesenthal.com/site/pp.asp?c=gvKVLcMVIuG&b=395043; accessed September 3, 2012.

3   Campbell, *Middle Passages*, 117.

4   Campbell, *Middle Passages*, 117.

5   Max Domarus, *The Essential Hitler: Speeches and Commentary* (Wauconda:

And, scientists played a central role in killing Jews and other supposedly inferior races. According to Professor Goede, it is

a myth that the Nazis applied force to subdue German scientists and science journalists. Not only did they for the most part voluntarily follow the party line, they even surpassed party officials. More than 60 years after the end of WW II historians are producing new and shocking evidence that...Germans enjoyed more liberties than previously assumed! Why did the scientific community and journalists support Hitler's ideology, the war and the Holocaust?[6]

Factors involved in the large number of people that accepted Darwinism in Nazi Germany include forced exposure to his ideas in the German public schools and colleges, the loss of Christian faith and a social environment that supported Darwinism and its offshoot, eugenics.[7] Support from leading scientists was critically important as well. On January 30, 1940, Hitler proclaimed,

this war will not end as the Jews imagine, namely, in the extermination of the European-Aryan peoples; instead, the result of this war will be the annihilation of Jewry.... And the more the fighting expands, the more anti-Semitism will spread—let that be said to world Jewry. Anti-Semitism will be fed in every prisoner-of-war camp, in every family enlightened to the reason why, in the end, it has to make this sacrifice. And the hour will come when the most evil enemy of the world of all time will at least be finished with for the next millennium.[8]

In short, on September 1, 1940,

Bolchazy-Carducci, 2007), 412.

6 Wolfgang Goede, "Science under the Swastika," *The Pantaneto Forum*, Issue 32 (October 2008): 1.

7 Wilhelm Niemöller, *Kampf und Zeugnis der Bekennenden Kirche* (Bielefeld: Ludwig Bechauf Verlag, 1948). [In English: *Struggle and Testimony of the Confessing Church*.]

8 Cited in Domarus, *The Essential Hitler*, 401.

a brutal new Darwinism broke over Europe: the Nietzschean triumph of the strong over the weak could at last begin. The weak who could be useful would be brutally enslaved, all others would be murdered. What seemed so offensive to the international community—that Hitler would take the territory of the Polish people by force—was nothing compared to what the Nazis were doing. Their racial ideologies demanded more than territory, Poland must become a giant slave labor camp. The Poles were to be treated as *Untermenschen* (sub-humans). Their lands would not merely be occupied, they themselves would be terrorized and broken into utter docility, would be dealt with as beasts. The Germans would not tolerate the possibility of failure or the slightest manifestation of mercy. Brutality and mercilessness would be aggressively cultivated as virtues.[9]

Hitler made it clear that his end goal was nothing less than total annihilation of those ethnic groups that he regarded as the enemy of the so-called "Aryan race," including what he regarded as all "inferior" races—which was every ethnic group but the Aryans. He stated, in regard to ethnic Russians, that the war against them "is a war of annihilation. If we do not grasp this, we shall still beat the enemy, but thirty years later we shall again have to fight the Communist foe. We do not wage war to preserve the enemy."[10]

The best summary of the major cause of Hitler's race war comes from a young girl who lived through it:

One of the central planks in Nazi theory and doctrine was, of course, evolutionary theory—equally a central plank in Marxist doctrine today. The Nazis were convinced, as are Communists today, that evolution had taken place, that all biology had evolved spontaneously upward, and that inbetween links (or less evolved types) should be actively eradicated. They believed that

---

9 Eric Metaxas, *Bonhoeffer—Pastor, Martyr, Prophet, Spy: A Righteous Gentile vs. The Third Reich* (Nashville: Thomas Nelson, 2010), 351–352.

10 Cited in Ian Kershaw, *Hitler 1936–45: Nemesis* (New York: W.W. Norton, 2001), 356.

natural selection could and should be actively *aided*, and therefore instituted political measures to eradicate the handicapped, the Jews, and the blacks, whom they considered as "underdeveloped." They wanted to raise the Nordic status of the German people by importing Scandinavian girls to breed with the SS (*Lebensborn E.V.*). They wanted to create German *Herrenvolk* to rule over the world.[11]

She added,

Christians knew all about this later on.... As soon as Christians became convinced of the real purpose of the Nazi policy, resistance commenced. Hiding of Jews in houses became common, and thousands of both Christians and Jews were thrown into the horrors of the concentration camps.[12]

The Nazi plan, drafted by agronomists and other scientists, was to

colonize Eastern Europe with the aim of deporting 30 million people. Germans were to settle this region while the local population was to be taken to concentration camps or killed. The scientists developed the plans entirely on their own without any pressure from functionaries.... The prestigious "German Research Society" DFG (*Deutsche Forschungsgemeinschaft*) financed this project with 500,000 Reichsmarks—10 percent of its budget.[13]

The director of the Master Plan

was professor Konrad Meyer. About a dozen different scientific disciplines such as geology, climatology and urban planning were involved in the initial planning stage.... In a separate study, just

---

11 Beate Wilder-Smith, *The Day Nazi Germany Died: An Eyewitness Account of the Russian and Allied Invasion of Germany* (San Diego: Master Books, 1982), 31.

12 Wilder-Smith, *The Day Nazi Germany Died*, 31–32.

13 Goede, "Science under the Swastika": 2–3.

recently initiated, the DFG admits that as of 1933, it "wholeheartedly supported the NS [Nazi] regime," that it participated in banning Jewish and democratic scientists from academic life [and]...sponsored "criminal research" and financed sterilization experiments at the Auschwitz concentration camp as well as Josef Mengele's research on twins.[14]

In 2011, University of Minnesota Professor Paul Zachary "PZ" Myers wrote the following in response to a debate on Christian radio about whether Darwinism influenced Nazism. It illustrates the misinformation existing about the topic of this book:

> one of the points the Christian fool trotted out was the tired old claim that the Nazis were no true Christians—no True Christian™ would ever commit such horrible acts. It's an annoyingly feeble and unsupportable argument, but it has a lot of life in it, unfortunately.[15]

His "True Christian™" is a way of mocking Christianity. Professor Myers adds that this argument was been covered previously in an

> evolution column for the *Philly Inquirer*, and has gone on through several articles thanks to that hack from the Discovery Institute, Richard Weikart. It started with an article titled "Severing the link between Darwin and Nazism," which cited real scholars like Robert Richards and Daniel Gasman to ably refute Weikart's ridiculous claim that Nazism was inspired by Darwin. The Nazis banned Darwin's books and rejected the idea that Aryans could have evolved from the lower orders.... So Flam got a contribution from...Scott Gilbert, who pointed out that biology and Darwinism were not factors in Hitler's rise to power: the Lutheran and Catholic churches were.... Nazism

---

14 Goede, "Science under the Swastika": 2–3.

15 P.Z. Myers, "Hitler Was a True Christian™," October 27, 2011 (http://scienceblogs.com/pharyngula/2011/10/hitler_was_a_true_christian.php; accessed September 3, 2012).

was not science-based. It was pseudo-scientific religious dogma, tightly tied to the German culture of the time, which was almost entirely Catholic and Lutheran. All you have to do is look at Hitler's own words.... You cannot blame the horrors of the Third Reich on Darwin.... If you wanted a lever to shift public opinion on anything in the 1930s, religion was where you applied your force.[16]

These irresponsible, but common, claims have been carefully refuted by this and hundreds of other well-documented books. It is true that many Christians supported the Nazi Party during, and before, World War II, and one major reason was because they were convinced that both Darwinism and eugenics were true and scientifically proven. Actually, churches and ministers were a major source of support of eugenics, both in the Northern United States and in Germany.[17] The German church's response to Darwinism and the eugenics movement is not only well documented, but also provides much insight into the results of uninformed and uncritical acceptance of hypothetical and unproven scientific theory.

The church in Hungary defined Jews as a race and "not only did the priesthood [in Hungary] not speak up against the use of the term 'race' to define a group of citizens in order to discriminate [against] them legally—it even supported this approach."[18] Even many active Christians, some who were ordained Christian clergy and held at some level to Jewish ethics, were deceived by Darwinism.

Herczl documented that there was resistance by some church leaders to the treatment of Christians of Jewish background.[19] The very groups that should have strenuously opposed Darwinism and eugenics, on the grounds that it is blatantly contrary to basic Christian

---

16 Myers, "Hitler Was a True Christian™."

17 Jerry Bergman, "The Church Preaches Eugenics: A History of Church Support for Darwinism and Eugenics," *Journal of Creation*, Vol. 20, Issue 3 (December 2006): 54–60.

18 Moshe Y. Herczl, *Christianity and the Holocaust of Hungarian Jewry*, trans. Joel Lerner (New York: New York University Press, 1993), 47.

19 Herczl, *Christianity and the Holocaust of Hungarian Jewry*, 202.

teaching, all too often rejected biblical teaching and accepted the so-called "scientific" theory of Darwinism.[20]

Professing German Christians even produced publications supporting eugenics. One full length book by a Protestant theologian, published in 1940, that attempted to justify Nazi eugenics was *Erbpflege und Christentum : Fragen der Sterilisation, Aufnordung, Euthanasie, Ehe* (*Eugenetics and Christianity: Questions about Sterilization, Nordic purity, Euthanasia, Marriage*). Since many Germans admired the "Northern race," the word *Aufnordung*, was created, which could be translated as "to advance people to become like the northern race," meaning more "Arian." The word was popularized by Hans F.K. Günther, a national socialist ideologue who got the term from Ludwig Ferdinand Clauß, a psychologist and race theorist of the era.

The book argued that Christians should support the Nazi programme of eugenics in order to achieve racial purity. This book, although placed on the Catholic Index of censored books, "received high praise from Protestant circles in Germany."[21] In the end, the efforts of church leaders to appease or even support the Nazi movement did not deter the Nazis from their long-term goal of eliminating Christianity from Germany.

Another example was a religion textbook titled, *Licht and Leben* (*Light and Life*), that advocated eugenics. Yet another example was a booklet called *Blut und Rasse im Licht der Bibel* (*Blood and Race in Light of the Bible*) by Max Slawinsky, which supported eugenics and the need to apply it to society. He used the same rationale for his conclusions as the Nazis did, including that it was "scientific."[22] These books show that many German pastors bought into Darwinian eugenics, and this was one other reason why so many Christians supported Nazism. Unfortunately, the societal and church mistakes that led up to the Third Reich in Germany are now a worldwide problem.

---

20 Christine Rosen, *Preaching Eugenetics: Religious Leaders and the American Eugenics Movement* (New York: Oxford University Press, 2004).

21 Doris L. Bergen, *Twisted Cross: The German Christian Movement in the Third Reich* (Chapel Hill: The University of North Carolina Press, 1996), 41.

22 Bergen, *Twisted Cross*, 41.

HITLER'S DECEPTIONS

Hitler, although he "willingly appeared to be religious at times…he saw organized religion as a threat to his power."[23] For example, on January 1, 1945, in his last proclamation made only a few months before he committed suicide, Hitler wrote

> I cannot close this appeal without thanking the Lord for the help that He always allowed the leadership and the *Volk* to find, as well as for the power He gave us to be stronger than misery and danger. If I also thank Him for my rescue, then I do so only because through it I am happy to be able to continue dedicating my life to the service of the *Volk*. In this hour as the spokesman of Greater Germany, I therefore wish to make the solemn avowal before the Almighty that we will loyally and unshakably fulfill our duty also in the new year, in the firm belief that the hour will come when the victory will favor for good the one who is most worthy of it, the Greater German Reich.[24]

This oft-quoted passage has been frequently used to prove that Hitler was a strong Christian, but it actually proves that he was a consummate liar if it served his purpose—as did his entire proclamation, such as his boast in 1945 that he had no doubt that Germany would win the war, when it was very clear they could not. The fact is, Hitler and the Nazi movement did distort and exploit Christianity just as others have in our time. His real feelings were made clear in words he spoke in private to his close associates. He once said about Christians:

> For the moment, I am just keeping my eye upon them: if I ever have the slightest suspicion that they are getting dangerous, I will shoot the lot of them. This filthy reptile raises its head whenever there is a sign of weakness in the state, and therefore it must be stamped on. We have no sort of use for a fairy story invented by the Jews.[25]

---

23 Domarus, *The Essential Hitler*, 426.

24 Cited in Domarus, *The Essential Hitler*, 425–426.

25 Cited in Alan Bullock, *Hitler, A Study in Tyranny* (New York: Harper & Row, 1964), 6–7.

THE ROLE OF THE PHYSICIANS AND SCIENTISTS

As documented in chapters 5–7, both medical doctors and university professors played a major role in the Nazi movement and the Holocaust, especially in laying the foundation in the 1920s of the eugenics movement.[26] Goede noted that although some physicians tried to resist being part of Hitler's killing machine, sometimes successfully, most

> physicians did not even make the attempt, despite their oath. They engaged in the most awful medical tests on humans. For example, placing prisoners in ice water in order to observe the moment of death or implanting slivers of wood and glass into bodies to study the development of infection—all this, of course, with the purpose of "enhancing medicine." The Robert Koch Institute infected people with typhus and plague in the pursuit of suitable vaccines.[27]

The result was that almost 250,000 innocent people were murdered, including 80,000 handicapped people. For these crimes, as noted in previous chapters, twenty medical doctors and three Nazi functionaries were tried in Nuremberg in 1946 and

> 8 were sentenced to death, 7 received a life sentence—most were released by 1954. Professor Hubertus Strughold, highest ranking doctor in the German Air Force, was not tried but taken to the USA with his research where he became the father of space medicine. Why did hundreds, perhaps thousands, of physicians kill people? Although incomprehensible to us, scientific curiosity must have been one of their motivations. Still, the majority shared the ideological and racist belief in eugenics and euthanasia.... The topic remains controversial: in the spring of 2008, German doctors rewarded 92-year-old Hans-Joachim Sewering for his merits as one of Germany's leading physicians. He had been a member of the SS and had allegedly contributed to the euthanasia program.[28]

---

26 Loren R. Graham, "Science and Values: The Eugenics Movement in Germany and Russia in the 1920s," *American Historical Review*, Vol. 82, No. 5 (1977): 1133–1164.

27 Goede, "Science under the Swastika," 3–4.

28 Goede, "Science under the Swastika," 3–4.

DARWINISM'S ROLE IN THE HOLOCAUST

That Darwinism played a critical role in the Holocaust and World War II is not debatable, only its relative influence is. The Nazi regime's leaders had sealed their fate with Hitler's version of Darwinism and, as a result, the "regime's genocide and other untold acts of inhumanity" occurred. Numbers do not tell the whole story, only individual people do. When the war was over the Nazis had only their

> own collective suicide in an inexorably lost war to contemplate. But like a mortally wounded wild beast at bay, it fought with the ferocity and ruthlessness that came from desperation. And its leader, losing touch ever more with reality, hoping for miracles, kept tilting at windmills—ready in Wagnerian style in the event of ultimate apocalyptic catastrophe, and in line with his undiluted social-Darwinistic beliefs, to take his people down in flames with him if it proved incapable of producing the victory he had demanded.[29]

As a result of Hitler's Darwinian beliefs and those of his leading disciples, plus the German people's passiveness, never before

> in history has such ruination—physical and moral—been associated with the name of one man.... Hitler's name justifiably stands for all time as that of the chief instigator of the most profound collapse of civilization in modern times. The extreme form of personal rule, which an ill-educated beerhall demagogue and racist bigot, a narcissistic, megalomaniac, self-styled national savior was allowed to acquire and exercise in a modern, economically advanced, and cultured land known for its philosophers and poets, was absolutely decisive in the terrible unfolding of events in those fateful twelve years.[30]

The fact is, Hitler and his close disciples were "the main author" of a war that cost over 55 million lives and left millions more grieving

---

29 Kershaw, *Hitler 1936–45*, 615.
30 Kershaw, *Hitler 1936–45*, 841.

over their lost loved ones. Those that survived were forced to attempt to do the impossible, namely

> put their shattered lives together again. Hitler was the chief inspiration of a genocide the likes of which the world had never known, rightly to be viewed in coming times as a defining episode of the twentieth century. The Reich whose glory he had sought lay at the end wrecked.[31]

Ironically, Hitler's

> arch-enemy, Bolshevism, stood in the Reich capital itself and presided over half of Europe…in its maelstrom of destruction Hitler's rule had also conclusively demonstrated the utter bankruptcy of the hyper-nationalistic and racist world-power ambitions (and the social and political structures that upheld them) that had prevailed in Germany over the previous half a century and twice taken Europe and the wider world into calamitous war.[32]

In the end, one of the worst and most ruthless slaughters in all of history, surpassed only by Stalin and Mao with their equally anti-theistic materialism underpinned by evolution, were the product of Hitler and his loyal Darwinian disciples and followers.

MARTIN LUTHER: THE GERMAN REFORMER
No discussion of the factors that caused the Holocaust and the rise of Hitler is complete without a discussion of Martin Luther (1483 –1546). Luther was a German priest, professor of theology and major instigator of the Protestant Reformation. His translation of the Old and New Testament Bible into German, the language of the people (instead of Latin), made the Bible far more accessible, resulting in a major impact on the church and German culture. It also fostered the development of a standard version of the German language and influenced the translation of the Bible into English.[33]

---

31 Kershaw, *Hitler 1936–45*, 841.
32 Kershaw, *Hitler 1936–45*, 841.
33 Bernt Engelmann, *In Hitler's Germany* (New York: Pantheon, 1986).

EXAMINING THE CLAIM THAT LUTHER WAS RESPONSIBLE FOR THE HOLOCAUST

To the claim that Hitler was a Christian is often added the allegation that Martin Luther was a racist anti-Semite, and that this claim reflects the church's view during the Nazi era. A typical example is Professor Giberson's claim that more blame for the Holocaust lies

> at the feet of Martin Luther than Charles Darwin. Luther had described Jews as "poisonous envenomed worms" and encouraged Christians to destroy them, inaugurating hostilities that continued unabated into the twentieth century.[34]

This, at best, is a very distorted view. A main source of this claim is a single mention of Luther in Hitler's Bible of Nazism, *Mein Kampf*, where Hitler wrote:

> the great warriors in this world who, though not understood by the present, are nevertheless prepared to carry the fight for their ideas and ideals to their end.... To them belong, not only the truly great statesmen, but all other great reformers as well. Beside Frederick the Great stands Martin Luther as well as Richard Wagner.[35]

Hitler said nothing about Luther and Jews in *Mein Kampf*, but that Luther was a man who fought for his ideas, a conclusion that is true regardless of whether one agrees with Luther. Obviously, whether or not Luther's views about the Jews inspired Nazism is, at best, only indirectly related to Christianity's validity. However, the question has come up so often that this chapter examines this claim. Eric Metaxas wrote that, as a younger man,

> Luther's attitude toward the Jews was exemplary, especially for his day. He was sickened at how Christians had treated Jews. In

---

34 Karl W. Giberson, *Saving Darwin: How To Be a Christian and Believe in Evolution* (New York: HarperOne, 2008), 77.

35 Adolf Hitler, *Mein Kampf* (Cambridge: Houghton Mifflin/The Riverside Press, 1962), 213. See also Eric W. Gritsch, *Martin Luther's Anti-Semitism: Against His Better Judgment* (Grand Rapids: Eerdmans, 2012).

1519 he asked why Jews would ever want to become converted to Christianity given the "cruelty and enmity we wreak on them— that in our behavior towards them we less resemble Christians than beasts?"[36]

A few years later in an essay titled, "That Jesus Christ Was Born a Jew," Luther wrote

If I had been a Jew and had seen such dolts and blockheads govern and teach the Christian faith, I would sooner have become a hog than a Christian. They have dealt with the Jews as if they were dogs rather than human beings; they have done little else than deride them and seize their property.[37]

In his later years, Luther's attitude toward Jews, and many other things, had changed drastically. It must be stressed that Luther's concern was not Jews as a nationality but Judaism as a religion. The Nazis major concern was Jews as a race, not their religion. Jews who were baptized Christians, even those that were ordained ministers or priests in a Christian church, were usually sent off to the camps like every other Jew.

Jewish historian Nachum T. Gidal concluded that Luther's fulminations against the Jews

found little response either among the populace or in the world of humanists scholarship.... Luther's Bible [the translation into German] gave the people access to Jewish religion and history, which had previously been unfamiliar to them and had therefore inspired unease and distrust.... In this way many non-Jews were actually drawn closer to the Jews by reading Luther's Bible.[38]

He added that Luther "felt a close bond with the Old Testament."[39]

---

36 Metaxas, *Bonhoeffer—Pastor, Martyr, Prophet, Spy*, 92.

37 Cited in Metaxas, *Bonhoeffer—Pastor, Martyr, Prophet, Spy*, 92.

38 Nachum T. Gidal, *Jews in Germany: From Roman Times to the Weimar Republic* (Cologne: Könemann Verlag, 1988), 83.

39 Gidal, *Jews in Germany*, 83

Martin Luther (1483-1546)

Luther's later writings about Jews while a very sick man have haunted his legacy. Sadly, these ravings were seized upon by the Nazis and used in their propaganda to influence others against the Jews.

LUTHER'S ILLNESS CONTRIBUTED TO HIS INTOLERANT RHETORIC ABOUT THE JEWS

Metaxas claims that

> Luther seemed to have an absolutely torrid love affair with all things scatological. Not only were his linguistic flourishes styled along such lines, but his doctors seem to have followed suit: for one of his ailments, they persuaded him to take a draught of "garlic and horse manure," and he infamously received an enema—in vain—moments after he had departed this world. So it is in this larger context that one has to take his attitude toward the Jews, which, like everything else in his life, unraveled along with his health.[40]

Luther's attacks on Jews evidently began in 1528 when, after consuming a

> large meal of kosher food, he suffered a shattering attack of diarrhea. He concluded that the Jews had tried to poison him. By that time he was making enemies everywhere. In his last decade, his list of ailments ballooned to include gallstones, kidney stones, arthritis, abscesses on his legs, and uremic poisoning.[41]

Furthermore, these health issues only added to his many other health problems, some that were very serious, including:

> constipation, hemorrhoids, a cataract in one eye, and a condition of the inner ear called Meniere's disease, which results in dizziness, fainting spells, and tinnitus. He also suffered mood swings and depression. As his health declined, everything seemed to set him off. When a congregation sang anemically, he called them "tone-deaf sluggards" and stormed out.[42]

---

40 Metaxas, *Bonhoeffer—Pastor, Martyr, Prophet, Spy*, 93.

41 Metaxas, *Bonhoeffer—Pastor, Martyr, Prophet, Spy*, 92. See also Gritsch, *Martin Luther's Anti-Semitism*.

42 Metaxas, *Bonhoeffer—Pastor, Martyr, Prophet, Spy*, 92.

It was at this time that his nastiness hit its peak. He "wrote the vile treatise *Von den Juden and ihren Lügen* (*On the Jews and Their Lies*), and the man who once described the Jews as 'God's chosen people' now called them 'a base and whoring people.'"[43]

Nonetheless "Luther's foulest condemnations of the Jews were never racial," as was the Nazi's, but clearly religious.[44] Furthermore, to be fair, Luther was "an equal opportunity insulter…attacking everyone with equal fury, including Jews, Muslims, Catholics, and fellow Protestants." Metaxas listed some examples including:

> He attacked King Henry VIII as "effeminate" and blasted his theological opponents as "agents of the devil" and "whore-mongers." His language waxed fouler and fouler. He called the pope "the Anti-christ" and "a brothel-keeper above all brothel-keepers and all lewdness, including that which is not to be named." He blasted the Catholic church's regulation of marriage and accused the church of being "a merchant selling vulvas, genitals, and pudenda." Expressing his contempt for the devil, he said that he would give him "a fart for a staff." He viciously mocked Pope Clement III's writings: "Such a great horrid flatus did the papal arse let go here! He certainly pressed with great might to let out such a thunderous flatus—it is a wonder that it did not tear his hole and belly apart!"[45]

In the end, what he wrote about the Jews "would rightly haunt his legacy for centuries and would in four centuries become the justification for such evils as Luther in even his most constipated mood could not have dreamed."[46] Specifically:

> At the very end of his life, after becoming a parody of his former cranky self, Luther said and wrote some things about the Jews that, taken on their own, make him out to be a vicious anti-

---

43 Metaxas, *Bonhoeffer—Pastor, Martyr, Prophet, Spy*, 93.
44 Metaxas, *Bonhoeffer—Pastor, Martyr, Prophet, Spy*, 94.
45 Metaxas, *Bonhoeffer—Pastor, Martyr, Prophet, Spy*, 92–93.
46 Metaxas, *Bonhoeffer—Pastor, Martyr, Prophet, Spy*, 93.

Semite. The Nazis exploited these last writings to the utmost, as though they represented Luther's definitive take on the matter, which is impossible, given what he'd said earlier in life.[47]

His infamous rants against the Jewish religion were written a mere three years before his death, when he was very ill, suffering from serious, painful illness. This is when Luther wrote that Christians should set

fire to their synagogues and schools, destroying their houses, confiscating their prayer books, taking their money, and putting them into forced labor. One may only imagine what Luther's younger self would have thought of such statements. But Goebbels and the other Nazis rejoiced that Luther's ugliest ravings existed in writing, and they published them and used them with glee, and to great success, giving the imprimatur of this great German Christian to the most un-Christian and—one can only assume—demented ravings. The hundreds of thousands of sane words he had written were of little interest to the men in brown.[48]

SUMMARY

Among the many factors that influenced the Holocaust and the Nazi movement, Jewish author Ray Comfort concluded that the

evolutionary philosophies espoused by Charles Darwin were at the core of Hitler's ideology, and this belief in the superiority of the Aryan race motivated the Third Reich to implement the practices of eugenics, euthanasia, forced sterilization, and racial extermination. As Nazi Leader Rudolf Hess admitted, "National Socialism is nothing but applied biology."[49]

---

47 Metaxas, *Bonhoeffer—Pastor, Martyr, Prophet, Spy*, 92. See also Christopher J. Probst, *Demonizing the Jews: Luther and the Protestant Church in Nazi Germany* (Bloomington: Indiana University Press, 2012).

48 Metaxas, *Bonhoeffer—Pastor, Martyr, Prophet, Spy*, 93. See also Probst, *Demonizing the Jews: Luther and the Protest Church in Nazi Germany*.

49 Ray Comfort, *Hitler, God & the Bible* (Washington: WND Books, 2012), 100.

Clearly, racism was central to the Nazi's Final Solution, the Holocaust.[50] Fortunately, today more attention is now being given to the problem of the philosophy of Darwin and its implications than during the last several decades, especially in books written for laypeople.[51] This was a major goal of this work.

---

50 George L. Mosse, *Toward the Final Solution: A History of European Racism* (New York: Howard Fertig, 1978).

51 For example see Sharon Sebastian and Raymond G. Bohlin, *Darwin's Racists: Yesterday, Today and Tomorrow* (College Station: VBW Publishing, 2009); Carl Wieland, *One Human Family: The Bible, Science, Race & Culture* (Atlanta: Creation Book Publishers, 2011).

Bibliography

Books

Astor, Gerald. *The Last Nazi: The Life and Times of Joseph Mengele*. New York: Donald Fine, 1985.

Aycoberry, Pierre. *The Nazi Question: An Essay on the Interpretations of National Socialism, 1922–1975*. New York: Pantheon, 1981.

Azar, Larry. *Twentieth Century in Crisis*. Dubuque: Kendall Hunt, 1990.

Barber, John and Andrei Dzeniskevich. *Life and Death in Besieged Leningrad, 1941–44*. New York: Palgrave Macmillan, 2005.

Bard, Mitchell Geoffrey, ed. *The Complete History of the Holocaust*. San Diego: Greenhaven Press, 2001.

Barzun, Jacques. *Darwin, Marx, Wagner: Critique of a Heritage*. New York: Doubleday Anchor Books, 1958.

Baur, Erwin. *Eugen Fischer and Fritz Lenz, Human Heredity*. New York: MacMillan, 1931.

Bendiscioli, Mario. *Nazism versus Christianity*. London: Skeffington & Son, 1939.

Berenbaum, Michael, ed. *Witness to the Holocaust*. New York: HarperCollins, 1997.

Bergen, Doris L. *Twisted Cross: The German Christian Movement in the Third Reich*. Chapel Hill: The University of North Carolina Press, 1996.

Bernstein, Jeremy. *Hitler's Uranium Club: The Secret Recordings at Farm Hall*. 2nd ed. New York: Copernicus Books, 2001.

Bettelheim, Bruno. *The Informed Heart: Autonomy in a Mass Age*. New York: Free Press, 1960.

Beyerchen, Alan D. *Scientists under Hitler: Politics and the Physics Community in the Third Reich*. New Haven: Yale University Press, 1977.

Binding, Karl and L. Alfred Hoche. *The Release of the Destruction of Life Devoid of Value: It's* [sic.] *Measure and It's* [sic.] *Form* (1920). Trans. Robert L. Sassone. Santa Ana: privately published, 1975.

Black, Edwin. *War against the Weak: Eugenics and America's Campaign to Create a Master Race*. New York: Four Walls Eight Windows Press, 2003.

Blackburn, Gilmer W. *Education in the Third Reich: A Study of Race and History in Nazi Textbooks*. Albany: State University of New York Press, 1985.

Block, Maxine, ed. *Current Biography: Who's News and Why*. Vol. 2. New York: H.W. Wilson, 1942.

Boteach, Shmuel. *Moses of Oxford: A Jewish Vision of a University and Its Life*. London: André Deutsch Ltd, 1995.

Boyle, David. *World War II: A Photographic History*. The Netherlands: Metro Books, 2001.

Breitman, Richard. *The Architect of Genocide: Himmler and the Final Solution*. New York: Alfred Knopf, 1991.

Brinkley, Douglas. *World War II, 1939–1942: The Axis Assault*. New York: Times Books, 2003.

Brohmer, Paul. *Der Unterricht in der Lebenskunde*. 4th ed. Osterwieck-Harz: A.W. Zickfeldt, 1943.

Browning, Christopher R. *Remembering Survival: Inside a Nazi Slave-Labor Camp*. New York: W.W. Norton, 2010.

Browning, Christopher R. *The Origins of the Final Solution*. Lincoln: University of Nebraska Press, 2004.

Bruinius, Harry. *Better for All the World: The Secret History of Forced Sterilization and America's Quest for Racial Purity*. New York: Knopf, 2006.

Bullock, Alan. *Hitler, A Study in Tyranny*. New York: Harper & Row, 1964.

Burleigh, Michael and Wolfgang Wippermann. *The Racial State: Germany, 1933–1945*. New York: Cambridge University Press, 1991.

Bytwerk, Randall L. *Julius Streicher: The Man Who Persuaded a Nation to Hate Jews*. New York: Dorset Press, 1983.

Calic, Edouard. *Reinhard Heydrich: The Chilling Story of the Man Who Masterminded the Nazi Death Camps*. Trans. Lowell Bair. New York: William Morrow, 1985.

Campbell, James T. *Middle Passages: African American Journeys to Africa, 1787–2005*. New York: The Penguin Press, 2006.

Cantor, Geoffrey and Marc Swetlitz, eds. *Jewish Tradition and the Challenge of Darwinism*. Chicago: The University of Chicago Press, 2006.

Carr, Firpo. *Germany's Black Holocaust, 1890–1945: The Untold Truth!* Los Angeles: Scholar Technological Institute, 2003.

Cecil, Robert. *The Myth of the Master Race: Alfred Rosenberg and Nazi Ideology*. New York: Dodd and Meade, 1972.

Cesarani, David. *The Final Solution: Origins and Implementation*. New York: Routledge, 1996.

Chase, Allan. *The Legacy of Malthus: The Social Costs of the New Scientific Racism*. New York: Alfred Knopf, 1980.

Chiders, Thomas. *The Nazi Voter: The Social Foundations of Fascism in Germany, 1919–1933*. Chapel Hill: The University of North Carolina Press, 1983.

Chown, Marcus. *The Magic Furnace: The Search for the Origins of Atoms*. New York: Oxford University Press, 2001.

Clark, Robert. *Darwin: Before and After*. Grand Rapids: Grand Rapids International Press, 1958.

Cohn, Norman. *Warrant for Genocide: The Myth of the Jewish World Conspiracy and the Protocols of the Elders of Zion*. New York: Scholow Press, 1981.

Comfort, Ray. *Hitler, God & the Bible*. Washington: WND Books, 2012.

Conklin, Edwin G. *The Direction of Human Evolution*. New York: Scribner's, 1921.

Constable, George, ed. *The New Order*. Alexandria: Time Life, 1990.

Conway, John S. *The Nazi Persecution of the Churches, 1933–1945*. New York: Basic Books, 1968.

Cornwell, John. *Hitler's Scientists: Science, War, and the Devil's Pact*. New York: Viking, 2003.

Corvaja, Santi. *Hitler and Mussolini: The Secret Meetings*. Trans. Robert L. Miller. New York: Enigma Books, 2008.

Crook, Paul. *Darwinism, War and History*. New York: Cambridge University Press, 1994.

Darwin, Charles. *The Descent of Man, and Selection in Relation to Sex*. London: John Murray, 1871.

Darwin, Charles. *The Descent of Man, and Selection in Relation to Sex*. 2nd ed. London: John Murray, 1874.

Darwin, Charles. *The Life and Letters of Charles Darwin*. Ed. Francis Darwin. New York: D. Appleton, 1896.

Davidson, Eugene. *The Trial of the Germans: An Account of the Twenty-two Defendants before the International Military Tribunal at Nuremberg*. Columbia: University of Missouri Press, 1997.

Dawkins, Richard. *A Devil's Chaplain: Reflections on Hope, Lies, Science, and Love*. Boston: Houghton Mifflin, 2003.

Dawkins, Richard. *The God Delusion*. Boston: Houghton Mifflin, 2006.

Dederichs, Mario R. *Heydrich: The Face of Evil*. London: Greenhill Books, 2006.

Deichmann, Ute. *Biologists under Hitler*. Trans. Thomas Dunlap. Cambridge: Harvard University Press, 1996.

Deuel, Wallace. *People under Hitler*. New York: Harcourt, Brace and Company, 1942.

Dietrich, Donald. "Racial Eugenics in the Third Reich: The Catholic Response." In *The Churches' Response to the Holocaust*, edited by Jack R. Fischel and Sanford Pinsker. Greenwood: Penkevill Publishing Company, 1986.

Dimont, Max I. *Jews, God and History*. New York: New American Library, 1994.

Domarus, Max. *The Essential Hitler: Speeches and Commentary*. Wauconda: Bolchazy-Carducci, 2007.

Douglass, Paul. *God among the Germans*. Philadelphia: University of Pennsylvania Press, 1935.

Duncan-Jones, Arthur. *The Struggle for Religious Freedom in Germany*. London: Victor Gollancz, 1938.

Dutch, Oswald. *Hitler's 12 Apostles*. New York: Robert M. McBride & Company, 1940.

Evans, Richard J. *The Coming of the Third Reich*. New York: The Penguin Press 2004.

Evans, Richard J. *The Third Reich at War*. New York: Allen Lane, 2008.

Feely, Raymond T. *Nazism versus Religion*. New York: The Paulist Press, 1940.

Fest, Joachim C. *The Face of the Third Reich: Portraits of the Nazi Leadership*. New York: Pantheon, 1970.

Fischel, Jack R. and Susan M. Ortmann. *The Holocaust and Its Religious Impact: A Critical Assessment and Annotated Bibliography*. Westport: Praeger, 2004.

Frankl, Viktor E. *The Doctor and the Soul: From Psychotherapy to Logotherapy*. 3rd ed. New York: Vintage Books, 1986.

Gallagher, Nancy L. *Breeding Better Vermonters: The Eugenics Project in the Green Mountain State*. Hanover: University of New England Press, 1999.

Ganzenmüller, Jörg. *Das belagerte Leningrad 1941–1944*. Paderborn, Germany: Ferdinand Schöningh Verlag, 2005.

Garbe, Detlef. *Between Resistance & Martyrdom: Jehovah's Witnesses in the Third Reich*. Trans. Dagmar G. Grimm. Madison: The University of Wisconsin Press, 2008.

Gasman, Daniel. *The Scientific Origin of National Socialism*. New York: American Elsevier, 1971.

Gassert, Philipp and Daniel S. Mattern. *The Hitler Library: A Bibliography*. Westport: Greenwood Press, 2001.

Gerlach, Wolfgang. *And the Witnesses Were Silent: The Confessing Church and the Persecution of the Jews*. Lincoln: University of Nebraska Press, 2000.

Gerstenmaier, Eugen. "The Church Conspiratorial." In *We Survived: Fourteen Histories of the Hidden and Hunted in Nazi Germany*, edited by Eric H. Boehm, 172–189. Boulder: Westview Press, 2003.

Giberson, Karl W. *Saving Darwin: How To Be a Christian and Believe in Evolution*. New York: HarperOne, 2008.

Gidal, Nachum T. *Jews in Germany: From Roman Times to the Weimar Republic*. Cologne: Könemann Verlag, 1988.

Gilbert, Martin. *Kristallnacht: Prelude to Destruction*. New York: Harper Collins, 2006.

Gillette, Aaron. *Racial Theories in Fascist Italy*. New York: Routledge, 2002.

Goldhagen, Daniel Jonah. *Hitler's Willing Executioners: Ordinary Germans and the Holocaust*. New York: Knopf, 1996.

Gould, Stephen Jay. *Bully for Brontosaurus: Reflections in Natural History*. New York: Norton, 1991.

Gould, Stephen Jay. *Ontogeny and Phylogeny*. Cambridge: Harvard University Press, 1977.

Goure, Leon. *The Siege of Leningrad*. Palo Alto: Stanford University Press, 1981.

Grabowski, John. *Josef Mengele*. Farmington Hills: Lucent Books, 2004.

Graf, Jakob. *Biologie für Oberschule und Gymnasium, Band 4, Ausgabe für Knabenschulen.* München: J.F. Lehmanns Verlag, 1942.

Gritsch, Eric W. *Martin Luther's Anti-Semitism: Against His Better Judgment.* Grand Rapids: Eerdmans, 2012.

Grunberger, Richard. *The 12-Year Reich: A Social History Of Nazi Germany, 1933–1945.* New York: Holt, Rinehart and Winston, 1971.

Haeckel, Ernst. *Eternity: World War Thoughts on Life and Death, Religion, and the Theory of Evolution.* New York: Truth Seeker, 1916.

Haeckel, Ernst. *The Evolution of Man.* New York: Appleton, 1920.

Haeckel, Ernst. *The History of Creation: Or the Development of the Earth and Its Inhabitants by the Action of Natural Causes.* New York: Appleton, 1876.

Haeckel, Ernst. *The Riddle of the Universe.* New York: Harper, 1900.

Haeckel, Ernst. *The Wonders of Life: A Popular Study of Biological Philosophy.* New York: Harper, 1905.

Hale, Christopher. *Himmler's Crusade: The Nazi Expedition to Find the Origins of the Aryan Race.* New York: Wiley, 2003.

Haller, John S. Jr. *Outcasts from Evolution: Scientific Attitudes of Racial Inferiority, 1859–1900.* Urbana: University of Illinois Press, 1971.

Hamann, Brigitte. *Hitler's Vienna: A Dictator's Apprenticeship.* New York: Oxford University Press, 2010.

Harris-Zsovan, Jane. *Eugenics and the Firewall: Canada's Nasty Secret.* Winnipeg: Shillingsford, 2010.

Hawkins, Mike. *Social Darwinism in European and American Thought, 1860–1945.* New York: Cambridge University Press, 1997.

Heiber, Helmut. *Goebbels.* New York: Hawthorn Books, 1972.

Heilbron, J.L. *Dilemmas of an Upright Man: Max Planck and the Fortunes of German Science.* Cambridge: Harvard University Press, 1986.

Herczl, Moshe Y. *Christianity and the Holocaust of Hungarian Jewry.* Trans. Joel Lerner. New York: New York University Press, 1993.

Herman, Stewart W. *It's Your Souls We Want.* New York: Harper, 1943.

Hesse, Richard. *Abstammungslehre und Darwinismus.* 7th ed. Leipzig: B.G. Teubner, 1936.

Hickman, Richard. *Biocreation.* Worthington: Science Press, 1983.

Hillel, Marc and Clarissa Henry. *Of Pure Blood.* New York: McGraw-Hill, 1976.

Hillenbrand, Laura. *Unbroken: A World War II Story of Survival, Resilience, and Redemption.* New York: Random House, 2010.

Himmelfarb, Gertrude. *Darwin and the Darwinian Revolution.* New York: Doubleday, 1959.

Hitler, Adolf. *Hitler's Secret Conversations, 1941–1944.* Trans. Norman Cameron and R.H. Stevens; intro. H.R. Trevor-Roper. New York: Farrar, Straus and Young, 1953.

Hitler, Adolf. *Mein Kampf.* Cambridge: Houghton Mifflin/The Riverside Press, 1962.

Hitler, Adolf. *The Speeches of Adolf Hitler, April 1922–August 1939.* Ed. Norman Baynes. New York: Oxford University Press, 1942.

Höhne, Heinz. *The Order of the Death's Head: The Story of Hitler's SS.* Trans. Richard Barry. London: Pan Books, 1969.

Hooton, Earnest Albert. *Why Men Behave Like Apes and Vice Versa; or, Body and Behavior.* Princeton: Princeton University Press, 1941.

Höss, Rudolf. *Commandant of Auschwitz: Autobiography of Rudolf Höss.* Cleveland: World Publishing Company, 1959.

Hughes, Matthew and Chris Mann. *Inside Hitler's Germany: Life under the Third Reich.* New York: MJF Books, 2000.

Hutton, Christopher. *Race and the Third Reich.* Cambridge: Polity, 2005.

Irving, David. *Goebbels: Mastermind of the Third Reich.* London: Focal Point, 1996.

Jackel, E. *Hitler's Weltanschauung.* Middletown: Wesleyan University Press, 1972.

Jackson, John, Jr. and Nadine M. Weidman. *Race, Racism, and Science: Social Impact and Interaction.* Santa Barbara: ABC-CLIO, 2004.

Johnson, Eric A. *Nazi Terror: The Gestapo, Jews, and Ordinary Germans.* New York: Basic Books, 1999.

Johnson, Paul. *A History of Christianity.* New York: Atheneum, 1976.

Jones, Greta. *Social Darwinism and English Thought: The Interaction between Biological and Social Theory.* Atlantic Highlands: The Humanities Press, 1980.

Kater, Michael H. *Doctors under Hitler.* Chapel Hill: The University of North Carolina Press, 1989.

Keith, Arthur. *Essays on Human Evolution.* London: Watts & Co., 1946.

Keith, Arthur. *Evolution and Ethics.* New York: G.P. Putnam's Sons, 1946.

Kellogg, Vernon. *Headquarters Nights: A Record of Conversations and Experiences at the Headquarters of the German Army in France and Belgium.* Boston: Atlantic Monthly Press, 1917.

Kershaw, Ian. *Hitler 1936–45: Nemesis.* New York: W.W. Norton, 2000.

Kevles, Daniel J. *In the Name of Eugenics: Genetics and the Uses of Human Heredity.* New York: Knopf, 1985.

Keysor, Joseph. *Hitler, the Holocaust, and the Bible.* New York: Athanatos, 2010.

Kinder, Hermann and Werner Hilgemann, eds. *The Penguin Atlas of World History.* Trans. Ernest A. Menze. Harmondsworth: Penguin Books, 2003.

King, James. *The Biology of Race.* Berkeley: University of California Press, 1981.

Klicka, Christopher J. and Gregg Harris. *The Right Choice: The Incredible Failure of Public Education and the Rising Hope of Home Schooling.* Gresham: Noble Publishing Associates, 1992.

Kramp, Peter and Gerhard Benl, eds. *Vererbungslehre, Rassenkunde und Rassenhygiene: Lehrbuch für die Oberstufe Höherer Lehranstalten.* 2 vols. Leipzig : G. Thieme, 1936.

Krausnick, Helmut, ed., Hans Buchheim, Martin Broszut and Hans-Adolf Jacobsen, contrib. *Anatomy of the SS State*. Trans. Richard Barry, et. al. New York: Walker & Company, 1968.

Kubizek, August. *The Young Hitler I Knew*. London: Greenhill Books, 2006.

Kühl, Stefan. *The Nazi Connection: Eugenics, American Racism, and German National Socialism*. New York: Oxford University Press, 2002.

Kunz, Dieter and Susan D. Bachrach, eds. *Deadly Medicine: Creating the Master Race*. Chapel Hill: The University of North Carolina Press, 2006.

Laffin, John. *Hitler Warned Us*. New York: Barnes & Noble Books, 1998.

Lagnado, Lucette Matalon and Sheila Cohn Dekel. *Children of the Flames: Dr. Josef Mengele and the Untold Story of the Twins of Auschwitz*. New York: William Morrow, 1991.

Lenz, Johannes. *Untersuchungen über die künstliche Zündung von Lichtbögen unter besonderer Berücksichtigung der Lichtobogen-Stromrichter nach Erwin Marx*. Braunschweig: Hunold, 2004.

Lewis, Brenda Ralph. *A Dark History: The Popes: Vice, Murder, and Corruption in the Vatican*. New York: Metro Books, 2011.

Lichtenberger, Henri. *The Third Reich*. Trans. and ed. Koppel S. Pinson. New York: Greystone Press, 1937.

Liebster, Simone Arnold. *Facing the Lion: Memoirs of a Young Girl in Nazi Europe*. New Orleans: Grammaton Press, 2000.

Lifton, Robert Jay. *The Nazi Doctors: Medical Killing and the Psychology of Genocide*. New York: Basic Books, 1986.

Lochner, Louis. *What about Germany?* New York: Dodd, Mead & Co., 1942.

Longerich, Peter. *Heinrich Himmler. Biographie*. München: Siedler Verlag, 2008.

Longerich, Peter. *Holocaust: The Nazi Persecution and Murder of the Jews*. New York: Oxford University Press, 2010.

Lüdecke, Kurt. *I Knew Hitler: The Story of a Nazi Who Escaped the Blood Purge*. London: Jarrolds, 1938.

Ludmerer, Kenneth, ed. *The Encyclopedia of Bioethics*. New York: Free Press, 1978.

Lukas, Richard. *The Forgotten Holocaust: The Poles under German Occupation 1939–1944*. New York: Hippocrene Books, 1997.

Lutzer, Erwin W. *Hitler's Cross: The Revealing Story of How the Cross of Christ Was Used as a Symbol of the Nazi Agenda*. Chicago: Moody Press, 1995.

Magne, Charles Lee. *The Negro and the World Crisis*. Hollywood: New Christian Crusade Church, 1972.

Manvell, Roger and Heinrich Fraenkel. *Heinrich Himmler: The Sinister Life of the Head of the SS and the Gestapo*. New York: Skyhorse Publishing, 2007.

Marrs, Jim. *The Rise of the Fourth Reich*. New York: William Morrow, 2009.

Mazower, Mark. *Hitler's Empire: How the Nazis Ruled Europe*. New York: The Penguin Press, 2008.

McGovern, James. *Martin Bormann*. New York: William Morrow, 1968.

McGovern, William Montgomery. *From Luther to Hitler: The History of Fascist-Nazi Political Philosophy.* Cambridge: Riverside Press, 1941.

Medawar, Jean and David Pyke. *Hitler's Gift: The True Story of the Scientists Expelled by the Nazi Regime.* New York: Arcade Publishing, 2001.

Metaxas, Eric. *Bonhoeffer—Pastor, Martyr, Prophet, Spy: A Righteous Gentile vs. The Third Reich.* Nashville: Thomas Nelson, 2010.

Meyer, Erich and Karl Zimmermann. *Lebenskunde: Lehrbuch der Biologie für höhere Schulen.* Vol. 2. Erfurt: Verlag Kurt Stenger, 1940.

Millikan, Robert. *The Autobiography of Robert A. Millikan.* New York: Prentice-Hall, 1950.

Milner, Richard. *Darwin's Universe: Evolution from A to Z.* Berkeley: University of California Press, 2009.

Milner, Richard. *The Encyclopedia of Evolution.* New York: Facts on File, 1990.

Miskolczy, Ambrus. *Hitler's Library.* New York: Central European University Press, 2003.

Mosse, George L. *Nazi Culture: Intellectual, Cultural, and Social Life in the Third Reich.* Madison: University of Wisconsin Press, 1981.

Mosse, George L. *Toward the Final Solution: A History of European Racism.* New York: Howard Fertig, 1978.

Müller-Hill, Benno. *Murderous Science: Elimination by Scientific Selection of Jews, Gypsies, and Others, Germany, 1933–1945.* Oxford: Oxford University Press, 1988.

Murdoch, Stephen. *IQ: A Smart History of a Failed Idea.* New York: Wiley, 2007.

Nicholas, Lynn H. *Cruel World: The Children of Europe in the Nazi Web.* New York: Alfred A. Knopf, 2005.

Niemöller, Wilhelm. *Kampf und Zeugnis der Bekennenden Kirche.* Bielefeld: Ludwig Bechauf Verlag, 1948.

Nordenskjöld, Erik. *The History of Biology.* Trans. Leonard Bucknell Eyre. New York: Tudor Publishing Company, 1935.

Nova, Fritz. *Alfred Rosenberg: Nazi Theorist of the Holocaust.* New York: Hippocrene Books, 1986.

Numbers, Ronald L. *Science and Christianity in Pulpit and Pew.* New York: Oxford University Press, 2007.

Overy, Richard. *Goering: Hitler's Iron Knight.* New York: Barnes and Noble Books, 1984.

Phillips, Kevin. *Post-Conservative America: People, Politics, and Ideology in a Time of Crisis.* New York: Random House, 1982.

Poewe, Karla. *New Religions and the Nazis.* New York: Routledge, 2006.

Poliakov, Leon. *The Aryan Myth.* New York: Barnes & Noble, 1996.

Posner Gerald L. and John Ware. *Mengele: The Complete Story.* New York: McGraw Hill, 1986.

Pringle, Heather. *The Master Plan: Himmler's Scholars and the Holocaust.* New York: Hyperion, 2006.

Probst, Christopher J. *Demonizing the Jews: Luther and the Protestant Church in Nazi Germany.* Bloomington: Indiana University Press, 2012.

Proctor, Robert N. *Racial Hygiene: Medicine under the Nazis.* Cambridge: Harvard University Press, 1988.

Redlich, Fritz. *Hitler: Diagnosis of a Destructive Prophet.* New York: Oxford University Press, 1998.

Rees, Laurence. *Auschwitz: A New History.* New York: Public Affairs Press, 2005.

Reid, Anna. *Leningrad: The Epic Siege of World War II, 1941–1944.* New York: Walker and Company, 2011.

Reimann, Viktor. *Goebbels.* Trans. Stephen Wendt. Garden City: Doubleday, 1976.

Reuth, Ralf Georg. *Goebbels.* New York: Harcourt Brace, 1993.

Rhodes, James M. *The Hitler Movement: A Modern Millenarian Revolution.* Stanford: Hoover Institution Press, 1980.

Rich, Norman. *Hitler's War Aims.* New York: W.W. Norton & Co., 1973.

Riess, Curt. *Joseph Goebbels: A Biography.* Garden City: Doubleday, 1949.

Rigg, Bryan Mark. *Hitler's Jewish Soldiers: The Untold Story of Nazi Racial Laws and Men of Jewish Descent in the German Military.* Lawrence: University of Kansas, 2002.

Riley, William Bell. *Hitlerism or the Philosophy of Evolution in Action.* Minneapolis: Irene Woods, 1941.

Röder, Thomas, Volker Kubillus and Anthony Burwell. *Psychiatrists: The Men behind Hitler.* Los Angeles: Freedom Publishing, 1995.

Roland, Paul. *The Illustrated History of the Nazis.* Edison: Chartwell Books, 2009.

Rose, Jonathan. *The Holocaust and the Book: Destruction and Preservation.* Amherst: University of Massachusetts Press, 2001.

Rosen, Christine. *Preaching Eugenics: Religious Leaders and the American Eugenics Movement.* New York: Oxford University Press, 2004.

Rosenberg, Alfred. *The Myth of the Twentieth Century.* Torrance: The Noontide Press, 1982.

Rossner, Ferdinand. *Der Weg zum ewigen Leben der Natur: Gegenwartsfragen der biologischen Lebenskunde.* 2nd ed. Langensalza: Verlag von Julius Beltz, 1937.

Rudorff, Raymond. *Monsters: Studies in Ferocity.* New York: The Citadel Press, 1969.

Rummel, Rudolph J. *Death by Government.* New Brunswick: Transaction Publishers, 2008.

Ryback, Timothy W. *Hitler's Private Library: The Books That Shaped His Life.* New York: Knopf, 2008.

Rychlak, Ronald. *Hitler, the War and the Pope.* Rev. ed. Huntington: Our Sunday Visitor Books, 2010.

Salisbury, Harrison Evans. *The 900 Days: The Siege of Leningrad.* New York: Da Capo Press, 1969.

Santayana, George. *Persons and Places.* New York: Charles Scribner's, 1944.

Schleunes, Karl A. *The Twisted Road to Auschwitz: Nazi Policy toward German Jews, 1933–1939.* Urbana: University of Illinois Press, 1970.

Schmittroth, Linda and Mary Kay Rosteck. *People of the Holocaust.* Vol. 1: A-J. Detroit: Gale, 1998.

Sebastian, Sharon and Raymond G. Bohlin. *Darwin's Racists: Yesterday, Today and Tomorrow.* College Station: VBW Publishing, 2009.

Semmler, Rudolf. *Goebbels: The Man Next to Hitler.* London: Westhouse, 1947.

Sewell, Dennis. *The Political Gene: How Darwin's Ideas Changed Politics.* London: Picadon, 2009.

Shirer, William L. *The Rise and Fall of the Third Reich.* New York: Simon and Schuster, 1960.

Shub, Borris and Bernard Quint. *Since Stalin: A Photo History of Our Time.* New York: Swen Publications Company, 1951.

Sime, Ruth Lewin. *Lise Meitner: A Life in Physics.* Berkeley: University of California Press, 1996.

Smith, Bradley. *Heinrich Himmler: A Nazi in the Making, 1900–1926.* Stanford: Hover Institution Press, Stanford University, 1971.

Snyder, Louis L. *Encyclopedia of the Third Reich.* New York: Paragon, 1989.

Snyder, Louis L. *Hitler's German Enemies: Portraits of Heroes Who Fought the Nazis.* New York: Hippocrene Books, 1990.

Speer, Albert. *Inside the Third Reich: Memoirs by Albert Speer.* Trans. Richard and Clara Winston. New York: MacMillan, 1970.

Spitz, Vivien. *Doctors from Hell: The Horrific Account Of Nazi Experiments on Humans.* Boulder: Sentient Publications, 2005.

Staemmler, Martin. *Rassenpflege und Schule.* 3rd ed. Langensalza: Hermann Beyer und Söhne, 1937.

Stanton, William. *The Leopard's Spots: Scientific Attitudes toward Race in America, 1815–1859.* Chicago: University of Chicago Press, 1960.

Steigmann-Gall, Richard. *The Holy Reich: Nazi Conceptions of Christianity, 1919–1945.* New York: Cambridge University Press, 2003.

Steinberg, Jonathan. *All or Nothing: The Axis and the Holocaust, 1941–1943.* New York: Routledge, 1990.

Steinweis, Alan. *Kristallnacht 1938.* Cambridge: Harvard University Press, 2009.

Steinweis, Alan. *Studying the Jew: Anti-Semitism in Nazi Germany.* Cambridge: Harvard University Press, 2006.

Tenenbaum, Joseph. *Race and Reich.* New York: Twayne, 1956.

Tobach, Ethel and John Gianusos, Howard R. Topoff and Charles G. Gross. *The Four Horsemen: Racism, Sexism, Militarism, and Social Darwinism.* New York: Behavioral Publications, 1974.

Trevor-Roper, Hugh R. *The Last Days of Hitler.* 3rd ed. New York: MacMillan, 1962.

Victor, George. *Hitler: The Pathology of Evil.* Washington: Brassey's, 1998.

Von Lang, Jochen. *The Secretary: Martin Bormann, the Man Who Manipulated Hitler.* Trans. Christa Armstrong and Peter White. New York: Random House, 1979.

Waite, R.G.L. *The Psychopathic God.* New York: Basic Books, 1977.

Walker, Bruce. *The Swastika against the Cross: The Nazi War on Christianity*. Denver: Outskirts Press, 2008.

Wegner, Gregory. *Anti-Semitism and Schooling under the Third Reich*. New York: RoutledgeFalmer, 2002.

Weikart, Richard. "The Impact of Social Darwinism on Anti-Semitic Ideology in Germany and Austria. 1860-1945." In *Jewish Tradition and the Challenge of Darwinism*, edited by Geoffrey Cantor and Marc Swetlitz. Chicago: The University of Chicago Press, 2006.

Weikart, Richard. *From Darwin to Hitler*. New York: Palgrave Macmillan, 2004.

Weikart, Richard. *Hitler's Ethic: The Nazi Pursuit of Evolutionary Progress*. New York: Palgrave MacMillan, 2009.

Weinding, Paul. *Health, Race and German Politics between National Unification and Nazism, 1870-1945*. Cambridge: Cambridge University Press, 1989.

Weinert, Hans. *Entstehung der Menschenrassen*. 2nd ed. Stuttgart: Fredinand Enke Verlag, 1942.

Weinreich, Max. *Hitler's Professors*. 1946 ed. Reprint, New Haven: Yale University Press, 1999.

Weiss-Wendt, Anton, ed. *Eradicating Differences: The Treatment of Minorities in Nazi-Dominated Europe*. Newcastle: Cambridge Scholars Publishing, 2010.

Weiss, Sheila Faith. *Race Hygiene and National Efficiency: The Eugenics of Wilhelm Schallmayer*. Berkeley: University of California Press, 1988.

Welch, Claire. *Rise & Fall of the Nazis*. London: Magpie Books, 2008.

Wertham, Frederic. *A Sign for Cain: An Exploration of Human Violence*. New York: Macmillan, 1966.

Whisker, James Biser. *The Philosophy of Alfred Rosenberg: Origins of the National Socialist Myth*. Torrance: The Noontide Press, 1990.

Whitehead, John. *The Stealing of America*. Westchester: Crossway, 1983.

Wiehle, Hermann and Marie Harm. *Lebenskunde für Mittelschulen. Fünfter Teil. Klasse 5 für Mädchen*. Halle: Hermann Schroedel Verlag, 1942.

Wieland, Carl. *One Human Family: The Bible, Science, Race & Culture*. Atlanta: Creation Book Publishers, 2011.

Wiggam, Albert Edward. *The New Dialogue of Science*. Garden City: Garden City Publishing Co, 1922.

Wilder-Smith, Beate. *The Day Nazi Germany Died: An Eyewitness Account of the Russian and Allied Invasion of Germany*. San Diego: Master Books, 1982.

Wolf, Abraham. *Higher Education in Nazi Germany*. London: Methuen, 1944.

Wolpoff, Milford and Rachel Caspari. *Race and Human Evolution: A Fatal Attraction*. New York: Simon and Schuster, 1997.

Yahil, Leni. *The Holocaust: The Fate of the European Jewry, 1932-1945*. New York: Oxford University Press, 1990.

Zentner, Christian and Friedemann Bedürftig, eds. *The Encyclopedia of the Third Reich*. New York: Da Capo Press, 1997.

Magazine and journal articles

Anonymous. "German Martyrs." *Time* 36, Vol. 26 (December 23, 1940): 38–41

Bergman, Jerry. "Darwinism and the Nazi Race Holocaust." *Creation ex nihilo Technical Journal* 13 (November 1999), No. 2: 101–111.

Bergman, Jerry. "Darwinism as a Factor in the Twentieth-Century Totalitarianism Holocausts." *Creation Research Society Quarterly* 39, Vol. 1:47–53.

Bergman, Jerry. "The Church Preaches Eugenics: A History of Church Support for Darwinism and Eugenics." *Journal of Creation*, Vol. 20, Issue 3 (December 2006): 54–60.

Bergman, Jerry. "The Jehovah's Witnesses' Experience in the Nazi Concentration Camps: A History of Their Conflicts with the Nazi State." *Journal of Church and State* 38, No. 1 (Winter 1996): 87–11.

Blackburn, Gilmer W. "The Portrayal of Christianity in the History Textbooks of Nazi Germany." *Church History* 49, Vol. 4 (December 1980): 433–446.

Brücher, Heinz. "Lebenskunde." *Nationalsozialistische Monatshefte* (1937), 8:190–192.

Campbell, Philip. "Germany Rising." *Nature* (September 30, 2010), 467.

Caplan, Arthur. "Deadly Medicine: Creating the Master Race." *The Lancet* 363, No. 9422 (May 22, 2004): 1741–1742.

Dawidowicz, Lucy S. "The Failure of Himmler's Positive Eugenics." *Hastings Center Report*, Vol. 7, Issue 5 (October 1977): 43–44.

Goede, Wolfgang. "Science under the Swastika." *The Pantaneto Forum*, Issue 32 (October 2008): 8.

Graham, Loren R. "Science and Values: The Eugenics Movement in Germany and Russia in the 1920s." *American Historical Review*, Vol. 82, No. 5 (1977): 1133–1164.

Gray, Paul. "Cursed by Eugenics." *Time* (January 11, 1999): 84–85.

Haas, Peter J. "Nineteenth Century Science and the Formation of the Nazi Policy." *Journal of Theology* 99 (1995): 6–30.

Heineman, Elizabeth D. "Sexuality and Nazism: The Doubly Unspeakable?" *Journal of the History of Sexuality*, 11, No. 1 & 2 (January/April 2002): 22.

Hull, David. "Uncle Sam Wants You. A review from the book *Mystery of Mysteries: Is Evolution a Social Construction?* by Michael Ruse." *Science* 284 (1999): 1131–1132.

Jones, E. Michael "Darwin and the Vampire: Evolution's Contribution to the Holocaust." *Culture Wars* 17 (November 1988): 18–29

Linder, H. and R. Lotze. "Lehrplanentwurf für den biologischen Unterricht an den höheren Knabenschulen. Bearbeitet im Auftrag des NSLB. Reichsfachgebiet Biologie." *Der Biologe*, Vol. 6 (1937): supplement, 239–246

Lorenz, Konrad. "Nochmals: Systematik und Entwicklungsgedanke im Unterricht." *Der Biologe* 9 (1940): 24–36.

Numbers, Ronald L. "Creationism in 20th-Century America." *Science* 218 (November 5, 1982): 538–544

Olasky, Marvin. "Darwinian Siege." *World Magazine* (April 11, 2009): 22.

Pringle, Heather. "Confronting Anatomy's Nazi Past." *Science* (July 16, 2010): 274–275.

Schiermeier, Quirin. "Dispute Erupts over Nazi Research Claims." *Nature*, Vol. 398, No. 6725 (March 25, 1999): 274.

Smith, Kingsbury. "The Nuremberg Trials: The Execution of Nazi War Criminals." *International News Service* (October 16, 1946): 1.

Spielvogel, Jackson and David Redles. "Hitler's Racial Ideology: Conflict and Occult Sources." *Simon Wiesenthal Center Annual*, Vol. 3, Chapter 9 (White Plains: Kraus, 2009), 228.

Stein, George. "Biological Science and the Roots of Nazism." *American Scientist* 76, No. 1 (Jan–Feb 1988): 50–58

Thompson, Larry V. "Lebensborn and the Eugenics Policy of the Reichsführer-SS." *Central European History*, 4, No. 1 (March 1971): 54–77.

Washington, Ellis. "Nuremberg Project: Social Darwinism in Nazi Family and Inheritance Law." *Rutgers Journal of Law and Religion* (Fall 2011).

Videos

Charles Darwin. Architects of Modern Thought series. Produced by W. Rowan. Toronto: Canadian Broadcasting Corporation, 1955.

Visit us online at

www.joshuapress.com

Other titles available from Joshua Press...

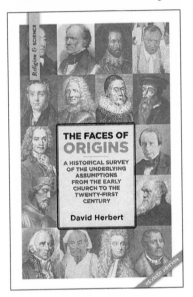

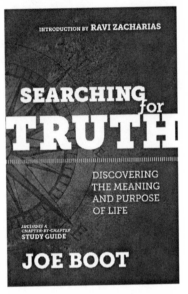

THE FACES OF ORIGINS

A historical survey of the underlying assumptions from the early church to the twenty-first century
By David Herbert

THIS IS NOT just another book presenting evidence in favour of creationism as opposed to evolutionism. Herbert explores the philosophical presuppositions behind Western worldviews throughout history, with a focus on origins.

ISBN 978–1–894400–45–9

SEARCHING FOR TRUTH

Discovering the meaning and purpose of life
By Joe Boot

BEGINNING WITH a basic understanding of the world, Joe Boot explains the biblical worldview, giving special attention to the life and claims of Jesus Christ. He wrestles with questions about suffering, truth, morality and guilt.

ISBN 978–1–894400–40–4

Visit us online at www.joshuapress.com

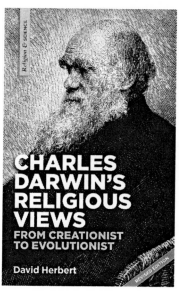

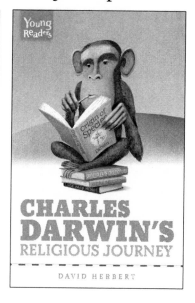

CHARLES DARWIN'S RELIGIOUS VIEWS

From creationist to evolutionist

By David Herbert

A SPIRITUAL BIOGRAPHY that focuses primarily on the religious experiences of Charles Darwin's life—demonstrating how Darwin's rejection of the Bible led him to adopt the naturalistic assumptions that were foundational to his belief in evolutionism.

ISBN 978–1–894400–30–5

CHARLES DARWIN'S RELIGIOUS JOURNEY

By David Herbert

WRITTEN FOR YOUNG PEOPLE, this book traces Charles' life— from his voyage around the world on HMS *Beagle* to his research and experiments on his return to England. Complete with maps and photos.

ISBN 978–1–894400–34–3

A companion workbook is also available:
ISBN 978–1–894400–35–0

Other titles available from Joshua Press…

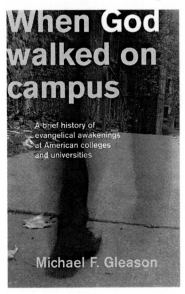

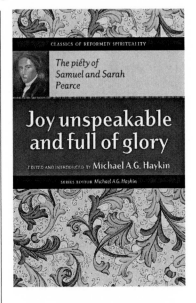

WHEN GOD WALKED ON CAMPUS

A brief history of evangelical awakenings at American colleges and universities

By Michael F. Gleason

FROM THE academic halls of Princeton, Yale, Harvard, Dartmouth, Middlebury, Union, Bethel, Wheaton, Williams, Trinity, Ashland—and many others—comes the stirring stories of awakening and revival.

ISBN 978–1–894400–16–9

JOY UNSPEAKABLE AND FULL OF GLORY

The piety of Samuel and Sarah Pearce

By Michael A.G. Haykin

SAMUEL PEARCE played a key role in the formation and early days of the Baptist Missionary Society in eighteenth-century England—helping to send William Carey to India. Through Samuel and Sarah's letters and writings, we are given a window into their rich spiritual life and living piety.

ISBN 978–1–894400–48–0

Visit us online at www.joshuapress.com

SOCIAL JUSTICE THROUGH THE EYES OF WESLEY
John Wesley's theological challenge to slavery
By Irv A. Brendlinger

THOUGH LITTLE has been written about this dimension of Wesley's life, he was the first Christian leader of world renown to take a decisive stand against slavery—and his contribution was significant in bringing about its demise.

ISBN 978–1-894400-23–7

A FOUNDATION FOR LIFE
A study of key Christian doctrines and their application
Editor: Michael A.G. Haykin

CURIOUS OR CONFUSED about what the Christian faith is all about? This book brings together contemporary pastors and church leaders to help explain the basic doctrines of the Christian faith in an easy, understandable way.

ISBN 978–1-894400-17–6

Deo Optimo et Maximo Gloria
To God, best and greatest, be glory

www.joshuapress.com

CPSIA information can be obtained at www.ICGtesting.com
Printed in the USA
BVOW080519290313

316783BV00002B/2/P